THE LAST COMMISSIONER

A BASEBALL VALENTINE

Fay Vincent

Simon & Schuster

New York   London   Toronto   Sydney   Singapore

SIMON & SCHUSTER
Rockefeller Center
1230 Avenue of the Americas
New York, NY 10020

For information about special discounts for bulk purchases,
please contact Simon & Schuster Special Sales:
1-800-456-6798 or business@simonandschuster.com

Designed by Leslie Phillips

Manufactured in the United States of America

1   3   5   7   9   10   8   6   4   2

Library of Congress Cataloging-in-Publication Data
Vincent, Fay.
The last commissioner : a baseball valentine / Fay Vincent
p.   cm.
Includes index.
1. Vincent, Fay.   2. Baseball commissioners—United States—Biography.
3. Baseball—Anecdotes   I. Title.
GV865. V56   2002
796.357'092—dc21
[B]   2002029431
ISBN 0-7432-4452-4

For RALPH BRANCA, *great player;*
BRUCE FROEMMING, *superb umpire;*
and SLICK SURRATT, *true hero.*

With affection and respect.

C O N T E N T S

Chapter Five

Chapter Six

Chapter Seven

Chapter Eight

Chapter Nine

*The longer one lives, the more one's pleasures
are conditioned by memory.*

—MONSIGNOR RONALD KNOX

INTRODUCTION

I BORROWED THE TITLE of this book from a column by George Vecsey of *The New York Times*. I became the commissioner of baseball in September 1989, succeeding my great friend Bart Giamatti, who died six months into his commissionership, just as the pennant races were heating up. I resigned as commissioner three years later, forced out by owners who didn't want me or my ultimate goal for the game, which was to get the players and owners to work together with the best interests of baseball in mind. George came to visit me shortly after I left baseball. I was visiting in England and he was covering Wimbledon. We talked, and in his piece he called me "the last commissioner." I hope he proves not to be correct. Baseball needs a commissioner who has only the welfare of the game in mind, who works to protect the interests of players, owners, and, most significantly, fans. In the near-decade since I left baseball, I don't think we've had a real commissioner. Someday I hope that will change. For now, I'm the last.

Don't get the wrong idea: It's not my intent in this book to redress old grievances. Time has done that well enough. This book is not only about my three years as commissioner; it's about a lifetime in the game. It's a book many of us could have written. It is a baseball book by a fan.

The subtitle was a gift from the late and legendary Hollywood literary agent, Swifty Lazar. I knew Swifty from a previous life, when I was head of Columbia Pictures. Later, when I became commissioner of baseball, he urged me to write a "valentine to baseball." I have loved the game all my life, but in my years in baseball, and in the years immediately afterward, I lost my capacity to think of baseball in the sweet terms the game deserves. Some years ago I started a memoir, about my career in business and baseball, but I abandoned it. I wanted to do what Swifty had suggested—I wanted to celebrate the game— but the thunder from my stormiest days in baseball still rang in my ears. I wasn't ready.

Seasons came and went. A century closed and a new one began. I found myself drawn again to the game of my boyhood. A friend, the courtly Don Logan, knew my baseball stories and urged me to get them down. One day I realized it was time to write a different book. I was ready.

I want to share with you my life in baseball. Getting Connie Mack's autograph as a boy; being admitted to (then ejected from, then readmitted to) Joe DiMaggio's circle of friends as an adult; catching Giant first baseman Will Clark when I was *trying* to catch a World Series foul ball. These are, to me, little treasures from a life in and around baseball. Of course, not all my experiences in the game filled me with joy. I dueled with Pete Rose and George Steinbrenner and certain team owners. But I realize now, as I make the transition from middle age to old man, that these are significant episodes, within the cloistered world of baseball, and I learned from them and maybe others will, too. Those episodes, tart as they may be, are here, too, as they must be.

All through my life, I have been a collector of stories. I enjoy hearing good stories and I like to tell them, too. I know of no sport that produces stories the way baseball does. Bart used to say, "Tell me a funny basketball story." The pause is long. Baseball is filled with funny stories. I am fortunate to be able to recall stories and dialogue, and I've relied on that memory here. If you had been lucky enough to happen upon Stan Musial at a church one Sunday in Cooperstown, New York, you'd remember the scene and its lines in vivid detail, too. They say you remember the things that interest you.

I have tried to be as accurate as possible in retelling these stories.

But I am sure there are errors. Where they exist, they are wholly unintentional; to those whom they offend, I offer my sincere apologies. My goal has been to entertain, to enlighten, and to give back something to a game that has given so much to me. All of my proceeds from this book are going to the surviving Negro League alumni, a group of baseball-loving gentlemen dear to me.

I am grateful to David Black and to all his colleagues at his literary agency, who made me, a rookie author, feel like a big-league veteran. I am profoundly thankful to my editor, the wise Jeffrey Neuman, a veteran, a pro—a man with an eye to rival Musial's.

And, of course, a special thanks to my wife, Christina.

Finally, but most important, I have written this book with a partner, Michael Bamberger, a senior writer for *Sports Illustrated* and an old friend. He has taken my stories and helped mold them into a book. The content is mine; the shape, form, and elegance—where it exists—are his. I am very grateful to him for his diligence, patience, and solid good judgment. It has been a joy to work with him.

I have lived the experiences and heard the stories that compose the heart of this baseball valentine. I have committed the experiences and the stories to paper in the hope you will enjoy them as I have. I would be pleased if you would pass them on. Baseball is in the public domain. The game is ours.

Fay Vincent
February 14, 2002

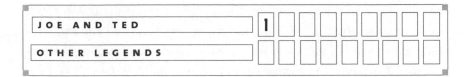
CHAPTER ONE

Joe and Ted

MOSTLY, I'VE BEEN LUCKY. I came of baseball age in the late 1940s, when Ted Williams and Joe DiMaggio were at the height of their powers. My family lived in southern Connecticut, in New Haven, a train ride away from Boston and a train ride away from New York. You could get the Red Sox games on the radio. But the Yankee games you could get—if you actually had one—on TV. We had a DuMont TV, black-and-white, about the size of a breadbox; my father, a frugal New Englander, had won it at a raffle at a Polish Catholic church in New Haven. I rooted for DiMaggio's Yankees, much to my father's chagrin. His team was the Philadelphia Athletics of Connie Mack. "Rooting for the Yankees," he'd say, "is like rooting for General Motors." The Red Sox, anchored by Williams in left, embodied the New England spirit: frugal, never flashy, successful, but not wildly so. When the Sox and the Yankees played, our little world slowed down. How many hits for DiMaggio? How many hits for Williams? Who won? Up and down Orange Street, where we rented the first floor of a three-family house, that's what people wanted to know. All the ballplayers were heroes, and these two men were the giants among them. They were in your dreams at night, on the sports page the following morning, they followed you up to the plate in our sandlot games as we tried to imitate their batting stances.

Later, I became the commissioner of baseball. As I say, I've been lucky. Forty years after Orange Street I was the commissioner of baseball and Williams and DiMaggio were still alive and well and active in the game I was charged with running. I found myself with a legitimate role in their lives, which, even as an idea, took some getting used to. When I became commissioner—after the death of my great friend, Bart Giamatti, late in the 1989 season—I remember walking on the grass at Wrigley Field and having the feeling that somebody would chase me off, that somebody would realize I was an interloper. But nobody did, and in fact people were very nice to me: I was the commissioner of baseball. And because I was the commissioner of baseball, I got to know DiMaggio and Williams, the heroes of my boyhood. The title came with remarkable privileges.

One day, I was able to spend several hours with them in a Washington hotel room, talking baseball. The two men respected each other, but they were never pals, they were not close friends, and now I had the two of them in a single room. As far as I know, it was the longest conversation the two of them ever had, the most time they had ever spent together. When this remarkable session was over, I did something smart: I got out a notebook and started writing things down as fast and as accurately—I'm blessed with a good memory—as I could.

I had met DiMaggio first, a few years earlier, in Baltimore, at a meeting of the Orioles board of directors. Eli Jacobs, the owner of the Orioles, did a smart thing: People he liked, he put on his board in ceremonial positions. DiMaggio was on that board. Howard Baker, the former Senate majority leader. George Will, the writer. An interesting group. I was invited to attend a meeting, as commissioner. I met DiMaggio and sat next to him during the game that followed. I knew enough to know that one had to be very careful, very respectful, when approaching DiMaggio on any subject.

"May I ask you a fan's questions?"

"You are the commissioner of baseball. You can ask me anything you want, Mr. Commissioner. I'll answer."

I warmed him up with some innocent questions. But then:

"How come you never hit 400?" I asked.

"Now that is a question almost nobody asks me," he said.

"They're afraid. I know you won't yell at me."

"It's a good question," DiMaggio said. This was a pleasing thing, to be able to ask DiMaggio—the great DiMaggio, as Ernest Hemingway called him in *The Old Man and the Sea*—a good question. "In 1939, I was going to hit .400. Right around the first of September, we clinched the pennant. We always clinched around the first of September. Right about then, I was hitting .408.

"I was going to hit over .400 that year. Then I got an eye infection. Couldn't see out of the infected eye. Our manager was Joe McCarthy. Every day, McCarthy puts me in the lineup. Commissioner, that guy made out a lineup card in April and he never changed it. Every day I'd go to the ballpark, every day my eye is getting worse and worse, and every day I'm in the lineup. I couldn't hit. My average starts falling. Finally, the eye gets so bad they have to give me an injection in the eye. And McCarthy still has me in the lineup. I wouldn't say anything to him. Now I did not have a bad year, Commissioner. I batted .381. But with my eye amost closed I had to open my stance. The infection was in my left eye, the lead eye. So I had to swing my left foot around to try to see the ball, but I couldn't. I had trouble and my average fell. That was my year to bat .400 and I didn't do it."

My little interview was going all right, so I asked the follow-up question: "Joe, did McCarthy ever tell you why he kept you in the lineup every day with the eye infection?"

"Yes, one time," Joe said. "We were in Buffalo, speaking together. He says, 'Joe, did you ever wonder why the hell I kept you in the lineup that year, when you had the bad eye?'

"I said, 'Yes, I did.'

"He says, 'Because I didn't want you to be a cheese champion.' "

"Cheese champion?" I asked. "What does that mean?"

"I don't know, Commissioner," Joe said. "I never asked."

From then on, I loved talking to Joe because he seemed interested in talking to me. This was all a function of my job, and I was grateful for it—about the greatest unexpected benefit a job could have. My office was in New York, where Joe spent a lot of time. Every so often, my secretary would say, "Mr. Vincent, Mr. DiMaggio is here. He wonders if you could see him." I would say, "There is always time in the commissioner's life for the Yankee Clipper." He loved that. He would say, "I was in the building and just stopped by." He was around a fair bit, because he had a great friendship with his old teammate Dr. Bobby Brown, the American League president who was also a physician.

With DiMaggio, all the great questions were long-simmering, and he went to his grave with many of them unanswered. Bobby had the same fascination with Joe that I had, that a great many of us of my generation had. Bobby used to tell the story of a game in which Joe hit two long shots to deep center—it might have been Joe's brother, Dom, of the Boston Red Sox in center, I'm not sure—and both times the centerfielder made the catch. Now he comes up a third time, same thing. Three huge blows, three outs, Joe comes into the dugout and there's an ice bucket. He kicks it as hard as he can. But the ice bucket is jammed up against a pole in front of the dugout. The bucket doesn't budge. "Every heart in the dugout stopped because he's our meal ticket," Bobby said.

"Now I'm in medical school. I know he has to be hurting like mad, he's probably broken at least a toe. But he shows no emotion. We don't say a word and he doesn't say a word. He just walks down the dugout and sits down. Doesn't rub his foot, doesn't touch it, nothing.

"Years later, we're in Japan together. I say to him, 'Joe, there's a question I've been wanting to ask you for years. Do you remember the game where you hit those three shots to center and made three outs, came into the dugout, and kicked the ice bucket?'

" 'Oh yeah, I remember. My foot hurt for weeks. Jesus, I thought I had broken it. But I couldn't let you guys know I was hurting. I couldn't do that.' When someone asks how Joe led that team, that's the story I tell."

I once said to DiMaggio, "People are always asking you about your successes. May I ask you a question about failure?"

DiMaggio nodded.

We had been talking about All-Star games.

"What's the biggest failure you ever had in an All-Star game?"

"My first one, 1936," DiMaggio said, without pausing. He knew his career like nobody's business, the good times and the bad, not that there were many of those. "I was playing right field, at Fenway. Earl Averill, from Cleveland, was in center. He was senior to me. I was a rookie. Schoolboy Rowe was warming up along the right-field foul line for us. Gabby Hartnett, the Cubs' catcher, comes up to bat for the National League.

"I hear Rowe saying to me, 'Back up, kid, this guy hits out here.' I backed up a little bit. 'Back up, rookie. He's gonna hit it out here.' I knew how to play the outfield, and I didn't like to play deep, but I backed up a little more. I'm a rookie, I'm not going to show up Schoolboy Rowe.

"Hartnett hit a shallow line drive. I went charging in for it. I never dove for a ball in my life, Commissioner, and I didn't dive then. The ball went right under my glove. The ball got by me, went to the wall, and we lost. Everybody ripped me, except one guy. Commissioner, do you know who that was?"

"Who?"

"Damon Runyon. Runyon was the Yankee beat writer. He was the only guy who didn't rip me."

In 1991, the All-Star game was to be played in Toronto and I invited President Bush—the first President Bush, older brother of my high-school classmate and friend Bucky Bush—to be my guest at the game. The president's son, George W., was then the president of the Texas Rangers.

I was in my office when the phone rang and the White House operator said, "Mr. Vincent, the president would like to speak to you. Are you available?" When the president of the United States calls, your heart skips a beat. Of course you are available. A minute later, George Bush was on the phone. His voice was very upbeat. He said, "I have an idea. You've invited me to the All-Star game. Why don't you come here with Williams and DiMaggio before the game, we'll have a ceremony midday in the Rose Garden, I'll give them the Presidential Medal of Freedom and then we'll all fly to Toronto? I'll meet with the Canadian prime minister. It will be the first time a president has ever gone to a ballgame outside the United States and it could be the first time a ballgame has been used for a diplomatic meeting." I could hear the excitement in his voice. It was wonderful.

We agreed that he would call Williams and I would call DiMaggio. A couple of days later, the president called again. "We have a problem. DiMaggio has already received the Medal of Freedom. Williams doesn't have it but DiMaggio does." I had already called DiMaggio, who neglected to mention that fact to me. I said to the president, "Go look in the closet. There must be another award you can give him." He laughed. "That's exactly what we'll do," he said.

When I called DiMaggio, I received a tremendous insight into his world. The moment I asked him if this was something he'd like to do, DiMaggio said, "Do you want me to come, Commissioner? Is it personal to you?" He was making a mental note, depositing a chit from me into his account. Now he'd have a favor in the bank if he ever needed one from me. I realized that he lived in a world where he would do you a favor, but in doing so you created a debt. If I was having a problem with George Steinbrenner, the Yankees owner, and I had plenty of those, Joe would say, "Mr. Commissioner, I think I can be helpful to you." And he tried to be, but all the while he was depositing a chit in his account with me. Maybe the whole world works that way, but with DiMaggio it was more evident.

Anyway, we began to make the arrangements for our day at the White House and our trip to Toronto, and nothing is easy when you're traveling with the president of the United States, to say nothing of the Yankee Clipper. He gave the impression of not being excited about doing anything. That was central to his character. At one point, I was telling Bobby Brown of our plans. Now Bobby had known DiMaggio for decades. He said to me, "Fay, let me tell you how the day will go. Joe will do everything you would like him to do. He will have a great time. When it's all over, he will say, 'I had a good time, I enjoyed my-self, it was a very nice day. I will never do it again.' "

The night before the Rose Garden ceremony, I went to Washington, spent the night in a beautiful, large suite at the Madison Hotel. The next morning at about half past seven, the telephone rang. It was DiMaggio, asking if I'd like to join him for breakfast. I invited him up to the suite for breakfast; he said he'd be up in fifteen minutes. I put the phone down, it rang again. It was Williams. I told him that DiMaggio was coming up for breakfast and asked if he would do the same. He had his son, John Henry, with him. I said John Henry was wel-come, too.

We were due at the White House around noon. We had the entire morning. I knew then it was, for a serious baseball fan, a historic oc-casion: two of the greatest ballplayers of all time, two players who de-fined a generation, sitting together and talking baseball in more detail and at greater length than they had ever before. I can see the table in my mind, the four of us sitting at it, eating eggs and bacon, as clearly as I can see my hand in front of my face. DiMaggio was dressed beau-tifully as he always was, tailored sport coat, pressed pants, each of his perfect silver hairs in place, nails neatly manicured. Williams looked much more like a professor of hitting. If the barber had had an off day the day he was working on Williams, Ted didn't care. DiMaggio was calculated, reserved, always "on," soft-spoken, measured. Williams was effervescent. Williams took the lead. He brought DiMaggio out.

He said, "Joe? Joe! Did you ever use a lighter bat when you got older? Jesus Christ, I did, and it made such a difference. How 'bout you, Joe? Did you ever use a lighter bat?"

And DiMaggio answered, "No, you know, I never did that, Ted."

And Ted was surprised. "Really, Joe? Because I did, and it made such a difference." It was Williams as an expert interviewer, on his fa-vorite subject, hitting.

"Well, maybe, once. In the World Series, in 1951. My last season."

DiMaggio was talking now, and you could hear a breakfast spoon drop on the plush Madison carpeting between his carefully chosen words.

"Fifty-one series, and I couldn't get a hit. Hitless in the first three games against the New York Giants. We trailed, two games to one. Game Four was rained out. I spent that day with Lefty O'Doul, my manager from my minor-league days in San Francisco. O'Doul told me to use a lighter bat. I had used a thirty-seven-ounce bat my whole career. This one was thirty-four. I did what Lefty told me. Had a single and a homer in Game Four, which we won. Few more hits in Game Five, which we won. Few more in Game Six, which we won. The Series was over and I was done. The only time I ever used a lighter bat."

Williams was wonderful, drawing DiMaggio out, but it wasn't always easy. Williams's intuitive understanding of DiMaggio was extraordinary. I had the strong sense that the two men, these two greatest living baseball icons, hardly knew each other, and here I was, playing a role in getting the two of them together. At one point, Ted said to Joe, "Do you remember Ned Garver, that little righthander for the Browns?"

"I remember him," DiMaggio answered.

"I had trouble with that son of a bitch. He could throw anything up there and get me out."

"I think I did all right against him," DiMaggio said.

At one point Williams said, "At Griffith Stadium, Joe, did you feel like you were hitting uphill? Did you feel like the whole park was tilted against you?"

"No," said Joe. "I never noticed that, Ted. I liked that ballpark, hit very well there."

Whenever there was a lull in the conversation, I was ready with a question. I asked, "Could you guys hit the knuckleball? When you guys played, didn't Washington have five knuckleballers?"

"Of course, Commissioner, I could hit the knuckleball," Williams said.

"That's right, we could hit the knuckleball," DiMaggio said.

"Hitting a knuckleball is like swatting a goddamn fly, dancing around," Williams said. "You don't lunge at it, you wait. You're going to miss some, and you're going to hit some."

"How about knockdown pitches," I asked. "Did guys throw at you?" Williams jumped at that question.

"Oh, it was stupid to throw at us. The one thing you didn't want was for Joe or for me to get mad. Not smart." I thought it was very charming, the way Ted included Joe, speaking for Joe in the least presumptuous way. "You hoped that we didn't feel good, that we had a cold, that for some reason we didn't care. The one thing you don't want to do is get us mad. Now you throw a ball at me and I am going to go down, but I'm going to get back up. And now I'm going to be angry. You don't want me angry. You want me daydreaming, you want me not caring. Now I'm angry. The next strike you throw, I'm going to hit it."

I was like a kid in the candy store, knowing he can eat all the candy he wants and that he will not get sick. I asked them, "Did you guys guess? Were you guess hitters? Did you try to guess whether the next pitch would be a fastball or a curve?"

"That's not the way I would put it, Commissioner," Joe said. "I calculated the odds, what you think is going to happen, which is not guessing. You're pitching to me, you've got me a little behind in the count, a ball and two strikes. You have a really good fastball and you've got a curve. I can't afford to take the chance that you're going to slip the fastball by me. So I've got to look for the fastball and be ready to adjust to the curve. On the other hand, if I'm ahead in the count, I know you're going to throw me a fastball and that gives me a terrific advantage, because I can hit a fastball. I can hit it quite hard if I'm expecting it. It's all a case of expectations."

Bart Giamatti used to say that you had to be really smart to be an excellent hitter, that a Williams or a DiMaggio had an enormous, calculating brain. At that moment, I understood exactly what he was talking about. I had the feeling that if you gave these guys an IQ test that was geared toward sheer intelligence, the ability to come up with the correct answer on the basis of presented data, they would both be off the charts. Being with them in that room, for three uninterrupted hours, was one of the great experiences of my life.

The rest of the day was memorable, too. (Every encounter I ever had with DiMaggio or Williams was memorable, as commissioner and in the years after I left the office, too.) At the Rose Garden ceremony, it was obvious what true affection President Bush had for these two men. He awarded them . . . nothing. Just a nice ceremony on a beautiful July day to honor two baseball icons on the day of the All-Star game. President Bush was a great baseball fan, and a great fan of both players. Everywhere we went that day, the power of DiMaggio and Williams together was staggering. I had been the chairman of Columbia Pictures and saw Dustin Hoffman, Warren Beatty, Candice Bergen, great stars, in action, in public. The response to DiMaggio and Williams was clearly at a higher and deeper level. As we entered the Oval Office, a tall, crisp Marine officer in white gloves said to me, "Would Mr. DiMaggio and Mr. Williams be willing to sign my glove? I could go to the brig for this, but I don't care. Those two are great heroes." John Sununu, President Bush's chief of staff, asked DiMaggio and Williams to sign four dozen balls, which is a lot. DiMaggio, in his life, probably never signed forty-eight balls in one sitting—flat objects, yes, many more than that. They were terrific about it, and with every signature and every little conversation they had, their stature just continued to grow. I complimented them on how they handled themselves in public. Williams said, "You work at it. It's not an accident." DiMaggio said, "You have to be very aware of every public thing you do."

But even on that day, I could see the private DiMaggio was different. When Sununu presented him with the balls, DiMaggio looked at me and said, "Is he kidding?"

"He's not kidding," I said.

"I'm going to do it, Commissioner, but I don't like it."

But this was all private, between Joe and me. Sununu and the president had no idea what DiMaggio was thinking.

At some point, I became very aware that I would not likely ever again have a day like this, and that I had better take full advantage of it. After being at the White House, DiMaggio, Williams, and I rode out to Andrews Air Force Base, a forty-five-minute drive, to take *Air Force One* to Toronto for the All-Star game. I got in as many questions as I could, particularly to DiMaggio. You could always talk to Williams about baseball, hitting particularly. That was his life's work. DiMaggio had to be in the correct setting to want to talk, and this entire day was the correct setting.

"Joe," I said, "could you tell me about Lazzeri?" Tony Lazzeri was a second baseman on the 1927 Yankees—the greatest baseball team ever, many people think, I among them. Lazzeri was from San Francisco, like Joe, and he was closing out his career when Joe was beginning his. He was a legend, in part because he played with Ruth and Gehrig and DiMaggio, in part because he was a Yankee. "He was a great second baseman," DiMaggio said. DiMaggio was spare, and not often generous, in his analysis of others, so when he said words like those, it was truly startling. "He had epilepsy," DiMaggio said. "He had a seizure, fell down the basement steps, and died. Did you know that?" I did not.

I asked Joe, "Who is not in the Hall of Fame that should be?"

"Joe Gordon," DiMaggio said. "Joe Gordon never made a mistake. He was a terrific hitter, but beyond that, he always did the right thing. He never made a bad throw. He never threw to the wrong base. Joe Gordon." Gordon succeeded Lazzeri at second for the Yankees. He was a .268 career hitter and a .970 career fielder. In an eleven-year career, he played in the World Series six times, five with the Yankees, one with the Cleveland Indians in 1948.

I asked DiMaggio about Kenny Keltner, the Cleveland third baseman who basically ended DiMaggio's historic fifty-six-game hitting streak of 1941. For what would have been game fifty-seven, Keltner positioned himself directly on the third-base line and stopped two bullets, sure doubles, with two remarkable plays. "Keltner told me later he wasn't trying to stop the streak," DiMaggio said. "He was trying to stop me from getting doubles." What DiMaggio didn't say was the next day he began a sixteen-game hitting streak. He knew I knew. He said what he thought you needed to know, and no more. In his own way, he was an amazing conversationalist, a study in economy.

We flew on *Air Force One* to Toronto, and Williams was fascinated. He had been a fighter pilot in Korea and he was captivated by planes. "Look at the size of these engines," he said. "My little plane in Korea had two thousand pounds of thrust. I have to find out how much thrust these engines have." We made arrangements for Williams to go up to the cockpit and talk to the pilots; when he came back he said, "Jesus Christ, this plane has two hundred thousand pounds of thrust in each engine. That's a big, big plane."

Later, Williams, DiMaggio, and I were invited to sit with the president, in a conference room aboard the plane. We were at a large table with about fifteen big armchairs all around it, very well appointed, and there was a phone at each seat. We were all in a playful mood and the idea came up that we should have President Bush call somebody. I suggested he call the person who beat one of us for class president in grade school, or the girl who turned us down for the prom, something like that. But I couldn't come up with a name. So President Bush called Ted's daughter in Boston, out of the blue. He said, "Cornelia, this is President Bush. I'm in *Air Force One* with your father, Joe DiMaggio, and Fay Vincent. I just wanted you to know that he's doing fine and we're off to Toronto to go to the All-Star game." She, of course, thought it was some sort of prank.

The game itself was not as memorable for me. My walking for most of my life has been poor, owing to an injury I sustained in college, so it was very important for me to pace myself. During the pregame ceremonies, I stayed up in the press level, while the president and DiMaggio and Williams went to the clubhouses. I can see the scene in my mind's eye: Jose Canseco and Joe Carter and Lenny Dykstra and Roger Clemens and other players standing in such proximity to three great heroes of the war generation, standing in awe. I know it had to be in awe, because those three men had that effect on most everybody.

When it was all over, Bobby Brown proved prophetic. As Joe and I waited for a car after the game, I turned to him and said, "Well, Joe, that was quite a day, wasn't it?"

"It was a very nice day, Commissioner," DiMaggio said. "But I will never do it again." That was pure Joe.

○   ○   ○

A FEW WEEKS LATER I was in Cooperstown, for the annual induction of players into the Hall of Fame, and on a Sunday at 6:00 A.M. I was going down the elevator on my way to an early Mass. The elevator door opened at the lobby level and who should be there? Ted Williams. All the players and officials stay at the Otesaga, so you see everybody if you're there that weekend. Everybody but DiMaggio, that is. Joe had no use for Cooperstown, he was angry at them over something, and nobody could hold a grudge like Joe DiMaggio.

"Commissioner!" Williams said. "How about some breakfast!"

I was happy to defer Mass for an hour or two. When Ted Williams invites you to breakfast on a Sunday morning, you know it's an invitation to the Church of Hitting, and you can't—or the twelve-year-old in you, anyhow, cannot—pass it up.

We sat down for breakfast.

"Commissioner," Ted said, "have I told you how stupid pitchers are?"

"Really, Ted?" Williams was past seventy, but sounding still like an everyday player.

"Let me tell you why. Almost every pitcher in American Legion ball has a pretty good fastball. A few of 'em get to the big leagues with that fastball. Nine out of ten big-league pitchers have good fastballs." His intensity was white-hot by this point. "Then Ted Williams comes to the plate. But remember, I got to the big leagues because I could hit that fastball. Pitchers forget that. They throw me a fastball and I knock the hell out of it.

"Then the pitcher says to himself, 'Nobody hits my fastball that hard. I just didn't get it in the right spot. I had it too far up. Next time, I'll get it down.' So the next time it's a little down. I hit it again. I make my living hitting fastballs pitchers think they can get past me. You can't, especially when I've got a pretty good idea that it's coming."

At this point, Warren Spahn entered the dining room. He is the winningest lefthanded pitcher in baseball history, 363 wins. Ted called out: "Hey, Spahnie, I'm telling the commissioner how dumb pitchers are."

"Yeah," Spahn said dryly. "But not as dumb as hitters."

"He wasn't so dumb," Williams said.

Spahn had been through this before. But it was obvious he wanted to hear more from Ted.

"I remember Spahnie at the end of his career. He's in the National League, so I don't see him that much, but I remember this. He had this horseshit screwball." That's the primary epithet for players of that generation, maybe because so many of them came from the farm. "If a righthanded hitter is up with a man on first or first and second with less than two outs, Spahnie always threw him that horseshit screwball. And you can't hit that pitch."

Spahn grinned. Now remember, Williams was describing a pitcher in the other league, from forty or more years earlier, and he's thinking of the whole situation as a righthanded hitter, when of course Williams batted from the left. That's why I say his intelligence was so superior.

"Now Commissioner, when he throws you that horseshit screwball, there's only two things you can do with it. You can hit a grounder to second, in which case Spahn gets a double play. Or you pop it up to right. There's nothing you can do with that horseshit pitch. Now you tell the commissioner, Spahnie, am I right?"

"He's right. I had the screwball. I threw it to righthanded hitters only when I had men on base. It was a good pitch for me," Spahn said. "Ninety-nine percent of the time, they'd hit a grounder to second or pop it up."

Williams was pleased with himself. He understood Spahn's tactics as well as Spahn himself did. Almost. Spahn had to add something to get the last lick in.

"But I would have never thrown him that horseshit screwball."

When I was a kid, growing up in Connecticut, worshiping the Yankees but never really despising the Red Sox, I had the idea, mostly from the newspapers, that Williams was a curmudgeon, nasty, aloof. Spending time with him, I had a totally different impression. Williams himself was aware of how different his image and his actual self were.

Every year at Cooperstown, there's a private dinner for the returning Hall of Famers—DiMaggio was very seldom, if ever, among them—and the commissioner of baseball. Nobody else is allowed in the room. They take turns speaking, and in this setting, Williams is clearly the pope among all his cardinals. One year at the dinner, Williams stood and told a fishing story.

"You guys will like this story," he said. "You guys all know I like to fish down in the Florida Keys, and when I'm down there, I don't use my real name. So I check into this hotel under the name Al Forster, our old groundskeeper at Fenway, who you all know. He's been there forever.

"Now I'm checking into the hotel and the clerk says, 'Are you really Al Forster? Because you look a lot like Ted Williams.'

"So I say to the desk clerk, 'Who the hell is Ted Williams?'

"The clerk says, 'You've never heard of Ted Williams?'

" 'No.'

" 'Well, Ted Williams was a great ballplayer for the Boston Red Sox, great lefthanded hitter, batted .406,' the clerk says.

"I say, 'Never heard of him. I don't follow baseball. Too slow.' So we talk a little more, he's being nice to me and I'm being nice to him. And as I'm walking away, the clerk calls me back. 'You know, Mr. Forster, I realize now you can't be Ted Williams.'

" 'Oh yeah? Why not?'

" 'Because you're really a nice guy and Ted Williams is a real pain in the ass.' "

With Williams, you could ask anything and not be afraid to do it. One year at Cooperstown, I asked Williams to give me his all-time starting eight, at each position. He had Bill Dickey of the Yankees catching, the greatest defensive catcher he ever saw and a superb hitter, too. He had Lou Gehrig of the Yankees at first. Williams said nobody hit more line drives than Gehrig. "He always hit it right on the button. No lift, like Joe or me." He put Charlie Gehringer of the Tigers at second, the smoothest-fielding second baseman Williams had seen and a superb hitter. (DiMaggio once told me he copied his swing from Charlie even though Gehringer hit lefthanded.) He put his teammate Joe Cronin at shortstop, although Cronin was also his manager. He put Jimmie Foxx, also a teammate, at third, although he played more first in his career, but Ted said he had to get him in there somewhere. His comment on Foxx was that, had it not been for Jimmie's battles with alcohol, he would have broken just about every hitting record there is. In right, he put Babe Ruth, of course. In center he put Joe DiMaggio, but he might have been tempted to put his teammate Dom DiMaggio there, because he loved Dom like a brother and thought he was a better fielder than Joe, thought he was one of the best center-fielders ever. But Joe was superb at everything. When he got to left field he said, "Modesty forbids," and moved on. Clearly, he had reserved left for himself, and properly so.

Another time at Cooperstown I asked Williams about the foul pop he hit that gave Allie Reynolds, the great righthander on Casey Stengel's Yankees, the last out of his second no-hitter in the 1951 season. He was the first American League pitcher to throw two no-hitters in the same season.

"Tell me about Reynolds's second no-hitter," I said to Williams. Whenever I was around him, I felt like a cub reporter.

"Oh, you want me to talk about that, I hate talking about that."

Just then Yogi Berra came by. Yogi played a crucial role in the second no-hitter, so Williams called him over.

"Hey, Yog," Williams said. "I'm telling the commissioner about that goddamn pop-up. You know what happened."

Now Williams dwarfs Yogi, but Yogi's his own man. Still, he fulfills Williams's demand. Ted said, "Commissioner, Allie Reynolds was a tough cookie. He already had the one no-hitter. Now he's going for the second one at Yankee Stadium. He gets two outs in the ninth and now I'm up. I'm supposed to be the last out. I step in on him and say to myself, 'That son of a bitch is not going to get his no-hitter on me.' Now he's got a great fastball, but I can hit it. I was sure I would get a hit.

"Yog, you tell the commissioner if I'm wrong. I never swung at bad pitches." At this point, he grabbed my cane and used it as a bat, recreating the at bat. "That son of a bitch throws me a high fastball right here"—he points under his chin—"and I swing at the goddamn pitch. I don't know why. I hit this lousy high pop, straight up, in foul territory. And the little Italian here"—he's pointing at Yogi, of course—"he drops the thing. I can't believe it. Now I've got another chance. I say to myself, 'I'm going to hit him this time.' Then he throws me the exact same pitch, in the exact same place, maybe a little harder, and I do the same damn thing, pop it straight up. This time Yogi staggers around and around and catches it. I'll tell you, in my life I don't think I ever swung at two bad pitches like that in a row. Yog, you tell the commissioner, am I telling the truth?"

Now it was Yogi's turn.

"Commissioner, you want to hear my side? He's got it right. He popped up the first one, and I dropped it. What you don't know is right after I dropped it, Reynolds stepped on my hand. He was mad at me, and he steps right on my hand. Casey motions me to go to the mound to talk to him, to calm him down. But not me. There's no way I'm going out there. He was really hot. Next pitch, Ted hits the same pop-up. I'm getting under it and the whole while Reynolds is screaming, 'You better catch this one, you fucking dago, or I'll kill you.' "

○   ○   ○

AFTER THAT CEREMONY in the Rose Garden, President Bush still wanted to give Williams the Medal of Freedom. DiMaggio had it, and the president felt Williams should have it. I know this because one day I received a call from John Sununu, the president's chief of staff.

"Commissioner, we need a favor from you," Sununu said. "It's about Williams."

I asked how I could help.

"The president wants to give him the Medal of Freedom. Ted doesn't have it, and the president feels he should. We wrote him a letter, inviting him to lunch and the ceremony, but he hasn't answered. There's a bunch of other people who will receive it that day, too. Why he won't answer, I don't know. Maybe you can reach him and find out what's going on?"

"John," I said, "what is the dress code for the ceremony?"

"Dress code?" the chief of staff said. "We don't care what he wears. I don't care if he comes in a T-shirt. We just want him there."

"Because you know he has this thing about wearing a tie," I said. "He hates ties."

"We want to honor him and the president will not care if he's not wearing a tie," Sununu said.

So I called Williams. I said, "Ted, do you have a letter from the White House—"

"Oh, Commisioner, I figured somebody would call about that," he said.

"Ted, come on, the president of the United States wants to give you the highest civilian honor he can and you won't answer the letter?"

"Commissioner, I'm sure this is going to be one of those black-tie deals and I can't do those things."

"Ted, this is not black tie. It's lunch. Have you ever seen a black-tie lunch?"

"Well, I'd still have to wear a tie."

"You would not have to wear a tie."

"Really?"

"Really."

"Then I'll go, but you have to go, too."

I said of course.

I called back Sununu, told him Williams was coming but without a tie. Sununu said the president would be delighted.

The morning of the ceremony arrived. I had told Williams I'd meet him at the White House, and we made arrangements for a good friend of mine, John Dowd, to pick up Williams at the airport and bring him to the White House. Dowd was a lawyer who worked for baseball on the Pete Rose investigation and also did some work for Williams, who admired him. Dowd was also, just like Williams, a retired Marine Corps captain. As Williams came off the plane, Dowd was there to meet him. Williams later told me what happened.

Dowd took one look at Williams and greeted him with, "Mr. Williams: Are you a retired captain of the United States Marine Corps?"

"Yes, sir, I am."

"Well that makes two of us. And let me tell you something, Mr. Williams. You are about to go to the White House, to be honored by our commander in chief, and you look like a bum. You are a disgrace to the Corps. So we are going to get you fixed up for our president."

Whereupon Dowd took Williams to a downtown store and bought him a jacket, shirt, and tie. When I saw Williams, he looked resplendent.

"Oh, Ted, may I have that tie?" I asked.

"You're pretty good, Commissioner, but Dowd gets the tie," he said. Williams had been shamed into it, Marine to Marine. It was odd, seeing Williams in a tie, but he was graceful about it. He stole the show as he always did. You could see during the ceremony how much the president, the commander in chief, loved Williams, how pleased he was to be in a place in his life where he could honor a man he considered a great hero. I felt very much the same way. Dowd told me later Sununu asked for and still has the tie!

o   o   o

IT'S A VERY SATISFYING THING, to get to know an icon and to discover the real human being underneath the shell of celebrity. This was harder to achieve with DiMaggio than with Williams because DiMaggio was an altogether more private, complex, enigmatic person. But no less fascinating. One day, fairly near the end of his life, he told me something I would have never expected to hear from him: a self-deprecating story. I was long out of baseball by this point and Joe and I were having lunch when I asked him about Lefty Gomez, the great Yankee pitcher. Gomez was a Californian, like DiMaggio, who had played in the minors for the San Francisco Seals, like DiMaggio. He was a veteran pitcher when DiMaggio came up as a rookie in 1936. On some very staid, serious Yankee teams, Gomez was a bright spot. He was famous for being a goofball, but also for his wit and his intelligence.

Joe said, "In my rookie year, Lefty and I both lived at the Mayflower Hotel, on Central Park West. Still there. He's a big star and I'm just coming up. He had a car, and I didn't, so he said I could ride with him to the Stadium, which I did, every day. This one Sunday, we're going to play a doubleheader against the Red Sox and there's a big article that morning in one of the New York papers about Tris Speaker."

Tris Speaker was a former Red Sox centerfielder, long retired by this point, in fact a year away from becoming the seventh inductee in the Hall of Fame. On his plaque at Cooperstown it says "greatest center-fielder of his era."

Joe continues: "The article says that Tris Speaker is the greatest centerfielder who ever lived because he played really shallow but still could go back on the ball.

"That day I get in the car with Lefty and I say to him, 'Did you see that story in the paper today about Tris Speaker being the greatest cen-terfielder who ever lived?' Lefty says, 'Yeah, kid, what of it?' Now I can't believe what I said next, Commisioner, but I said it: 'Lefty, I'm going to make people forget about Tris Speaker. I'm going to be the greatest centerfielder who ever lived.'

"Now remember, I'm a rookie and Lefty's a veteran. He doesn't say a word. We get to the Stadium. Lefty's pitching the second game and the next Tris Speaker is playing center, playing real shallow, just like Speaker. When you're young, you think you can get back for anything over your head. I told that kid Williams for the Yankees that he's play-ing too shallow—we all do it.

"Lefty gets himself in trouble, the game is close, the Red Sox get a couple guys on. Lefty looks back at me and he's motioning at me to move back, play deeper, I'm playing too shallow. He doesn't want a ball getting by me for a triple. But I'm the next Tris Speaker, I'm not mov-ing back. He keeps shaking his glove at me to get me back. I stay put.

"Well, wouldn't you know it, some guy hits a shot right over my head. While I'm chasing the ball out there two runs score on a triple and we lose the game.

"Now we have to drive home, Lefty and me. I don't say a word to him and he's not saying a word to me. But I'm thinking to myself, I got to say something to him. So when we're almost back at the hotel, I say, 'Lefty?'

"He says, 'What, kid?'

" 'I want you to know I'm still going to make them forget Tris Speaker.'

"Lefty pulls the car over to the curb. He looks at me and says, 'Kid, you keep playing like that, they're going to forget Lefty Gomez.'"

I treasured my relationship with DiMaggio, and not just because he was one of the heroes of my boyhood. You could say he was moody, surly, difficult, easily offended, whatever, and it might all be true, but he was Joe DiMaggio and he did a very difficult thing—play baseball—with an ease, a grace, and an excellence that have maybe never been matched. His teams always won, or so it seemed, and when the Yankees needed a big hit it was always Joe who came through.

He was extraordinary at holding grudges, too, and when I became the subject of one, I did everything I could to get back in his good graces. It wasn't easy.

When I was commissioner, I had a young man named Rick White running a division called Major League Properties. White was a very skillful, very smart young man, but one day he did something that was neither smart nor skillful: He insulted Joe DiMaggio. DiMaggio was visiting the baseball offices on Park Avenue. He went into the Properties office and met with White. For some reason, during a discussion of licensing some DiMaggio products, White said to him, "You are not doing enough for baseball. You should be more helpful to us."

I know this because about two minutes later, DiMaggio was in my office, saying, "I need to speak to you." I knew from his tone this was not the time to trot out my usual line, "There is always time in the commissioner's life for the Yankee Clipper." This was serious business. He pulled a chair around so that it was on my side of the desk and said, "Your guy upstairs just really insulted me. He said I'm not doing enough for baseball. You can't say that to me. That shows no respect. I am furious, at him and at you, because he's your guy."

I tried to apologize. I said it was a mistake on Rick's part to say that. I said that was not the view of baseball as I ran it. I told Joe he was an enormous asset to baseball and I didn't know what White was talking about. It was pretty futile. He left livid and told me I needed to conduct an investigation. And because he said that, I had to, because if you're the commissioner of baseball and you want to be effective in your job, you cannot afford to have Joe DiMaggio, the Yankee Clipper, mad at you.

My first call was to Rick. He acknowledged DiMaggio had the quotation correct. "He won't give us his permission to license a certain product," White said. It was a situation where baseball wanted something from DiMaggio and DiMaggio wanted something back. I said, "Rick, you can't strong-arm Joe DiMaggio. In the first place, if he goes out and tells a reporter that Major League Baseball is giving him a hard time, you're going to get killed. You can't take on Joe DiMaggio. If you want something from him, you have to do it more subtly. You can't win a fight with Joe DiMaggio. He'll get you fired if he pushes this. So the first thing you have to do is apologize to DiMaggio, which is not easy to do because he's an old tough Sicilian and it's almost inconceivable that you'll get him to accept an apology. There is no forgiveness in that man's church."

Well, DiMaggio simmered down, sort of. He didn't go public with White's quotation. But he said he would have nothing to do with him or his office. In fact, White had a deputy named Frank Simeo, who was in the room when White made his comment, and when Simeo left Major League Baseball to work for the Hall of Fame, DiMaggio stopped going to Cooperstown because Simeo was there. The man was world-class at holding grudges.

Months passed, years passed. I left baseball, White left baseball. More years passed. I'd see DiMaggio from time to time, and I'd always apologize for the White line, but there was very little acceptance from Joe. It was sad for me, because Joe was a hero to me, and even though I knew he was not being fair with me about this issue, fairness wasn't really the issue, because DiMaggio is DiMaggio, he has his ways, and you have to respect them if you want to have a relationship with him, which I did. I had had a relationship with him, it was tremendously gratifying and interesting, and later I did not, and it was frustrating.

DiMaggio and I had a mutual friend, a New York doctor named Rock Positano, a tremendously interesting person, someone who knew everybody, someone genuinely close to Joe. One day I said to Positano, "How can I clear the deck with Joe?" Positano got on the case. He was able to arrange for the three of us to have lunch. We met for lunch in New York, at a restaurant on the East Side Joe (and I) loved called Bravo Gianni.

We sat down for lunch and after just a few minutes DiMaggio said, "Doc, would you excuse the commissioner and me? Maybe you could take a little walk? We have a few things to talk about."

Rock left and DiMaggio said, "You know I like you but I'm still pretty angry about that episode." I went into my routine, for the hundredth time: Joe, I'm your biggest fan, I've always tried to be helpful to you, I have great respect for you, I love being in your company, you and I both loved Bart Giamatti, and so on.

And this time Joe said, "I forgive you. It's over. I wanted to have this meeting so that we could be friends again. And now everything is OK." Positano told me later that in his experience, it was the only time DiMaggio had ever let somebody back into the circle.

Several years later, DiMaggio was dead. Everybody knew his death was coming, but when it happened I still felt a great loss. Joe DiMaggio was a link to my own boyhood, to some of the joys of youth, to some sublime baseball moments. He was a central figure in my years as commissioner of baseball. He was the embodiment of excellence and grace. Of course he was a difficult man. That is not the point. He was Joe DiMaggio, a man I worshiped as a boy, a man who became a friend as an adult. When he died I was back in his good graces and that's one of the reasons I say I've been lucky in my life.

	Lineup: Other Legends
1.	Ralph Branca
2.	Johnny Bench
3.	Bob Feller
4.	Warren Spahn
5.	Stan Musial
6.	Johnny Vander Meer
7.	Hank Greenberg
8.	Ralph Kiner
9.	Johnny Mize

Other Legends

1. RALPH BRANCA

RALPH BRANCA, the old Brooklyn Dodgers pitcher from my boyhood, is today a great friend. We enjoy each other's company and talk almost every day. He is one of the truly "good guys" of baseball and remains very active in a charity dear to me, the Baseball Assistance Team, known as BAT, which helps out all manner of indigent baseball people—there are many of them—in various life struggles. His son-in-law is Bobby Valentine, another good guy and the longtime manager of the New York Mets.

Ralph's done many things well in his life. He was a basketball star at New York University in the 1940s. In 1947, the year Jackie Robinson joined his team, he won twenty-one games as a twenty-one-year-old pitcher for the Brooklyn Dodgers. But he is best known for a single pitch he threw in 1951.

The New York Giants, managed by Leo Durocher, and Charlie Dressen's Brooklyn Dodgers finished the season in a tie for first in the

National League. There was a best-of-three playoff for the National League title and the Dodgers and the Giants split the first two games. The third game, on the afternoon of October 3, was at the Polo Grounds, the Giants' home field, to see who would have the honor of playing the American League champs, the New York Yankees, in Joe DiMaggio's final season. This is why New Yorkers of a certain age, and those who lived within driving distance of the city, are so haughty about New York baseball in that era. That's about as good as it gets.

In the bottom of the ninth inning of the third game, Ralph came in from the bullpen to pitch to Bobby Thomson. There was one out and two on and Charlie Dressen chose Branca to face Thomson, a solid hitter who went from Glasgow, Scotland, to Staten Island, New York, to the Giants. Ralph threw him a good fastball right down the middle for strike one. The next pitch is among the most famous in baseball history: Thomson clubbed Ralph's offering for a three-run home run. Russ Hodges's call: "The Giants win the pennant, the Giants win the pennant. . . ." is still the most famous in baseball history. The Dodgers—Gil Hodges, Duke Snider, Jackie Robinson, Roy Campanella, and Ralph Branca among them—walked off the field in a daze. Their wait for next year had begun. The Giants, naturally, were jubilant. This was in the glory days of New York newspapering, when there were a dozen dailies in the city. Thomson's blast was grandly called "The Shot Heard 'Round the World." It still is.

Many years later, Ralph was a speaker at a dinner. He gave his talk and afterward a boy rose to ask the following question: "Mr. Branca, what pitch did you throw to Mr. Thomson and why?"

"I knew the kid wasn't setting me up," Ralph once told me. "He was a nice kid and he wanted his question answered. So I said, 'Sonny, let me tell you something. I could always get Thomson out with my curveball, low and away. He couldn't hit my curveball. But at that moment for some reason I decided I'd throw him a fastball up and in so the fastball would move him away from the plate and that would set up the next pitch, the curveball low and away, and I'd get him out.' The kid says, 'Thank you very much.'

"Now I'm at the buffet line loading up my plate and I feel a tap on my shoulder. It's Sal Maglie. All he did for those Giants in 1951 was win twenty-three games. 'The Barber,' they called him, because he'd shave you with his pitches. Chin music. Time passes, and Sal and I got to be pals.

"Now it's years later, and he's heard me answer this kid's question. He looks me in the eye and says, 'Dago, if you're going to get him with the fuckin' curveball, throw him the fuckin' curveball.' For the rest of my life, I realized Sal Maglie had it just right."

It's a tremendous strategic lesson. I use it in business talks. Don't fool with an alternative. If you have a good strategy, follow it. Ever since Ralph told me that story, I've been preaching Sal Maglie's sage advice and trying to follow it as well.

A footnote: Years later, the baseball world learned the Giants were using a spyglass in the center-field Giant office to steal the catcher's signs. Thomson knew he was getting a fastball. But he still had to hit it, no small feat. Ralph bore the knowledge of the cheating for years but never talked about it for fear of being seen as a poor loser. In 2001, a half-century after the fact, *The Wall Street Journal* broke the story in fantastic detail. Still, Ralph took the high ground. Another reason I love him.

2. JOHNNY BENCH

I WAS NEVER A FAN of the so-called Big Red Machine, the great Cincinnati Reds teams of the 1970s, led by Pete Rose, Joe Morgan, Johnny Bench, George Foster, Tony Perez, Dave Concepcion, and Ken Griffey, and managed by Sparky Anderson. They played pugnacious baseball, and I was by then a Baltimore Orioles fan living in Washington, D.C. Later, I got to know some of the players individually and liked them very much. George Foster helped coach a local team in Greenwich, Connecticut, near my home, and later helped start the New England Collegiate Baseball League. I've enjoyed listening to Joe Morgan broadcast games. But the player from that group who has made the deepest impression on me is Johnny Bench, the catcher. I admire his playing career, his excellence behind the plate and while standing at it. He is in the tradition of Yogi Berra that way. Bench was a complete player. Off the field, he carried himself with class. He was big-league in every way. I was in Cooperstown when Bench was inducted into the Hall of Fame in 1989. I was deputy baseball commissioner then, grappling with Pete Rose and the mounting evidence that he gambled on baseball. Rose and Bench had a deep bond, because of the success of their Reds teams and because of their standing in the Cincinnati community. They even shared a lawyer, Reuven Katz. But his deepest bond was with the game, and that is why I respect him so. At Cooperstown that summer, somebody asked Bench if Pete Rose should someday be inducted into the Hall of Fame. "Pete Rose should be in the Hall of Fame when he is innocent," Bench answered.

Later, I said to him, "Johnny, you said it all." He said, "I mean it."

He reduced the issue to a single sentence, just as Sal Maglie had done. Bench got the whole debate down to thirteen words. He was able to answer that question so succinctly because he understood the issue innately and believed deeply in the correctness of his position. (No other Red wanted to turn against Rose.) Ballplayers, typically, don't like to be called smart. They prefer the word "crafty." Call it what you will; in my opinion, Bench's answer revealed a certain genius.

3. BOB FELLER

ONE DAY IN 2001, I spent four hours interviewing Bob Feller, the great Cleveland Indians righthander, for an oral history project I'm involved in for the Hall of Fame. We are pals, so this was a four-hour treat. Feller was raised on an Iowa farm by a baseball-loving father who taught him to pitch at a young age. One day, the father was catching the son. The father called for a curveball. The son, barely a teenager, threw a fastball. The father's rib was broken. Soon after, the boy pitcher was signed by the Indians, for whom he pitched from 1936, breaking in at age seventeen, through 1956, except for four seasons in the prime of his career, which he spent on the battleship USS *Alabama* in the Pacific, as a turret gunner, during World War II. He won eight battle stars in the Pacific in nearly four years in the service. He has led an exemplary life.

Feller was signed by the legendary scout Cy Slapnicka, who was eager to show him off to the Indians brass. The Indians were playing an exhibition game against the St. Louis Cardinals in Cleveland. The St. Louis team in those days was known as the Gashouse Gang. Pepper Martin was the third baseman, Leo Durocher was the shortstop, Dizzy Dean was the ace, Ducky Medwick was the leftfielder, and the manager and second baseman was Frankie Frisch. Later, Frisch would take his .316 career batting average to the Hall of Fame; on this day he was facing a teenager he had never heard of, throwing gas the likes of which he had never seen before.

Feller threw two untouchable fastballs past Frisch, who was quickly in the hole, no balls and two strikes. Frisch, the old Fordham Flash, then backed out of the batter's box and headed for the dugout, barking over his shoulder at the umpire: "Fuck this. You hit against that kid. I'm not."

Of the nine hitters he faced, Feller struck out eight. He never pitched in the minors. His legend was born.

4. WARREN SPAHN

THE MOST INTELLIGENT PITCHER I ever met, for pure baseball craftiness, was Warren Spahn. (The smartest hitter I ever met was Williams.) Spahn got most of his 363 wins for the Boston and Milwaukee Braves, he threw a no-hitter as a forty-year-old, he was a tremendous hitter and fielder, and he never threw a pitch without a purpose. He mapped out everything. He said he learned from watching hitters, not other pitchers, and that hitters will tell you what they can hit and what they cannot. He'd come out early to watch other teams take batting practice just to see the hitters show the BP pitcher where they wanted it. In the modern era, Spahn once told me, the only pitcher he saw doing that was Greg Maddux. What a surprise.

Ted Williams thought about hitting the way Spahn did about pitching. They played in different leagues, so Williams and Spahn didn't face each other very often, but when they did it was memorable: the greatest lefthanded hitter of all time facing the greatest lefthanded pitcher of all time. (Koufax fans please note: Sandy was more dominating in his prime than Warren, but his flame, though it burned brightly, burned briefly. Spahn went on and on and on. Only four pitchers—Cy Young, Grover Alexander, Walter Johnson, and Christy Mathewson—have won more games, and don't forget those years lost to war.) Spahn once told me a story I love about matching wits with Williams:

"In the '54 All-Star game, I faced Williams," he said. "I got a couple of strikes on him and threw him a fastball up and in and he missed. I was really pleased with myself. Williams hit lefties, righties, he didn't care. Any time you got him out, it was good stuff.

"The following spring training, we're playing the Red Sox in an exhibition game. I'm out in left field running my sprints and out comes Ted. He comes busting across the field to see me. I'm asking myself, 'What does he want?'

"He says, 'Spahnie, remember what you did to me last year at the All-Star game? That was really a good pitch, up and in. That's a hell of a pitch, with two strikes on a lefthanded hitter. You got to keep using that.'

"Of course I make a note of it. Now it's the next year, 1956. I'm facing him in the All-Star game again. I get two strikes on him. I say to myself, 'He doesn't like that pitch up and in,' so I throw it. Williams hits it about 450 feet. Home run. As he's rounding second base, I yell at him, 'You son of a bitch, you conned me!' He just grinned and nodded his head up and down."

One other Spahn story. In Spahn's first months in the majors, in 1942 with the Boston Braves, his roommate was Paul Waner, also known as Big Poison, older brother of Lloyd Waner, Little Poison, both of whom are in the Hall of Fame. Big Poison was at the tail end of a career in which he would bat .333. One morning, Spahn woke up to see Waner drinking hard liquor, straight from the bottle. No words were spoken.

Soon after, Spahn saw Waner drinking for breakfast again. Waner looked at him and said, "Rook, let's just keep this our little secret. Nobody on the team needs to know about this."

The next time, Waner said this: "Rook, I've got an astigmatism. If I don't have a drink in the morning, I see two balls coming at me and I can't hit either one. If I have a drink, I see just one ball and I can hit the hell out of it."

5. STAN MUSIAL

WHEN BASEBALL FANS of my generation speak of the great mid-twentieth-century hitters, the conversation always turns back to DiMaggio and Williams. Really, it was a threesome of greats: Joe and Ted and Stan the Man. At age forty-one, Stan Musial batted .330. He hit as he fielded and he fielded as he played his beloved harmonica, with all the assuredness in the world. He was a folk hero in the Polish-American community, and had his career played out in New York, he would no doubt be on the same New York pedestal as Gehrig and DiMaggio and Berra and Mantle. But he was a modest man who played all his 3,026 games for the St. Louis Cardinals. Throughout the country's heartland, wherever the powerful waves of KMOX can be heard, Musial remains baseball's truest icon.

I've been fortunate to get to know him. Early one Sunday morning, when I was commissioner, I went to church in Cooperstown during the Hall of Fame induction weekend. It was an 8:00 A.M. Mass. Musial was in the back of the church, sitting with his great friend and former teammate, Red Schoendienst. (I can spell that name from memory because I wrote it so many times as a kid on All-Star ballots, in the days when you filled in the names of your favorite players. Today, of course, you punch a hole on your ballot for a computer to read.) The priest recognized Stan and Red and welcomed them to his church.

After Mass, Schoendienst and Musial stood patiently at the door of the church and signed autographs for every parishioner who wanted one. They must have signed hundreds. I signed a few, too, and as I stood beside them I found myself in awe of their graciousness. I complimented them on it. Musial shrugged and Red said, "It's our pleasure." They're old-school gentlemen.

Several times a year, Eli Jacobs and I organize a baseball dinner for friends in New York. A wide range of people come to the dinner, from academia and business and politics, many of them well known, but on the night of our dinners they have only one purpose: to talk baseball.

At each dinner, there's a special guest, a baseball person whom we honor. One night, Stan was our guest, escorted from St. Louis by my old friend Bucky Bush, brother of George H. W. Bush. In the company of Jerry Levin, George Will, Stephen Jay Gould, Herbert Allen, Tom Brokaw, and other powerful luminaries, Musial's demeanor was exactly as it was at the church that day: gentlemanly, gracious, comfortable with himself.

Musial was a lefthanded hitter with the most unusual crouched, awkward-looking stance baseball has ever seen from a great hitter. He peered over his right shoulder, coiled like a pretzel; how he hit from that position, both for power and for average, is a mystery. At that dinner, I asked: "Did anybody ever try to change your stance, in high school, in American Legion, in grammar school, anywhere?"

I think he was slightly bemused by the question. "Commissioner," he said, "why would they do that? I was always hitting .500."

The wonderful thing about Stan's answer, of course, is that he was dead serious.

6. JOHNNY VANDER MEER

BASEBALL FANS SPEAK of Joe DiMaggio's fifty-six-game hitting streak as the most untouchable baseball record. I'm not so sure. It is, of course, a mighty record; the second-longest hitting streak is the National League record, forty-four games, by Pete Rose. That's not really close. If anybody reaches even forty-six games, the pressure would mount almost exponentially over the final ten games.

There are records, though, that will never be broken. Nobody will ever again win 511 games, as Cy Young did. The game has changed too radically for that to happen. And I don't think anyone will ever again pitch back-to-back no-hitters, as Johnny Vander Meer did for the Cincinnati Reds in 1938, his second season in the bigs. The first was a 3–0 victory over the Boston Braves on June 11; the second was four days later, a 6–0 win over the Brooklyn Dodgers in the first night game ever played at Ebbets Field. It is one thing for a fire-throwing closer to pitch eighteen consecutive hitless innings. It is another for a starter to do it in back-to-back starts.

Vander Meer, of course, did other things in his life. He was a young man, just twenty-three years old, when he became The Dutch Master, Mr. Double No-Hit. But until the day he died, and in his every obituary, that's what he was known for and that's what he was known as. He was the man who threw consecutive no-hitters. It is a baseball feat of the highest order.

I met Vander Meer only once, at a BAT dinner in the late 1990s. He was an old man, about eighty, rail-thin but still tall. He told me his health was poor but he didn't have to. He was wearing a dark suit and smoking. He looked tired. But I was thrilled to be with him and to think about how dominating he had been one June week sixty years earlier, and to wonder what it must be like to carry such an accomplishment around with you for the rest of your days.

We chatted. I asked him what he remembered best from the second game. He said, "The Brooklyn fans. Toward the end, they were standing and cheering for me. They were on my side. They were hoping I'd get it. I'll never forget that."

I was touched by what he'd said. I asked him to sign a ball for me. He seemed pleased to be asked, proud to be recognized for his unique achievement. He died a few years later. I wished I had asked him about the next game. There were many things I wish I had asked him. It was just a brief visit, too brief. But I'll never forget it.

7. HANK GREENBERG

WHEN I BECAME commissioner of baseball, my first move was to hire Steve Greenberg as my deputy. It was also my best move. Steve, one of my closest friends today, had an extraordinary baseball pedigree: He was a star baseball (and soccer) player at Yale; he played minor-league baseball, rising to AAA ball; he was a well-respected lawyer and agent to a number of players; and his father was Hank Greenberg, the Detroit Tigers slugger and Hall of Famer who helped diminish American anti-Semitism and raise Jewish pride with every swing he took through the 1930s and '40s.

Hank Greenberg, the son of Orthodox Jews, was living proof to millions of first- and second-generation American Jews that a Jew could be faithful to his religion and be accepted by Christian America. He was proof that no profession was off-limits to Jews, even big-league baseball. He was among the first major leaguers to serve in World War II, which took nearly five seasons off his career but added immeasurably to his status as a hero. He did not play on Yom Kippur, the holiest day in the Jewish calendar. To American Jews, he could do no wrong.

From early 1942 through July 1945 he was an Air Corps officer in China and India, in charge of a B-29 bomber squadron. In other words, he wasn't there to rally the troops, he was there to lead. He returned to baseball in midseason as an Air Corps captain, then helped his team win the American League pennant and the World Series.

For many Americans, Greenberg represented a window into Jewish life. In 1938, he was hitting home runs at a record-breaking pace, trying to pass Babe Ruth's single-season mark for homers, 60. With five games left in the season, Greenberg had 58 homers, but then he got stuck. It was widely reported that Greenberg's mother—in a scenario likely conjured up by creative newspapermen—offered to make him 61 baseball-shaped servings of gefilte fish if he reached 61. That may not have been the best incentive. He finished the season with 58 after facing Bob Feller in Cleveland on the last day of the season without being able to catch up with that great fastball.

In the fall of 1934, the Tigers were trying to secure the American League pennant when a question arose: Would Greenberg play on Yom Kippur? In those days, particularly, many Jews chose not to be conspicuous about their religion. Many Jews changed their names to more Anglo-sounding names. If Greenberg didn't play and the Tigers lost, it would be bad for the Jews, many Jews said. Others said if Greenberg did play that would be worse. Debate raged.

Greenberg did not play. Detroit lost. And the country saluted him. A little newspaper ditty of the time, written by Edgar Guest, went, "Said Murphy to Mulrooney, 'We shall lose the game today! We shall miss him in the infield and shall miss him at the bat. But he's true to his religion—and I honor him for that!' " It helped that the Tigers, led by Greenberg, still won the AL pennant (but lost the World Series to the Gashouse Gang Cardinals). From then on, Greenberg was a mainstay of Yom Kippur sermons across the country, until Sandy Koufax chose God over the World Series on Yom Kippur, 1965.

I admired Hank Greenberg as a boy. I grew up knowing the legend of the man. He was an important symbol to all manner of observant baseball fans and I was a church-going Catholic. It was not until middle-age that I learned there was more to the story. There always is.

"My father got a lot of credit," Steve Greenberg told me once.

"How so?" I asked.

"For being so religious. The fact is, he was not religious at all. He didn't go to temple on Yom Kippur. When my brother and sister and I were young, he'd take us to the park or a museum on Yom Kippur, but never to a synagogue. That was not something he did."

Nobody knew that. The country didn't know the details of Hank Greenberg's spiritual life. What we knew was that he was not afraid to stand up and be counted, and that was more than enough.

8. RALPH KINER

HANK GREENBERG SPENT the final season of his career with the awful 1947 Pittsburgh Pirates, who tried to make Greenberg a gate attraction by building a short porch—a bullpen, actually—in left field at Forbes Field called Greenberg's Garden. Greenberg befriended a young, powerful righthanded-hitting outfielder named Ralph Kiner, and when Greenberg retired Kiner took over as the Pirates' main gate attraction. The Garden was renamed for the kid: Kiner's Korner. Kiner became a spectacular home-run hitter—in the first hundred years of baseball history only Babe Ruth hit homers at a faster pace—and after he retired as a player he became a Mets broadcaster for the original '62 team, and still holds that job forty years later. We live in the same town, in Greenwich, Connecticut. He's famous for his so-called Kinerisms. He comes out with some gems, including, "We'll be right back with Mets baseball right after this season is over." But I think he's a very good announcer because he's unpretentious and he knows the game. For years he conducted a postgame star-of-the-game interview program called Kiner's Korner. The player would receive a gift for being on the show, maybe a watch, if he was lucky, and was treated to

benign opening questions, such as, "How heavy is your bat?" Whenever I was on his show, we talked cigars first, baseball second. I love
the guy.

The night before new players are inducted into the Hall of Fame,
the baseball commissioner is the host of a dinner at the Otesaga Hotel
for all living Hall of Famers and the new inductees. You might have
forty men at the dinner and it's quite a fraternity. There's one long
U-shaped table and the commissioner sits at the bottom of the U, able
to see everything. Everyone sits on the outside of the table. One year,
out of the corner of my eye, I saw Kiner and Johnny Mize having an
animated conversation. Suddenly, they stood up and started making
phantom swings of the bat. Kiner from the right side of a make-believe
plate, Mize from the left. In 1947, each hit fifty-one home runs, tying
for the National League title. Maybe they were each trying to get in a
few more swings from that season. Whatever they were doing, it was a
sight, for neither of them had taken a swing at a live pitch, a game
swing, in nearly forty years. Yet here they were, two men in their seventies, still at it, even if their home plate was now a dinner plate.

After the dinner, I asked: "Ralph, may I ask you a question? I'm cu-
rious to know what you and Johnny were doing during the dinner.
Were you working on your swings for the great game in the sky?"

"Commissioner, I've admired Johnny Mize all my life because he
could hit inside fastballs to the opposite field and I could never do
that," Ralph said. "So during dinner, I asked: 'Johnny, how do you do
that?' And, as you know, he's always got an answer, on any hitting question he's always got something interesting to say. He told me:
'Righthanded hitter like you, you got to drop your left elbow way down
against your ribs and move your hands so you inside-out your swing.
But mostly you got to get that elbow down.' I don't know if I could have
done it but he really could and at least now I know how he did it."

The great ones never stop asking questions.

9. JOHNNY MIZE

JOHNNY MIZE was a great big southern country boy with a gorgeous,
smooth swing and drawl to match. He was born in Demorest, Georgia,

in 1913—born, I'd almost bet, talking. He was a Hall of Fame hitter and a Hall of Fame talker, although he wasn't enshrined in Cooperstown until 1981, twenty-eight years after he stopped playing, elected by the Veterans Committee. He had an extraordinary career. In nine of his first ten seasons, he batted over .300 and hit twenty-five or more homers seven times, but never played in a World Series. Then in his last five seasons he never batted better than .277, never hit more than 25 homers, but played in the World Series in five straight Octobers, from 1949 through 1953. That, of course, was because, after a decade with the St. Louis Cardinals and the New York Giants, he was a Yankee for those final five seasons. DiMaggio was his teammate for three of those seasons. Mize was as chatty as DiMaggio was reserved, but they were both students of hitting.

In his days as a Giant, Mize roomed with Bill Rigney, a light-hitting infielder, later a longtime manager. Rigney knew firsthand there was a shrewdness in his roomie that his country ways belied.

"One morning in Pittsburgh I wake up and I see Johnny looking out the hotel window," Bill Rigney once told me. "And I say, 'What are you looking at, big guy?'

" 'The flag over there.'

"Now usually he's got more to say than that, but he's just studying. I say, 'Now why would you be doing that?'

" 'Wind'll be blowing in from right today, Rig, no pulling the ball today, too tough. Have to go the other way today.' "

At that, of course—as Ralph Kiner and every smart National League pitcher knew—Johnny Mize was an expert.

Football takes brawn and basketball takes speed and hockey takes some of both. But baseball, in my opinion, is the best of the four big American sports, the best of all games, because it truly is a thinking person's game. I always knew its best fans were smart. When I got to know the players, I found the game's best performers were smarter yet. You can play it without either brawn or speed. The best play it with brains.

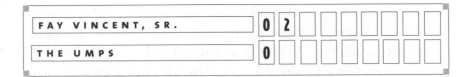

| FAY VINCENT, SR. | 0 | 2 | | | | | | | |
| THE UMPS | 0 | | | | | | | | |

C H A P T E R T W O

Fay Vincent, Sr.

BASEBALL IS PART of my genetic code. On the day I was born, my father was playing in a Connecticut baseball circuit called the Waterbury City Amateur League. They played quality baseball in that league, with many good college players along with some aspiring pros, some former pros, and men like my father. Spec Shea, the Yankee pitcher who was from nearby Naugatuck, played in that league. Later, Jimmy Piersall, the Red Sox centerfielder, played in the league. He was from Waterbury. He was a legend: the local boy who made it to the Red Sox. But my father, in certain neighborhoods and certain towns, was legendary too.

The City Amateur League was amateur in name only. The players, the good ones, were paid a few dollars a game, and that's why my father never missed one. He grew up with nothing, lived through the Great Depression, understood the value of a dollar as well as anybody I've ever known. There's a longtime *New York Times* reporter named Frank Litsky who was a batboy in that league. Litsky says my father was a generous man who gave him a dollar per game. I believe Litsky's memory is generous: a quarter, maybe, but not a dollar. He played on every occasion and in every league he could, inspired by the love of the game and the desire to be paid to play it. When he could make a few bucks playing ball, that went a long way toward paying the bills.

He started playing as a "professional" amateur in college, in violation of the collegiate rules for amateurism, but in that era there was widespread winking at some of the rules. He played first base, a solid fielder and a superb fastball hitter. Always, he hit fourth. Sometimes I think my memory is playing tricks on me, making his baseball accomplishments grander in my mind than they were. But the newspaper clippings I have from his playing days set me straight. He was class of '31 from Yale; he loved to read, about the Civil War and other history in particular, but his skill in football and baseball was what got him there. Money was tight and baseball helped pay for his books. There was a big mental hospital in upstate New York on Route 22 in Wingdale, New York, and the superintendent there was intent on sponsoring a winning baseball team, to provide entertainment for his patients on Sunday afternoons. So he recruited my father and other good ballplayers and paid them as much as five dollars a game to play under assumed names. The superintendent had a rule: If you went hitless for two consecutive Sundays, you weren't invited back. I once asked my father, "Did you ever get dropped?"

"Why would I do that?" he responded. "I needed that money. I got my hits." Years later, when I would play with him, long past his prime, he still got his hits. I rarely did. My mother was sympathetic. "He could *always* hit. He'd hit them right over third."

In Waterbury, during the Depression years, much of the city would show up for the City Amateur League games, filling Hamilton Park for cheap, good sporting entertainment. My father played for a team called the Tribunes, and one year he won the batting title, hitting .579. To mark this accomplishment he was given a gold Hamilton watch. That watch eventually came to me and I cherished it for years until one day, as a young New York lawyer, I fell down the steps of the subway station at Eighty-sixth and Lexington, on the Upper East Side of Manhattan. The watch strap broke, and in the commotion I didn't realize the watch was missing. My father's batting average was right on the back of that watch, and that gaudy statistic—.579—lingers in my memory still.

My father, like most fathers of that era, had high hopes for my baseball career. He started playing catch with me, with a real baseball, at an early age, probably five or six. He started me in football young, too. We lived in New Haven so Yale was nearby and I never missed an Eli game.

He loved both sports. He had been the captain of the baseball and football teams at Yale. He thought of football as work, as a hard game; baseball was a sublime pleasure, played in the loveliest time of year. Baseball was challenging and subtle. Football was about strength and speed. In their seasons, he thought both were great games, but he'd say, "When you practice football, you hate it. When you practice baseball, you love it. Practicing baseball is almost as much fun as playing baseball." No one could say that of football.

His team was the Philadelphia Athletics. Their manager was Connie Mack, who had once managed in Connecticut. My dad grew up rooting for the Irishman from his area. He could get the A's on the radio, in good weather, and on many summer nights he'd sit on our screened front porch with a cigar glowing in the dark listening to the game. I'd sit with him. I still remember the static from the broadcasts—my father ignored it—and the names from those A's teams of the late 1940s, managed by Mack: Fain, Suder, Joost, Majeski, going around the infield; Barney McCosky in left, Sam Chapman in center, Elmer Valo in right, always running into the outfield wall. The postwar A's were a pretty good team, though never able to beat the Yankees. When we went to Yankee Stadium, it was always for a doubleheader and it was always when the A's were in town. I can still see Connie Mack in my mind's eye, sitting in the dugout, lineup card in his hand, wearing a dark suit and tie and a stiff collar. Once, I got Mack's autograph. The Yankees always won and they were my team, much to my father's chagrin. When a Yankee homered, Bill "Bojangles" Robinson would jump up on the Yankee dugout and do a tap dance. I can still remember my first glimpse of the Stadium: the stark white of the home uniforms, the dark green grass, the deep blue sky, the heat shimmering off the field, the brightness of it all after emerging from the dark of the tunnel.

My father's father, Henry, had been a factory worker and occasional trolley car conductor in Torrington, Connecticut. His mother died when my father was nine years old. My father had one older brother, called Bunny, who died at nineteen from a burst appendix and bungled medical care. My father grew up poor. They had a small rented flat with no hot water and no plumbing. Henry Vincent worked six and a half days a week in the hardscrabble towns in the Naugatuck Valley, where there were numerous factories that prospered in good times, war times most particularly, and stagnated in bad. Torrington was heavily Irish-Catholic. Sports were played to win and at a high level. My father was a football and baseball star at Torrington High, but he never dreamed his skills at games would change his life. Like all his pals, his expectation was to go to high school, play his sports, and get a job in one of the metal shops like American Brass that dominated the town. There wasn't then the sense of movement and mobility there is in today's world.

Twenty-five miles and a world away from Torrington was a boys' prep school called Hotchkiss, in the idyllic village of Lakeville. Hotchkiss knew about Torrington and Torrington knew about Hotchkiss chiefly because of one man, Otto F. Monahan, the Hotchkiss athletic director. Once a year, Monahan would come to Torrington High and find one or two kids who excelled at football and baseball. He'd interview them, ask around about them, talk to the parents, and see if they were interested in attending Hotchkiss on scholarship. This was a well-known tradition in Torrington. Monahan wanted Torrington kids who could have a real impact on the Hotchkiss baseball and football teams, but the school also wanted to make an impact on the kids from Torrington, give them a chance they wouldn't have otherwise. A few years ahead of my father, Raymond "Ducky" Pond went from Torrington to Hotchkiss to Yale, where he later became the head football coach and hired as one of his assistants a Yale Law School student named Gerald Ford. When Ford became president in 1974, he promptly invited Pond to the White House. All of Torrington rejoiced.

My father was well aware of the Torrington-Hotchkiss connection, but I don't think attending Hotchkiss was ever his dream. For one thing, although as an adult he became a great reader of history, he was not studious as a boy. For another thing, going to boarding school would have meant leaving his father entirely alone. But a Torrington boy at Hotchkiss, Johnny Hoben, recommended my father to Monahan, and one day Monahan approached my father after a game: "Would you be interested in going to Hotchkiss? I can promise you it won't cost you a thing. It won't be easy, either. But if you keep your nose clean and behave as a gentleman, we'll get you a free ride through Hotchkiss and Yale."

As my father told the story, the real hero in this was his father. Henry Vincent could easily have said, "No, I need you to stay here and help me." Instead he said, "Go, fine—just don't ask me for help. I don't have a thing to give you." This was an act of great generosity on my grandfather's part. As I say, it was a different time.

At Torrington High, my father had been in the commercial classes. Now he took the Hotchkiss entrance examination. He scored a 16 out of 100 on the Latin exam. He scored a 25 in English. They told him not to be discouraged. They had a solution. Instead of entering Hotchkiss as a senior, he would enter as a sophomore, which at Hotchkiss is called the lower-mid year. This had the added benefit, for Hotchkiss, of getting two more years of a big, strong, experienced, talented athlete. For my father, the extra years allowed him to develop academically.

In those days, there was a class distinction between the scholarship boys and the other boys. His first year, my father lived in the village of Lakeville, in a house that rented rooms to scholarship boys. He walked a mile up the hill to school, worked in the dining room, played his sports, studied diligently, and loved it, all of it. Having three prepared meals a day and a bed with fresh sheets represented a vast improvement over life at home. There was some anti-Catholic bias at Hotchkiss. He put up with it. Some of the boys were rich-kid snobs. He endured them. He was two years older than most of the kids in his class, twenty when he graduated in 1927. He dealt with the age difference. He knew he was getting the chance of a lifetime, and he was grateful.

He got into Yale without a problem. Because of his sports prowess, and because of the Hotchkiss-Yale connection, the admissions path was smoothed for him. For the rest of his life, he remained grateful to Otto Monahan, his baseball and football coach. The feeling, I think, was mutual. Monahan was asked once to name the greatest athletes he had in forty years at Hotchkiss. As tackles, he named my father and another Yale great named Ted Blair. Whenever my father returned to Hotchkiss, he visited Monahan's gravesite and stood quietly in prayer. He was loyal.

Because he was the captain of the football and baseball teams at Yale, he was elected to Skull and Bones, the elite senior honor society. He struggled in the classroom, but he managed. He had problems in chemistry but was given a tutor, a little Jewish man who lived on Chapel Street in New Haven and taught generations of Yale athletes how to balance complex chemical equations. My father made it through chemistry, and all his other classes. His major was economics, and through his studies he developed a lifelong interest in finance and the stock market, an interest I inherited from my father, along with a batting stance.

My father still has the Yale baseball record for triples in a single season, seven, which tells you he could hit and he could run. His football exploits are probably better known, because Yale was a national power in football in those days and he was an honorable mention All-America as a senior, in 1930. He played in the East-West game that year and in the famous Army-Yale game of 1929, at the Yale Bowl. There were eighty-thousand people there, in the waning days of the Jazz Age. Both teams were very good. My father was a junior then, playing tackle on offense and defense. West Point, led by Chris Cagle, a superb halfback, built up a big lead. Then Albie Booth came in for Yale—Little Boy Blue, as he was called later. This was his first collegiate game. Booth scored three touchdowns and kicked three extra points and the legend began. One of Booth's touchdowns was a spectacular punt return and my father made the key block right in front of the Army bench. Yale won, of course. That game was on newsreels, in magazines, all over the newspapers. Howard Cosell kept the memory of that game alive for years, mentioning it often during his telecasts. It remains one of the most famous games in college football history.

As an undergraduate, my father got to know a man named Richard Joyce Smith, a law professor at Yale, a board member at Connecticut Light and Power, an Irishman, and a football fan. He and my father became friends. My father would get Smith tickets, as many as he needed, for the big games, against Army, against Harvard, excellent seats, right on the fifty-yard-line. And when my father graduated from Yale, he turned to Smith for a job. The Depression was on. It was miserable. There were no good jobs, even for celebrated Yale athletes. He got a job digging holes for electric light poles for Connecticut Light and Power. The fact that he was doing physical work, despite having a Yale degree, didn't bother my father; he was happy to have a job, and he knew the utilities rarely laid off employees. Eventually, he moved into the office. Later, in 1941, he took a job with another utility, the New England Telephone Company, in New Haven. He earned a living; he had job security. That was critical to him.

But his heart was always in sports, and when he could no longer play he took to officiating, both in football and in baseball. He worked NFL games starting in 1940. He worked college, high-school, and prep-school baseball games. He'd work any game he could, doubling his salary some weeks with his weekend work. In football, he was a superb official because he took it seriously, stayed in great shape, and could run. He was less good in baseball because he was not, as he put it, a good "plate man." It was from my father I learned how dedicated sports officials are and how badly they can be treated.

In some ways, he was way ahead of his time. He ran, as an adult, for exercise at a time when nobody did that. He'd run around our neighborhood, and he'd run through the local cemetery. The police would stop him, because people who ran at night were criminals. He'd come home, sweating and happy, and he'd say, "Cops stopped me again." In time, of course, they came to know him: Fay Vincent, the old guy who runs at night!

He was frugal, exceptionally so. That, of course, was a product of his childhood poverty and the Depression. For years and years, he would not buy a car. He walked or rode his bike, or took the bus. A car to him was a waste of money. "The most expensive thing you can own," he said. One Saturday he went into downtown New Haven, way down near the train station, five miles or so from our house, to a furniture store to buy a rocking chair for my mother for her birthday, which was the following day. But the store would not deliver the chair to our house until Monday. My father became upset.

"But her birthday is tomorrow!" he said.

"We're sorry, Mr. Vincent," the clerk said.

"Fine," he said. "Give me the chair." He hoisted the chair on his back and carried it all the way home, five miles. When my mother found out, she was appalled: "Everyone knows you all along the way. Now they know you're crazy." But of course she was proud of him, for his devotion to her, for his refusal to let anything stand in his way.

One day he was biking over to one of the Yale fields, to umpire a soft-ball game. He was dressed in his usual attire: tattered pants, old sneakers, forty-year-old Yale baseball cap. He's biking through a wealthy New Haven neighborhood, Westville, and he comes upon an old gent struggling with an air-conditioner lodged in the trunk of his car. The man stops my father and says, "Hey, could you help me?" He figured my father was a bum, a big strong bum maybe, but a bum. My father says, "Sure." He lugs the air-conditioner up to the second floor of the house, installs it, and on his way out the man hands him a dollar bill. My father loved telling that story, the story of how he managed to make a buck, literally, on his way to a ballgame. He saved the dollar bill as a memento.

For most of my first twelve years, my family—my mother and father, my two younger sisters, and I—lived in a rented house on Orange Street in New Haven. It was a three-story house and we had the first floor: three bedrooms, a living room, kitchen, dining room, and bathroom. Orange Street had a bus line and my father could ride to his office when he chose not to walk. The bus line was owned by Abe Podoloff, the first commissioner of the NBA, who lived two houses down. No one paid any attention; in those days, the NBA was way down from baseball in popularity.

My father was saving his pennies and my mother was teaching, so we might have afforded a house—we surely could have bought a car— but my father was just too cautious. He liked his money in the bank. He didn't incur big expenses; he never borrowed. He preached: "Save your money. Your dollar is your best friend."

We were happy where we were. We had a nice house in an interesting, mixed neighborhood. We had young Yale faculty members living near us, Jewish businessmen, including Podoloff, all manner of people. It was an ethnic stew: Irish, Italian, Polish, Jewish, Greek, although no blacks in those days. People got along, for the most part. The local school, Worthington Hooker, was superb and my parents wanted to be near it. There were corner bars, called "gin mills," and corner stores: a good place to grow up. Crime happened in other places. There were cops on motorcycles and we kids loved them.

My father often sent me to the store, owned by an old Greek named Nick Zarkos, to buy cigars, two at a time. He smoked a locally made cigar called Moneymaker. It was not an expensive cigar. Sales tax in those days began at twenty cents. The cigars were ten cents each. I was under strict instructions: buy one cigar, give Mr. Zarkos a dime, then buy the second cigar and give him the second dime. No tax on those sales. Zarkos was on to me early on: "Give me the twenty cents, I'll give you the two cigars," he'd say. I'd come home, a little embarrassed, and tell my father what the old Greek man had said. "Never mind," he'd say. "That penny's as good to me as it is to the state of Connecticut!"

When it came to money, he loved to tell the story of the Yale boxing coach, a tiny Jewish man named Moses King. Moses King dressed in old clothes, and he went everywhere by bike. The old Yalies pitied him. My father gave him his old sweaters because he knew Moses King would never buy his own. One day my father came home and said, "You won't believe what happened. You know who died? Moses King.

And you know what they found when they went looking around his apartment? Money. Stacks and stacks of bills, stacks of stock certificates. He could buy all of us." Moses King was my father's ideal: Live simply; flout nothing; save your money.

At Hotchkiss, my father picked up on the importance of having well-shined shoes. He was convinced that if your shoes were well-shined you were a gentleman and then it didn't matter what else you wore.

He was always looking for a bargain. If somebody gave him a good deal on a piece of cloth from one of the woolen mills in nearby Rockville, he'd have a suit made, a three-piece suit, by a tailor in Waterbury. The suit might end up costing more than if he had just gone out and bought a suit on sale at one of the New Haven department stores, but he didn't see it that way; he'd remember the deal he got on the piece of cloth. That's what brought him satisfaction. He was tight, but consistent. I admired him for that and am much like him.

Unlike a lot of people who came through the Depression, he believed in the stock market. He believed that owning stocks, owning pieces of American corporations, was the way to build wealth. He would buy stock in companies he had a feel for, as long as they paid a dividend. One of his stocks was Peter Paul, the candy manufacturers based in Naugatuck, Connecticut. Later Peter Paul became part of Cadbury Schweppes. Peter and Paul were two Armenian brothers, Peter and Paul Tatijian, who made Almond Joys and Mounds. At Christmas, they gave a box of candy to each shareholder. My father— trying, as usual, to outsmart the system—had shares registered in every name he could come up with: Francis T. Vincent, Sr., and Fay Vincent, Sr., for him. Alice Lynch Vincent and Alice Vincent for my mother. Francis T. Vincent, Jr., and Fay Vincent, Jr., for me. Joanna Vincent for my sister Joanna, and Susie Vincent, Joanna's nickname. Then more stock in my other sister's name, Barbara. Every name in which he bought stock represented a box of free candy at Christmas, and that delighted him. He'd show up at the annual meeting and say, "Remember to keep sending out those Christmas candies."

His frugality knew no bounds. He never had a checking account, because each check cost money. He paid his bills with his small dividend checks. If he received a fourteen-dollar dividend check from Kodak, he'd walk it down to Connecticut Light and Power and pay his thirteen-dollar bill with it and have a one-dollar credit. He'd walk miles paying his bills, all over town. By walking, he could avoid using stamps, which was a great incentive. It also helped keep him in wonderful shape.

Officiating was his great love. The one sadness in his life was that he couldn't make a living as a full-time official. He would have loved to be a major-league umpire, but he said his eye wasn't good enough for that. He admired big-league umps, particularly their ability not to blink when a bat was swung in their faces.

On Thanksgiving, he'd work two high-school football games, one at 10:00 A.M. in Waterbury and the other at 2:00 P.M. in Ansonia. My mother would say, "How can we have a Thanksgiving dinner if you're out all day?" He'd answer, "Eat without me." She'd say, "I'm not doing that, we're a family." She felt he led the life of a bachelor. It was fine for me, because I'd go wherever he had a game and often hold the down marker for him. But it was hard on my mother and my sisters. They knew they were loved. He just wasn't around that much. Football was a high priority for him.

He would work softball games at Blake Field in New Haven, where occasionally the teams would be virtually all black. My father was sometimes the only white man on the field. One day he made a tough call, as he would put it, in a Blake Field game, as all umpires are apt to do from time to time, and a group of players started hounding him. He just kept walking; he didn't believe in arguing with anyone. The offended players were calling him names and at one point he had heard enough. He turned around, put his hands on his hips, and said, "Go peddle your papers." To him that was the ultimate put-down. I started out toward him, just so he wouldn't be out there by himself. He was curt. "Leave me alone," he said. "I don't need help. I can handle this." And he could.

One of my father's favorite stories about his officiating came from a day he worked a high-school football game in Waterbury. A local schoolboy football hero returned a punt some ninety yards for a touchdown, but my father called it back because of a clipping penalty on the boy's team. In the stands a fan went crazy, yelling insults and turning vile. My father endured the abuse for the rest of the game. "Hey, ref," the middle-aged fan said when the game was over. "Don't be upset. It was my son who clipped and I was just standing up for him." My father looked the man in the eye and said, "Have a nice day."

Our annual trips to Yankee Stadium were special. We'd get tickets, not great ones but good ones, from a Yankee official my father knew, Jack White, who was from Connecticut. We'd arrive before the gates opened and we'd see all of batting practice. This was in the glory years for New York baseball, the late forties and the early fifties, when the Brooklyn Dodgers and the New York Yankees and Giants were all in their prime. He was as interested in watching the umpires as he was in the players. He was fascinated by the intricacies of the game. He'd say to me, "Watch the first baseman. Watch his feet on wide throws. He won't cross one foot over the other." He never had a great arm himself, and one of his favorite things was to watch a rightfielder throw a clothesline one-hopper to third. "That," he would say, "takes skill." He enjoyed watching Yogi Berra hit, even though Berra was a Yankee. He'd say, "Yogi looks like nothing up there, but wait 'til he gets a fastball. You can't throw a fastball by him."

He admired all the little things done well, because he knew it's the little things done well that make a good baseball team good. He'd say, "Watch the coach hitting fungoes. He can hit them anywhere he wants, straight up in the air if he wants." He admired control, in all things.

I was a pitcher. He'd say to me, "Watch the catcher. See the way the catcher throws the ball back to the pitcher so he never has to bend over or reach? That's the catcher doing his job, hitting the pitcher right in the letters."

Sometime, just about as I was entering Hotchkiss, we got our first TV, the one my father won in the St. Stanislaus church raffle. We'd watch baseball on TV together. Eventually, he bought a car and later a house. But he was frugal right to the end—not miserly, just careful.

He was generous, too, but never wasteful. When he retired, he contin-ued to work part-time, in a bank, just so he would have a place to go, a place to which he could walk. In the early eighties, when he was in his late seventies, he developed prostate cancer. He had already been a widower for a decade and then some; my mother had died in 1967, at the age of sixty-two. She took care of everybody else, but not herself. After she died, my father didn't retire from the world, as some men do. He kept busy. He was always doing things around the house. On the day he died, he was up on a ladder, painting the second story of his house. He grew tired, came in, sat on his favorite chair, had a heart attack, and died. He was seventy-eight. He was heading for some bad times. His death was surely a blessing; it was time to go and he knew it.

Naturally, just like his hero, Moses King, he died rather well off. He left an immense imprint not only on me, but on my two sisters as well: Joanna, a doctor, and Barbara, a teacher and librarian. (They are part of that socially active, progressive Catholic tradition that came of age in the 1960s, when helping the less fortunate was a core value.) When Joanna was a young doctor, my father would bid her off to work each morning with the same injunction: "Help some poor person today and don't charge him." And that's exactly what she did. My father was a Re-publican, went to Hotchkiss with boys from some of the richest fami-lies in the country. He was a Yalie. He was Skull and Bones. But at his core he knew he was the son of a working man and he never forgot the tough, corrosive world of the working poor: the inept medical atten-tion his brother received; the scarcity of fresh milk, the struggle to launder bedsheets regularly. He was a man who was comfortable in his own skin, whose motto was, "To thine own self be true." He remained true to his real self all the days of his life. To me, he was a true hero.

Near the end of his life, I was able to bring my father to a game at Shea. My friend Herbert Allen had a box right behind the visitors' dugout, and I took my father and my two boys. I'm sure they were the best seats my father ever had. The day was beautiful and sunny. I had no idea, of course, I would someday become commissioner. The thought would have never entered my head. I was just a fan, like my father, like my boys. I loved the game. I "caught" a foul pop hit by Rusty Staub (actually I picked it up when it fell at my feet) and my father got a big kick out of that—the ultimate souvenir, and free. (My son Bill has that souvenir today.) Terry Tata was the home-plate umpire and my father knew a relative of Tata's, Augie Guglielmo from Waterbury, who years earlier had been a National League umpire. My father watched Tata carefully, studying how Tata worked the plate and his game. Tata was good and it was an easy game and my father was filled with praise. Later, when I became commissioner, I got to know Tata and told him of my father's interest in his work in that game. Tata said, "Your father was thinking like an umpire." To an umpire, an easy game behind the plate is one in which there is no trouble, few complaints, no confrontation. Easy. Tata had my father exactly correct: He was always thinking like an umpire. He was always thinking about fair and foul, about making the correct call. A good way to go through life.

When my father died, Bart Giamatti came to the funeral. He was then the president of Yale and I was the president of Columbia Pictures and we were friends. He said, "When the last of your parents dies, you feel particularly pained because that is the end of the line. There is no longer anyone left between you and eternity." It was a sad, wonderful, truthful insight. I think Bart understood how close I was to my father. He had the same closeness to his father. That was one of the many things we shared.

o   o   o

I INHERITED MY FATHER's love of football and baseball (though not his skill in either sport), and I inherited his prep school, too. I was a good pitcher—as a boy I was big and strong and my fastball had some heat. Hitting the fastball was another matter. Hitting a good curve was out of the question. I played American Legion ball and some at Hotchkiss, but I didn't have the skill to play college baseball. I wasn't even good enough to dream. I remember once Ethan Allen, the Yale coach—a former big-leaguer with a thirteen-year career and a .300 lifetime batting average—pulling me aside. "Vincent, you will never hit because you keep moving your back foot," he said. "The pitcher releases the ball and your back foot dances. You've got dancing feet." My father said pretty much the same thing. "What the hell is the matter with you? I don't understand it. You just stand in there, get a good pitch, and hit it." If only it were that easy.

Sports at Hotchkiss weren't genteel—we played to win—but we were expected to behave like gentlemen. The headmaster was an imposing and inspiring man named George Van Santvoord—nicknamed "the Duke"—who had little interest in baseball but attended the games anyhow, because he knew there were lessons being taught there. Van Santvoord would not abide profanity. One game, a Hotchkiss player slid hard into third and broke his leg. He let loose a string of profanity. He was carried off to the infirmary and treated. Later that night, the Duke came to see him.

"I'm sorry about my language, sir," the boy said.

Van Santvoord was a beekeeper, among many other things. He pulled a jar of honey from behind his back.

"Here," he said. "Perhaps this will sweeten your tongue."

Football at Hotchkiss came easier to me than baseball. I was big and strong and better at football. I could not hit a baseball, not well, not consistently. (That explains some of my awe for DiMaggio.) My father could seldom come to games, because he was nearly always umpiring or officiating. But he came when he could, and maybe in watching me he saw a little of himself on the gridiron. At one game, he was cheering lustily for me, using my in-house nickname, which was Oscar. Mrs. Bush, the mother of the first President Bush and of my dear pal Bucky Bush, turned to him and said, "It must be so nice to have two boys at Hotchkiss, Oscar and Fay."

I took the name Fay from my father. We were both named Francis, for St. Francis, and I became "Little Fay" despite being six-three and 230 pounds at age fourteen. He claimed that every Irish boy in Torrington with the given name Francis was called Fay, but in my life I've only met one other Francis nicknamed Fay. It was a hardship to have a girl's name as a nickname. I was teased. I had a big head, a big body, and a girl's name. My mother, Alice, a reader, a quiet and wonderful and supportive mother, showed her spine when I complained about the size of my head or my nickname. "You may have a big head, but it's filled with brains," she'd say. "If someone calls you Miss Fay Vincent, smack them right in the mouth." I did, and it worked.

I could have gone to Yale after Hotchkiss; I was a good student and a decent football player and there was a pipeline between the two schools. But I decided after high school to make my first break from my father, with some encouragement.

One day in my last year at Hotchkiss, some friends and I were asked by our football coach, a Williams graduate, to drive up to Williams and have a look around. I met the coach, a charming old-timer named Len Watters.

"Are you going to Yale?" he asked.

"I think so," I said.

"Why do that?" he wondered. "If you go to Yale, you'll be competing with the legend of your father. Every year, he gets better. He's greater now than he ever was."

Watters was smart. He saw me, how big I was, and he knew I could help him. "Come here and you'll be a big fish in a small pond. Then when you go to graduate school, you can go to Yale."

He had made a strong case; I was sold. I went home and told my father. He was disappointed, but he held it in. That's how it was in those days, at least in our house. He said, "Williams is a good school and Watters is a fine coach." My father had officiated many games at Williams and knew Watters well. He had regularly worked the big Williams game, against Amherst, at the end of their seasons.

I think it was my father's plan to come to Williams in my sophomore year to watch me play football, when I would be on the varsity. As was required then, I played freshman football in my first year, in the fall of 1956. As it turned out, those were the final athletic experiences of my life as an active participant.

Up to that point, athletics had been the focal point of my life. Throughout southern New England, my father knew the fields, the schools, the coaches, and I was right at his side. Gridirons, baseball diamonds, field houses, dressing rooms, tracks, swimming pools— those were the churches of my youth.

I remember things well from that autumn of '56, when America was at peace and everybody I knew seemed to be happy and secure, and Casey Stengel's Yankees, *my* Yankees, won the World Series, four games to three, against the Brooklyn Dodgers. (Don Larsen won Game Five for the Yanks with his perfect game. DiMaggio was retired, but Mickey Mantle had picked up right where Joe D. had left off in centerfield.) While the Yankees were winning, we were practicing and playing. There are always small moments that stand out in one's memory: During a lull in practice, I was standing on the sidelines, looking around at the brilliant leaves and changing colors, the lovely, rolling hills, red and gold, with the crisp smell of a clear New England afternoon in fall. There was little to worry about. I recall thinking how happy I was. How lucky, too. Near the end of the season, we played Wesleyan. The varsity played in the afternoon so we played in the morning. At 10:00 A.M., it was cold. The field was covered with a thin layer of frost. You could see your breath. The coaches were as nervous as we were. I remember feeling young and strong and alive. I was part of a team and we shared a simple, reachable goal. We were as one. In a full life, few moments have been as rich as that one.

In those days, players worked both sides of the line, offense and defense, and that's what I did. I was a tackle, like my father. Against Amherst, our great rival, in a game we won easily, I remember tackling an Amherst back hard in front of the Amherst bench, under the brim of the Amherst coach's hat. I remember the Amherst coach screaming, "If you don't block that son of a bitch he's going to kill somebody!" It was a wonderful compliment. I cherish it still.

Our freshman football coach at Williams was Frank Navarro, who was not much older than we were. A few years earlier, he had been a star guard for Jim Tatum at Maryland. For a young man, he had keen insight into people and situations. One day a sophomore named Tommy Davidson came down to watch practice. Tommy was a good guy, from a great football family. His father, Gar Davidson, had been the football coach at West Point. But Tommy was too small to play. "You all see Tommy Davidson standing there," the coach said. "Tommy would love to be here, with you guys, playing football. He loves football. His family is all football. But he's not playing, and you are. You are lucky. You can play. You have health and you're doing something physical and doing it well. You are blessed. Remember that." I have.

The young coach, later the head coach at Columbia and Princeton, taught me a lesson I soon came to feel very sharply.

In the fall of my freshman year I lived with three friends, all from Hotchkiss, Bill Mead, Jon O'Brien, and Jim Ryan. The four of us got along very well. My social life that first semester was hanging around with Mead and O'Brien and Ryan. We were close.

We had a suite with a living room, one large bedroom with two beds in it, and two smaller bedrooms with one bed each. We were in a building called Williams Hall, room 24, on the top floor, up three flights of stairs. It was a Georgian brick building, shaped like an L, on a grassy quadrangle. It had a slate roof and copper gutters. Bing Crosby had a son in my class, Lindsay, and he lived in Williams Hall, too, and we all imagined that someday we would see a man with a fedora and a pipe come through the great wooden doors of our building singing a Christmas carol, maybe whistling. One day it did happen: Bing Crosby showed up for Parents Weekend. The father and son seemed so happy together, so enviable. You never know how a life will unfold. Lindsay's adult life was tragic and it ended in suicide some years after his family trust went dry. RIP.

My friend Bill Mead was mechanical. He could do anything with his hands. One day in December—December 10, it was—he and I were horsing around, as we called it, and he trapped me in my little bedroom, which was maybe five feet across and ten feet long. He removed the doorknob and locked me in there so I couldn't escape. I yelled at him to let me out and he said, playfully, "I'll be back." I could not kick the door down, because it opened in. Had I been smart, I would have taken the hinges off, but I didn't. I did what any freshman would do on a dark early winter afternoon. I took a nap. When I woke up two hours later, I had to go to the john. And this led me to the moment I still live with every day. I should have relieved myself in the wastepaper basket and waited for Mead to come back. Instead, I climbed out the window. There was a very thin ledge with a gutter attached to it. My idea was to edge my large freshman body the three feet or so and reenter the suite through Jim Ryan's unlocked window.

The ledge and the gutter were icy. I slipped and fell, from a height of forty feet. Halfway down, I hit a steel railing, which broke my back but probably saved my life. I landed on the ground, on my back, with a loud thud.

A junior, Brad Thayer, who was studying in a first-floor room, heard the thud and came out to find me. Brad took charge. He didn't move me, which was smart. An ambulance came and I was taken to North Adams Hospital, where I had emergency surgery to remove two crushed vertebrae. My spinal cord had been damaged. I was paralyzed from the midchest down. My life as an athlete was over.

I was placed in a Stryker Frame, which is like a stretcher with a piece of canvas under you. To turn you over, they put another piece of canvas over you and flip you over. I was flipped every two hours to keep my circulation active. I was in that Stryker for several months. I could move my arms. Everything below midchest was immobile.

After about ten days I was moved to the hospital in Waterbury, so I could be treated by a genius back surgeon there, Dr. Alfonso Dellapietra. He took bone from my hip and reconstructed the two missing vertebrae, in some fashion. I lost about an inch in height but I got back, over time, maybe half of my leg power. In other words, I could walk, sort of. The nerves began to regenerate. The body is an amazing thing.

My mother knew my athletic life would have no new chapters but she also knew there was much more to life. She loved books and music and poetry. She knew my father and sports had dominated the first eighteen years of my life. I was depressed, and she pondered how to help me. She saw an opening. One day, she brought a tiny record player into my hospital room and played Gershwin's "Rhapsody in Blue." I was in that godawful Stryker, just miserable and uncomfortable, and she was playing Gershwin loudly and saying above it, "Isn't that lovely? Isn't that beautiful?" I have never since enjoyed a piece of music as I did "Rhapsody in Blue" that afternoon in my hospital room. She had made her point. On that day I abandoned my life as an athlete, forced though the departure was, and embraced the life of the mind.

The accident was much harder for my father to accept. He felt sorry for me. He found it hard to imagine a life without exercise or games to play. Moreover, I was his lone son, with his name and his interests, and on a more modest scale, his talents. My two younger sisters weren't interested in sports. For my father, the idea of a life without active participation in sports was unspeakably sad. I continued to have a wonderful relationship with him until the day he died, but it was a different relationship after my fall. We came together to watch sports, not to play them. We talked about games past, games I had played in, more often games he had played in. When I think back to the day we sat together at Shea and I got the foul ball, it's with considerable happiness and some sadness. It's a wistful memory. He never saw me return to sports. He never saw me as the commissioner of baseball. How wonderful that would have been, to bring my father to a game as commissioner! To introduce him to DiMaggio and Williams and Terry Tata! That would have made him very proud. That he would have loved. So would I.

The Umps

1. AL BARLICK

I INHERITED FROM MY FATHER a love of umpires and umpiring, and when I got into baseball my friendships with the umpires came naturally. I became particularly close to Bruce Froemming, a stout man with a heart to match. Bruce broke into the majors under the watchful eye of Al Barlick, the legendary Hall of Fame umpire. At the beginning of the season, the umpires are placed into groups of four and they travel and work together the entire season. The most senior of the four is the crew chief, the boss. Froemming's rookie year was 1971 and Barlick was his crew chief. Bruce once told me the following story about Barlick and how he broke in the rookie Froemming.

"Barlick says to me, 'Look, Bruce, this is your first year in the big leagues. We want things to go smoothly for you. Now last year we had a bad episode and we want to make sure it doesn't happen again. We had a play where a ball was hit in left field in Cincinnati and it hit a goddamn bird in foul territory and the ball fell in fair territory. We had no ground rule to handle that situation. It was a big scandal for us, very embarrassing. We want to make sure it doesn't happen again. Every series, we want to know what the field has in the way of birds and pigeons and where they are. Then we'll come up with a ground rule for that ballpark. So if you wouldn't mind, Bruce, I'd like you to go out early, during batting practice, and report back to me and tell me whether you see any birds.'

"What do I know? I'm a rookie. It makes sense to me. So our first series is at Shea. First game, I go out early, watch for an hour. I report back to Al, 'No birds here, I think we'll be all right.'

"Barlick says, 'That's good, but we've got a three-game series here, so check before each game.' Al Barlick is my hero, the best umpire in the National League. I do what I'm told. Second game, same thing. Third game, same thing. No birds.

"Second series of the year, we're in Philadelphia for three games. Barlick wants me to continue my bird search. 'Of course,' I say. Three games, no birds.

"Now it's our third series of the year. We're in Cincinnati, Barlick says to me. 'Here's where we have to be really careful. This is where we had our problem last year. Let's be extra careful.'

"I go out for an hour during batting practice and son of a bitch if there isn't a flock of pigeons out in left field. So I go up to Barlick and say, 'Al, we've got a problem. There's a bunch of pigeons in left field.'

"Al says, 'No, actually, that's good. Now we can establish a ground rule before the game. We'll know what to do if a ball hits a pigeon and we won't have what we had last year. I'll tell you what, Bruce. You've got the plate tonight so you figure out what the ground rule should be. When we go over the ground rules you tell us what we should do with the damn pigeons.'

"So ten minutes before the start of the game we go out to home plate. Gil Hodges, the Mets' manager, comes out with his lineup card. Pete Rose, the Reds' captain, comes out with the Cincinnati lineup card. Barlick and I and the rest of the crew are standing at the plate. I start to go over the ground rules. I leave the pigeons for last. I say, 'One more thing—the pigeons.' Rose jumps right in: 'Yeah, what about those goddamn pigeons. Last year we had a ball hit one of those birds and you guys didn't know what to do.'

"Just then I see Barlick giving Hodges a little nudge with his elbow. I realize I'm being had. I see it. This is get-the-rookie time. But I don't let on. I say, 'Of course, there's two types of pigeons out there, male pigeons and female pigeons. Here's what we're gonna do. If a ball hits the male pigeon, it's two bases.

" 'Two bases if it's the male pigeon,' Rose says. 'OK—fine. What if it hits the female?'

" 'Ball hits the female,' I say, 'it's all you can get.'

"Everybody started laughing. From then on, Barlick left me alone. I had paid my dues."

2. BRUCE FROEMMING

OVER THE YEARS, I've asked various umpires about how a player or coach or manager gets thrown out of a game. We've all seen it. A guy is arguing with an umpire, the veins in his neck blue and bulging. For a while the umpire takes it, then he takes it some more, but at some point he reaches a breaking point and he tosses the guy. You wonder: What happened? Every umpire I've asked, I get the same answer.

"Guy says the magic words, he's gone," Bruce Froemming once told me.

"What are the magic words?" I asked.

"Anything with a 'you' before it," he said. " 'You blind fuck.' 'You're full of shit.' If a player says, 'That was a horseshit call,' he's fine. If a guy says, 'You're a horseshit ump,' you ring him up. He's gone."

It bears remembering. It also makes sense.

3. ED VARGO

THE PLAYERS, COACHES, and managers, of course, know about the magic words. Sometimes, they want to get thrown out of a game—a manager particularly. A bad call gets made, the manager goes out to argue it and he argues as if he thinks he's going to actually change the umpire's mind, which of course he never does. Maybe, if he argues the right way, he'll get a break on the next call. Maybe he wants to arouse his team or make a show of solidarity with his team and the team's fans. He uses the magic words. He gets himself tossed.

Ed Vargo, a longtime National League umpire and a good pal of mine, was once working a midsummer game in an impossibly hot stadium. It was probably in St. Louis, at Busch Stadium, when it still had artificial turf. On still days the turf would bake there in the broiling sun, and on-field temperatures on Sunday afternoons were often well over 120 degrees. The playing conditions were actually unsafe.

The catcher, on this particular day, started to give Vargo a lot of lip. He's doing everything he can to get himself thrown out. He's using the magic words. But Vargo's a pro. He knows what's going on.

"Every pitch I call, this guy is ragging me," Vargo told me. "Ordinarily, I would have thrown his ass out. But on this day, there's no way. After a couple innings I say to him, 'Let me tell you something. You can say whatever you damn want, today and never again, because I am not running you. I know it's hotter than hell. I know you want a cold shower. But no way. If I have to be here so do you.' The catcher just turned around and laughed."

4. BART GIAMATTI, NATIONAL LEAGUE PRESIDENT

THE LEAGUE PRESIDENTS, in the days when there were league presidents, used to preside over the umpires. They were the final arbiters of on-field disputes that could not be settled by the crew chief. They were authorized to levy fines and hand down suspensions when players, coaches, umpires, or managers misbehaved. If a game is played under protest, the league president sorts through the facts later before siding publicly with the crew chief of the game in question. When Bart Giamatti was president of the National League, from 1986 through 1989—the job he held before he became commissioner—he reveled in that role. He had been a student of umpiring since his high-school days, when the coach of the South Hadley High team would have Bart mon-

itor the umpires. Ed Vargo worked for him as the National League su-
pervisor of umpires. Bart learned a great deal about how umpiring
works from Eddie and they became very close pals. Bart was beloved
by the umpires. He understood the high purpose of their work: to
maintain the integrity of the game. Bart elevated the status of the umpires immeasurably by taking their role so seriously. He was the former
president of Yale, and he compared the role of the umpire in baseball
to the role of the dean at a university.

In 1987, sandpaper was found in the glove of Kevin Gross, a pitcher
for the Los Angeles Dodgers. He was scuffing balls with it so that their
aerodynamics would be uneven, making the flight of his pitches un-
predictable and the ball more difficult to hit. Bart suspended him for
ten days, with written comment, here slightly abridged:

"Acts of cheating are secretive, covert acts that strike at and seek to
undermine the basic foundation of any contest declaring a winner—
that all participants play under identical conditions. They destroy
faith in the game's integrity and fairness; if participants and spectators
alike cannot assume integrity and fairness, and proceed from there,
the contest cannot in its essence exist."

In a century and more of baseball, the umpires never had such an
eloquent defender.

5. AUGIE DONATELLI

AUGIE DONATELLI was a superb National League umpire who began his
umpiring career as a prisoner of war in a German stalag during World
War II. He reached the majors in 1958 and retired twenty-four years
later, but he was still around baseball working as a scout of umpires
when I got in the game. Whenever he was around, or whenever his
name came up, Augie stories poured out.

My favorite one goes back to 1969, when Leo Durocher was the
manager of the ill-fated Chicago Cubs, who were playing well that
year, looking to get into the World Series for the first time since 1945,
but the Miracle Mets won the National League East instead. Leo had
problems with umpires all his life, which is how he earned his nick-

name, Leo the Lip. One Saturday afternoon that season, with the Cubs trying to win their division, Durocher started arguing a play. He must have used the magic word—you—because Augie tossed him.

They were both good Catholics. The next morning, they both showed up at the same church in downtown Chicago. Durocher was in his pew, and Augie entered and sat next to the man he had thrown out the day before.

In the late 1960s, the Catholic Church was trying to make the Mass more participatory. Church officials were asking parishioners to greet one another during the Mass. You might say, God bless you. You might say, Peace be with you. The response might be, And also with you. Something along those lines. Something kind, warm, inviting, genial.

The priest in Chicago this Sunday morning invited the congregants to share a sign of peace with the person sitting beside them. Dutifully, Donatelli turned to Durocher and said, "Peace, Leo, peace."

To which Durocher responded, "War, Augie, war."

Their baseball characters and their life characters were one and the same.

6. BILL KLEM

THE GREATEST UMPIRE OF ALL time, by my informal polling, was a man named Bill Klem, a National League umpire from 1905 through 1940. My father knew about Klem and his accomplishments in the game the way I knew about DiMaggio and his hitting records. Klem was the inventor of the inside chest protector. He brought dignity to his profession. John McGraw, the legendary manager of the New York Giants, once threatened to have Klem fired. Klem said, "Mr. Manager, if it's possible for you to take my job from me, I don't want it." Klem once worked an entire season behind the plate because the job of an umpire on his crew was in jeopardy. The umpire was suffering from alopecia, a disease in which he was losing all his hair from the pressure of the job. The league president wanted him fired, said you couldn't have such an umpire stressed in so visible a way. Klem defended the umpire and offered to work home plate, the far more demanding assignment, every day—there were two-man crews in those days—if that would keep his partner on the job. So Klem took the plate every day and his partner's job was saved. That's why Klem remains a legend to all umpires.

When I was in baseball, there was an old-time baseball executive, a very close friend of mine, named Frank Slocum, who was also from the town of my birth, Waterbury, Connecticut. Slocum knew Klem well and told old Klem stories with special relish. Slocum's father, Bill Slocum, was a renowned New York baseball writer, so between the father and the son you had an entire century of baseball covered. I could ask Frank about anything. Frank had the same abiding respect for umpires I had. He told a story about umpire Klem that showed the stature of the man.

As commissioner, Kenesaw Mountain Landis—the autocratic Judge Landis—was vigilant about gambling in baseball. He had become commissioner, the game's first, in the wake of the 1919 Black Sox scandal and was determined to make baseball free of gamblers and gambling. He didn't want any baseball personnel involved in gambling, because gambling leads to debt and debt leads to corruption. Bill Klem presented a problem for Landis, because Klem loved to bet on the horses. He went to the track every day and he bet. He bet at the track, not with bookies. The track doesn't extend credit, you pay as you go, so you can't build up debts there. It's legal gambling. Still, Landis was not happy about it. He called Klem in.

"Mr. Klem, there is a strong suspicion in this office that you have been gambling on horses," Landis said, as Frank Slocum told me the story. "I want the facts about your gambling and I want them now."

At this, Klem, all five-foot-four of him, jumped out of his seat, slammed his fist on Landis's desk, and said, "Judge, I bet on horses every day, two dollars per race. I pay my debts as they come due. I have no intention of stopping."

Judge Landis was not accustomed to being addressed in this way. "Thank you, Mr. Klem," Landis said. "That will be all."

It is unimaginable that anybody else could have said those words to Landis and left the commissioner's office with his baseball life intact. In Bill Klem, Landis had met his match.

7. BILL MCGOWAN

BILL MCGOWAN was the Lou Gehrig of umpires. In one sixteen-year period, he is said to have worked 2,541 consecutive games. He was an
American League umpire for thirty years, and one of his most famous
decisions, ironically, involves Gehrig. In 1931, nobody hit more homers
than Gehrig, who hit forty-six, the same number as his teammate,
Babe Ruth. But Gehrig might have had forty-seven, were it not for a
famous call made by McGowan. On April 26, in Washington, Gehrig
hit a ball into the center-field bleachers. The ball landed in the stands,
but bounced back into play. A Yankee baserunner, Lyn Lary, didn't
know what was going on, and slowed down. Gehrig, by mistake,
passed him on the basepaths. McGowan made the tough call: He
ruled Gehrig out, and the early-season home run never happened, not
in the record books.

But he was not always so inflexible. Steve Greenberg once told me a
story about how McGowan worked the plate one day when Steve's father, the mighty Hank Greenberg, was standing at it.

"My father's batting. McGowan calls strikes on the first two pitches.
Then he calls a ball. My father hasn't taken the bat off his shoulder
yet. Now comes the fourth pitch. It's a perfect strike, except for some
reason my father doesn't swing and McGowan doesn't call it strike
three. He calls it ball two. The fans are screaming like crazy, 'You're
blind, that should have been strike three, get him out of there.' Mc-
Gowan and my father, they want both of them out of there. McGowan
very calmly goes around the catcher, sweeps off a perfectly clean home
plate with his brush. Still, he's sweeping it. He mutters to my father,
'Jesus Christ, Hank, you got to swing at a pitch like that.'"

From that day on, Hank Greenberg had a favorite umpire.

8. DUMMY HOY

WHENEVER I HANG OUT WITH major-league umpires. I learn something
new. The habits of umpires are highly particular and I have taken great
delight in studying them over the years. The third-base umpire, always
the third-base umpire, holds a pocket watch between innings. Why?

To keep track of the time to permit all the ads on TV to finish running. TV pays a lot of baseball salaries, and the umpires make certain the game does not resume until the ads are all shown. Why the third-base umpire? Because he's generally the umpire who has the fewest calls to worry about in an average game. Look carefully: You'll see the ump start his stopwatch once the third out is made.

Have you ever wondered why umpires use hand signals, most especially for called strikes? You might wonder: Why is it necessary for the umpire to turn his hand out like a turn signal every time a pitcher throws a called strike? Can't the catcher and the hitter and pitcher hear him bellow out, "Steerike!"? Everybody in the lower deck of the stands usually can.

The answer, I've learned from my umpiring friends, is no. Not everybody can hear the umpire say strike. There was a player in the late nineteenth century named William Ellsworth Hoy who was deaf and mute and was called, in an era much less sensitive to physical handicaps, Dummy Hoy. Hoy stood four inches over five feet, was a career .287 hitter over fourteen seasons, and lived in a world of silence. (Stephen Jay Gould, the late and eminent Harvard paleontologist who was also a baseball scholar, believed Hoy is a legit Hall of Famer.) After every pitch, Hoy would look at the umpire for a hand signal to confirm his suspicions. If the umpire's hand went up, it was a strike.

With my own limitations, accommodating the handicapped is an important issue to me. The courts and the federal government have been forced by public pressure to address issues of making workplaces accommodate the handicapped. The umpires did it all on their own. They helped make the game, and a profession, more accessible for a man who never had an easy day in his life.

9. DOUG HARVEY

WHEN BART GIAMATTI was in baseball, as president of the National League and as commissioner, and when I was in baseball, as deputy commissioner and later as commissioner, we were deeply committed to umpiring. We wanted better salaries for umpires and better working conditions, but more than anything, we wanted the profession to receive the respect it deserves. We worked hard to try to make that happen. We consulted the umpires, we included them, and I think, during our period in the game, we were successful. (Since 1993, the profession has been in decline again, and baseball's leadership should do something about it.) When I go to a game today, the umpires come by to say hello. I'm proud of that.

In 1991, when I was commissioner, the Atlanta Braves were in the World Series. During the Series, I was host for an umpire get-together, the umpires and their wives and some friends of mine congregating for dinner and adult refreshments at a fancy old-line Atlanta club called the Capital City Club. It was a wonderful party. Great baseball stories were told, the food was exquisite, everyone had a good time.

Toasts were made during the evening and at one point Doug Harvey stood to speak. Doug Harvey was a superb umpire in the National League who was called "God" by his fellow umpires and some managers because of the total authority with which he controlled a game. He was a tall, angular, white-haired man, and he was deeply respected even by difficult players.

The personality type of the umpire, by and large, is highly independent, much like my own. Umpires are resistant to authority, because they are the authority. They have bosses, as we all do in one manner or another, but they are loath to recognize them. At this party, Doug raised a glass and said, "In all my years in baseball, I will acknowledge working for only two people: Bart Giamatti and Fay Vincent. The other league presidents, the other commissioners, all the rest of them, I did not work for them. But for you and for Bart, I did."

I wish Bart could have been there to hear that. I know it would have moved him as it did me. The idea that Doug saw us as legitimate, that was important. The game and its rules were his ultimate master. What Doug was saying, I believe, is that we had earned his respect, that we were relevant to him, and that is what's gratifying. You have to give respect to get respect. You learn that by the third grade. If more people understood the critical role of the umpire in baseball and truly respected it, the great game would be improved. A civilization without laws and people to enforce those laws cannot be civil. Laws make us civil. Without rules and skillful umpires, baseball would be chaos. When the best umpires are working, when Doug Harvey and Bruce Froemming and Terry Tata and Jim Evans and Richie Garcia and Ed Montague are on the scene, you don't even notice them and the game is played as it should be.

CHAPTER THREE

Bart

IT IS RARE, I have noticed, for a man after forty to make new and close friends. In middle age, men tend to careers, families, lawns. Friends are something we already have. Few men are willing to take the time to cultivate a new and deep friendship. There is no need. But I was blessed: At forty, I made a great and new friend, a friend who enriched me, changed me, challenged me, fascinated me.

Bart Giamatti and I were both forty when we met. I was the new president of Columbia Pictures and he was the new president of Yale. Nine years later, Bart was named as the commissioner of baseball and made me his deputy. Before that, all I had been was a fan. It was Bart who brought me into baseball's sanctum sanctorum.

We met in the fall of 1978, after the Yale-Princeton football game, at Princeton. We had a mutual friend, a lawyer named Peter Knipe, an elegant and good-humored man. Peter had been in Bart's class at Yale, class of '60, and he was in my class at Yale Law School, class of '63. Bart and Peter were in a Yale senior society together, Scroll & Key. One of Knipe's clients was Peter Benchley, who wrote *Jaws* and *The Deep*.

Columbia had recently made *The Deep* into a movie. So the night after the Yale-Princeton game, Knipe invited Benchley and my wife at the time, Valerie, and me to his house for dinner. Knipe said to me, "Do you know Bart?"

"I know of Bart," I said. Around then, everybody knew of Bart. Yale, stodgy Yale, had a young, vibrant, fresh president with an Italian surname. My father had expressed his delight, saying Yale finally had a president whose ancestors hadn't come over on the *Mayflower*! Everywhere you turned, there was Bart—with Bryant Gumbel on the *Today Show,* or in *The New York Times*—talking about the importance of a classical education in a civilized society. With the help of the press, he was making himself into a national spokesman for education. He did this with a certain distinctive style. He was not the pompous university president from central casting, always pontificating; he was more like a charming professor who walked around his campus wearing the navy blue cap of his beloved Boston Red Sox and who just happened to be university president. When he was named president of Yale, he said, "All I ever wanted to be president of was the American League." American, because of the Red Sox. Eight years later, he was the president of baseball's ancient league, the National.

Knipe had told me: "You and Bart should know each other. You'd have lots in common. I'll invite him. You should meet." Each of us was in a new position of prominence, both sort of fast-track forty-year-olds, although with totally different styles. Bart had a job where he could have done his work behind the scenes, but he chose a public life. I had a job where I could have been a public person, but chose not to be. When you are the president of a Hollywood studio, an endless stream of invitations to premieres, parties, and dinners crosses your desk, and you could attend them all, if you were so inclined. I was not. When my college friend Herbert Allen made me the president of Columbia Pictures—he and his family firm controlled the company—we discussed whether I should run the company from New York or Los Angeles. We both agreed New York made more sense. "If you move to LA," Herbert had said, "you'll become one of them."

The evening after that 1978 Yale-Princeton game—Yale won—Bart and I met at the home of our mutual friend. It was a lovely evening, with a lot of verbal, witty people in attendance. Bart, who was there without his wife, Toni, stole the show. He was the star of the evening. He looked like a European movie star, with longish hair, black streaked with gray and combed straight back, dark skin, a deep, mellow voice and a flashing smile that always accompanied one of his verbal sallies. His use of the language was dazzling. There was a presence to him. I don't know if I had ever met a man who was more magnetic. I felt drawn to him immediately.

Bart spent much of the night teasing people he didn't know in a manner that was endearing and charming. I understood what he was doing immediately, because among men of our age, teasing was a way of developing intimacy and even affection, a way of showing interest, a way of showing off. For Bart, especially, it was a way of saying, "I want to know about your life." He could get inside a person quickly, largely because he kept probing, asking questions, showing curiosity. When Bart discovered that Valerie was from the Spring Glen section of Hamden, near New Haven, he was relentless. He was an expert on all things related to New Haven, where his father had grown up.

"Spring Glen," Bart said. "That's where rich people live."

"My father was a dentist," Valerie said.

"I could never make it in Spring Glen," Bart said. "No Italians lived in Spring Glen."

"I'm part Italian," Valerie said.

"You were a rich girl from Spring Glen," Bart said. Valerie loved him as I did. He was showing interest in her. She mattered to him.

You couldn't beat Bart at his game. He went after Benchley, who was at the height of his fame, erudite, handsome, stylish, a Harvard man, class of '61. His book *Jaws* was a great best seller and had made Benchley a fortune. So Bart played his trump card: the intellectual's avowed lack of interest in money. He would have you believe that living in the genteel poverty of academia, as he called it, was a high calling.

"Here we have a distinguished Harvard man who sets pen to paper to write not the Great American Novel but a paperback potboiler that scares little girls out of the ocean for fear they will be devoured by a shark!" Bart said. Benchley was up for the challenge and tried to impress Bart with the sales figures of his book; Bart would have none of it. He leapt on his prey. Commercial success, that was for commoners. A lack of interest in commercialism, that was the mark of excellence.

Then he turned to me. You could see immediately that he loved movies and the magic of their making. He subscribed to *Variety,* the movie trade magazine. He knew everything about my job, including what I was doing wrong. Columbia wasn't making enough Westerns. Nobody was making Westerns, Bart said, and it was the death of American movies. Make more Westerns, he urged.

"Indeed, I will write the next great Western for you," he said.

"You will?"

"Yes of course. Easily. I shall save you, sir. I will write it and Columbia will produce it and we will all make a lot of money."

He actually acknowledged the making of money as a goal.

"So I am to report to the board that President Giamatti is writing a Western for us and the company is saved. Correct?"

Somehow, we began to debate which of us had the more difficult job. Debate was his real love and argument was his lifeblood. He made his case: Academics are inherently contentious, he said. I tried to make the case that Warren Beatty, Dustin Hoffman, and their agents had to be more contentious than the Yale faculty. He would not hear of it. He was on a roll: Yale's nineteenth-century plumbing was ultimately his responsibility, the success of the football team ultimately fell to him, massaging the egos of dull, rich alumni who could not pronounce his surname was central to his job. I made the case that my job must be more difficult because they gave the Yale presidency to an English teacher. Of course, all the while I was referring to him as "Mr. President," while I was "Mr. Vincent." In the area of honorifics, and in almost every other way as well, I was at a disadvantage. I quickly realized I wasn't going to defeat Bart at his own game, so I got out.

"You may have the more difficult job," I told him, and for a moment he looked satisfied. "But at least I am paid for mine."

He feigned, like an actor, a look of deep hurt.

After that night, we started talking on the phone from time to time and inviting each other to various events. We discovered that our fathers were classmates at Yale, in the early 1930s. One day he called on me in my office in New York, looking for money for his university. Raising money was the worst and most important part of his job. He knew I had gone to law school at Yale and he was eager for me to make a gift to the law school.

"Fay, I'd like to talk to you this morning about making a substantial gift to your law school, Yale," he began. "I know how important Yale Law School is to you." He went on and on with his pitch. I let him go for about three or four minutes. Then I stopped him.

"Bart, before you came down here from New Haven today, didn't you do research about me?"

"Yes, of course."

"I assume you had somebody prepare a little paper on me?"

"Yes, one of my staff did exactly that."

"Well, I'd fire that person."

"What? Why?"

"Because I do not care for the Yale Law School."

"You do not?"

"Not a single warm cockle in my heart for Yale Law School."

Now he began to squirm a bit.

"Really," he said.

"My father, on the other hand, was class of '31 from Yale College, captain of his football and baseball teams. My father loved Yale, and I love my father."

"I know you do," Bart said, still trying to recover.

"If I were you, Bart, I would have come in here this morning and said, 'Mr. Vincent, I'd like to talk to you this morning about making a substantial gift to Yale College, for financial aid, in honor of your father, the great Yale athlete whom you love so dearly.' "

Bart jumped dramatically from his chair, bolted across the office and out the door, slamming it. I heard him in the vestibule talking to my secretary for a minute or two. Then there was a loud knock on my door.

"Yes," I said slowly.

Bart opened the door. "The president of Yale is here this morning to talk to Mr. Vincent about a gift to Yale College, in honor of his father, the great Yale athlete whom he loves so dearly."

"The president of Yale is now on the track," I said.

I wrote a check and began a scholarship in my father's name, which helps undergraduates attend Yale. They come from all walks of life— football players and violinists and math prodigies—and every year the recipients send me a very nice letter and when they do I of course think of my father, and the visit from Bart that began it all. In the meantime, my feelings for Yale Law School have evolved fully since Guido Calabresi, a friend of mine and a friend of Bart's, took over as dean and changed the entire tone of the place, making the school a much more full-bodied experience than it was in my day. I now support the Yale Law School as well.

That story might suggest that I had the upper hand in the friendship, but I didn't. I was dazzled by Bart, particularly by his ability to speak and to write, skills I valued. Our friendship deepened as we realized that we prized so many of the same things, language most particularly. He loved reading and reciting William Wordsworth, as did I. One morning, I woke up and, while reading *The New York Times*, discovered again why I was so impressed by Bart. The *Times* that morning had reprinted a letter Bart had written in response to a boy named Kempton Dunn, from a Yale family—the boy's grandfather played football with my father—who had written to Bart asking the value of studying Latin. In his reply, Bart addressed the young man as "noble Dunn," and emphasized that Latin is far from a dead language, as it lives on in the roots of all romance languages, and forms an essential piece of the history and heritage of Western civilization. His letter, which included such grace notes as *"Nosce teipsum* [know thyself], brave Dunn" and cited the Yale motto *Lux et veritas*, concluded by noting that Dunn's teacher's name (Mrs. Calderon) is "Latin," as is that of "your admirer, the undersigned." It displays many of the traits that explain why I liked Bart so much.

In 1985, I asked Bart to come out to California, to the Biltmore, a beautiful, secluded hotel in Santa Barbara, to speak at a Columbia Pictures management conference. He chose to speak about the end of the millennium. I offered to fly him out on the Columbia jet and initially he was hesitant; he had the idea, I gathered, that the plane would be a little prop job, flown by a guy wearing a leather helmet, goggles, and a white scarf. He might have asked something about the experience of the pilot.

"Pilots," I said.

"Oh," said Bart.

"Two pilots, flying a jet," I said.

Bart looked relieved. In the end, he saw, of course, that flying in an uncrowded private jet with two pilots and superb food and service directly to your destination is far superior to traveling on commercial airlines. I was starting to take this sort of corporate comfort for granted, so it was good for me to be reminded of the luxurious life I was leading. Bart, unaccustomed to it, clearly enjoyed his foray in the world of high luxury. We understood we were lucky, and how far we were from our roots. It was another bond.

In my introduction of him at the conference, I read his "noble Dunn" letter. Whether the 150 or so Hollywood executives understood it, I do not know, but I continue to believe it's a great letter, one that should be cited. Then came Bart. He had worked fanatically on his remarks, borrowing a typewriter at the hotel and rewriting it right up to the moment he was to go on. This was a chance for Bart to win over a new crowd, a challenge he enjoyed, particularly because he was speaking to movie people.

Bart began by noting that, historically, people tend to be frightened at the end of a millennium. One could see he loved his subject, the sweep of it; he was onstage, teaching again. The fright, Bart said, showed up when people turned inward and led lives in which they froze others out. Bart cited jogging with earphones as quintessential end-of-the-millennium behavior: Doing so, you're out in the world, but all by yourself, connecting to no one. In contrast, he preferred the movie-going experience, people coming together to watch the same film, to share something. That was a community. But he predicted that people would continue to withdraw from communities. He could not have imagined the rise of the Internet, but that's really what he was predicting: lives in which people sit in rooms with machines, having social intercourse with a screen instead of a person. It was a brilliant speech.

The next day, something special happened. Bart and I were having breakfast with a group of perhaps ten film executives and the conversation turned to baseball. The Dodgers were good then, Bart was knowledgeable, and you could see how truly impressed these business people were, that the erudite Yale president could talk about the end of a millennium one night and baseball the next morning. They saw what I saw from the day I met him: Bart was a modern Renaissance man.

With every passing year, Bart and I became closer. One thing we realized early on, without ever talking about it, was that there were things in my professional life that he envied and vice versa. I wasn't particularly interested in movies and Hollywood gossip and corporate politics. Bart loved all that stuff. I would have been very content leading the life of an academic, walking across a leafy campus, teaching, being surrounded by books and students. Bart grew up in that world—his father was a professor of romance languages at Mount Holyoke College—and had lived in it all his life. He was interested in the world beyond the shaded arboretum of the academy. I think he mostly wanted to be influential. He wanted to matter. At one point, trying to see into the future, we made a vow: Someday, we would work together. We joked about opening a bookstore together, on Chapel Street in New Haven, since we both loved books so much. We imagined we would have a full array of British detective novels, which Bart loved, and biographies for me, and big comfortable reading chairs, and coffee and bagels. When I brought up the issue of comfortable chairs, Bart said, "Those damnable wooden benches bookstores have. They are preposterous."

When middle-aged men talk openly to one another about their futures, that is a mark, I believe, of intimacy. We knew I wasn't going to stay at Columbia Pictures or Coke forever and that he wasn't going to stay at Yale forever and that we would both continue to do interesting things and it would be stimulating and fun to work together. We left it at that.

Then one day in 1986 Bart called and asked if we could get together for dinner. I went up to New Haven and we met at a spaghetti house on Wooster Street, and it was there he told me his secret: He was fed up with being the Yale president, tired of his fights with the unions and the constant fundraising and the petty, endless, unwinnable political squabbles and the lack of broad trustee support. He knew people who had real power or who were making big incomes or who had significant influence. He wanted a change. He said, "I want out. I want something different. Will you help me?" I was flattered. He wanted me to be his counselor, along with Max Frankel, then the op-ed page editor of *The New York Times*, and Franklin Thomas, who was then the head of the Ford Foundation. "I'll look to the three of you to guide me," he said.

I called some of the CEOs I knew and asked them to talk to Bart about a high-level corporate job. I called Jack Welch at General Electric, Dick Munro of Time, and Thornton Bradshaw of RCA. By that point, Columbia Pictures had been purchased by Coca-Cola, and I was an executive vice president at Coke. I talked to Roberto Goizueta, class of '53 from Yale, about hiring Bart, a man he admired, as Coke's head of public affairs. Everybody was willing to see him. They all knew about Bart Giamatti and respected him. Some of them had ties to Yale. But nobody was interested in hiring him. Perhaps some were intimidated by Bart, by his wit, his intellect, his charm, the breadth of his knowledge. They didn't know where to put him. Many of them said that Bart needed to be running his own show, not working for somebody else. Perhaps they thought having Bart Giamatti as a lieutenant would be impossible, like having Pavarotti in the chorus. I sympathized with them: Bart was not a man you could hide.

When I reported all this to Bart, his mood turned dark. It was the first time I had seen that. It would not be the last. His reaction was understandable. He was the president of Yale University. He could get the vice president of the United States, George Bush, on the phone. But he couldn't get anyone to see him as an executive, not in a business sense. He said, "What do these people think Yale is, a kindergarten?" It was frustrating.

I was hoping that one day I would be able to call him and say, "Something's come through," and hear his voice buoyant again. Then one day, in 1986, he called me.

"I need advice," he said. "What do you think of me as the president of the National League?"

It wasn't totally out of the blue. In 1984, some of the team owners, Bud Selig of the Milwaukee Brewers chief among them, approached him about becoming the commissioner of baseball, when baseball was looking for a successor to Bowie Kuhn. Bart couldn't talk about the job seriously then, he was too involved at Yale, and the commissionership went to Peter Ueberroth, who was coming off his great success running the '84 Olympic Games in Los Angeles. But Bart charmed Selig on their visits together with stories about his experience as the equipment manager of the South Hadley High School baseball team in the middle 1950s and with his humor:

Why is baseball so popular among intellectuals?
Because it goes so slowly they can understand it.

Charm and humor aside, the owners had seen Bart take a hard line with the Yale custodial union, a painful experience for him, but one that impressed the owners. Bart had kept his name in baseball, mostly by wearing a Red Sox cap around the Yale campus and by writing about the game. Bart wrote an essay on baseball that ran in *Harper's*. Its opening is probably his most oft-quoted passage:

> It breaks your heart. It is designed to break your heart. The game begins in the spring, when everything else begins again, and it blooms in the summer, filling the afternoons and evenings, and then as soon as the chill rains come, it stops and leaves you to face the fall alone. You count on it, rely on it to buffer the passage of time, to keep the memory of sunshine and high skies alive, and then just when the days are all twilight, when you need it most, it stops.

When baseball was having its horrid 1981 strike, Bart wrote a piece for the op-ed page of *The New York Times* that concluded with this:

O Sovereign Owners and Princely Players, masters of amortization, tax shelters, bonuses and deferred compensation, go back to work. You have been entrusted with the serious work of play, and your season of responsibility has come. Be at it. There is no general sympathy for either of your sides. Nor will there be. The people of America care about baseball, not your squalid little squabbles.

When the New York Mets dealt Tom Seaver to the Cincinnati Reds, Bart wrote an appreciation of the pitcher, praising his "dignitas" and writing:

On June 16, the day after Seaver was exiled to Cincinnati by way of Montreal, a sheet was hung from a railing at Shea bearing the following legend:

I WAS A

BELIEVER

BUT NOW WE'VE

LOST

SEAVER

I construe that text, and particularly its telling rhyme, to mean not that the author has lost faith in Seaver but that the author has lost faith in the Mets' ability to understand a simple, crucial fact: that among all the men who play baseball there is, very occasionally, a man of such qualities of heart and mind and body that he transcends even the great and glorious game, and that such a man is to be cherished, not sold.

We talked about the job, about what it would mean to be the president of the National League. I asked him, "Is it a real job?"

He said, "No. The league president is in charge of umpires and handles player fines and suspensions. There may be some interesting race issues, some drug issues. But there's not much to do."

"And what will they pay you?"

"Three hundred and fifty a year."

That would have represented about three times what Bart was making as Yale president. I congratulated him.

"What do you think?" he asked.

I told him what I thought. For the past six years, he had had a terribly demanding job, the Yale presidency, and had not been well paid. Now he could have an easy job, and get paid for it. The job would be in New York, so he could get some exercise and take better care of himself. Moreover, he would have plenty of time to write and give speeches. Then the day would come when Peter Ueberroth would want to leave baseball, and Bart would be a prime candidate to succeed him. He wanted out of Yale, and this gave him an ideal exit. I didn't need to say other options were not available.

"Do you think I should take it?" he asked.

"I think you should take it."

"Then I'll take it," Bart said.

o   o   o

A MONTH INTO his new job, Bart called.

"I am furious at you!" he said, bellowing.

"Hello, Bart."

"You son of a bitch, get me out of here! I am furious at you. I am bored! There's nothing to do. You got me into this, now get me out."

He was being mostly facetious, of course, but not entirely. He had already been talking to people about heading the Rockefeller Foundation, but they hired someone else. In time, I calmed him down. That was one of my roles in the friendship. I continued to remind him that his purpose in taking the job was to improve his health, to write, and to bide his time. Biding his time was not something Bart did well. Writing was something he did extremely well. During his National League presidency, and later as commissioner, he did some of his best writing. When he faced a decision whether to suspend someone—Kevin Gross of the Los Angeles Dodgers for hiding sandpaper in his glove for scuffing balls, Pete Rose for bumping an umpire—these were occasions for writing, and for teaching. When he taught, he was at his best, and teaching and writing were linked acts to him. Some of his writing appears in a slim book about baseball and the American love of games, called *Take Time for Paradise*. At one point, he sent me a draft of the book, in which he had included a Greek quotation but spelled phonetically, that is, using English letters.

"That Greek quote is bad," I told him. "You can't do it that way."

"What are you talking about," he said.

"The Yalie classicist who doesn't know Greek."

"I've seen other writers do it," Bart said.

"Sure, other writers with equally limited educations."

The better our friendship became, the more we could needle one another. We showed our appreciation in subtle ways. When the book came out, Bart wrote in the acknowledgments, "My friend Fay Vincent cast his literate eye over the whole, and made it better."

My favorite moment in the book is when Bart re-creates a baseball conversation he heard in the lobby of the Marriott Pavilion Hotel in St. Louis during the 1987 playoffs:

"So now Tebbets is catching in Boston, he tells me last winter, and Parnell is pitching, it's against New York, and it's a brutal day, no wind, hot, rainy, it's going to pour and they want to get the game in, and Joe Gordon splits his thumb going into second when Junior Stevens steps on his hand, he can't pivot, and now it's the eighth, tie score, and Bobby Brown comes up with two out and Bauer sitting on third and Birdie says to Ed Hurley who's got the plate, 'This is the Doctor, Ed, this is a lefthanded doctor . . . ' "

Bart captures not only the language perfectly there, but the tense. When baseball people gather to speak of their game they talk in the present tense. Bart picked up on that. Bart was by then part of baseball and he was very much living in the present tense, which suited him in the most elemental of ways, because he did not know what his own future would hold.

As National League president, Bart brought me into the game. One day, he invited me to Shea Stadium to watch the Mets with Fred Wilpon, the Mets co-owner, and Sandy Koufax, who had gone to high school in Brooklyn with Wilpon. Before the game, we had dinner together, the four of us, in Fred's dining room at Shea. Sandy was talking about guys who threw spitters, and how they got away with it. Anybody who really knows how baseball works knows that the spitball has been part of the game from the beginning. Not in Bart's book. "That's cheating!" Bart said. "I can't believe it." You could see poor Bart, struggling with the idea of cheating in his game. He was a romanticist.

During Bart's term as National League president there was an incident in which Pete Rose, the player-manager of the Cincinnati Reds, shoved an umpire, Dave Pallone, during a heated argument at first base. Pallone was reputed to be gay, so there were other issues under the surface. At that point, Bart held Rose in high esteem. He was Charlie Hustle, on his way to becoming the all-time hits leader. But when Rose put two hands on the chest of one of Bart's umpires and pushed him bodily, Bart was truly offended.

"Your father was an umpire," he said to me. "What would you give him?"

"I think you have to be very tough on him," I said.

"I agree with that, but that is not the question. The question is: How long is the suspension? I am looking for crispness."

"Ten days," I said.

"Ten days, Mr. Vincent? Mr. Vincent has wimped. He has missed the point. Mr. Rose will be suspended for thirty days by Mr. Giamatti. Nobody touches my umpires. I don't care who he is. I will teach him a lesson."

Rose accepted the punishment gracefully. He knew he had done wrong and he was ready to pay the price. Bart was impressed. In the end, Bart had to persuade Pallone, who was having trouble working with the other umpires, to leave baseball. Pallone later claimed the owners pushed him out, not Bart—but the fact is, Bart alone made the decision. He showed him the door, but in so artful a way that Pallone thought Bart had Pallone's best interests at heart. Baseball has enough lawsuits thrown its way; Bart wanted a settlement with Pallone. Bart could be very political.

In the spring of 1988, I left Coca-Cola. I had joined Coke when the company bought Columbia Pictures in 1981. By 1988, Columbia had not proven a good fit for Coke, which had decided to get out of the movie business. It was clear, too, that I had no future at Coke and was not going to become the CEO. I had returned to my old law firm, Caplin & Drysdale, and set up an office in New York. I had made enough money and I was deciding what to do next in my life when Bart intervened. I had a notion that I would divide my life into thirds: I'd practice law, I'd do pro bono work, and I'd teach. My office in New York was on East Fifty-fourth Street, between Park and Madison. Bart's baseball office was at Fifty-second and Park. We had lunch together almost every day. Sometime in 1988, the word was out that Ueberroth would soon being stepping down as commissioner and the owners wanted Bart to succeed him. He had a lot of support, particularly among the National League owners. Some of the American League owners wanted the doctor, Bobby Brown, whom they had known forever and who of course had played baseball. Ueberroth wanted Brown, too. But a commissioner never gets to name his successor. Besides, Bart's political instincts were far sharper than Bobby's. Bart's ability to say the right thing at the right time with the right words was unmatched. The last sentence of Bart's formal bibliographical note in his last book, *Take Time for Paradise,* reads, "I owe the reference to Jane Austen to Charles Bronfman of Montreal." Charles Bronfman of Montreal was a major shareholder of Seagram's, the liquor company; he also owned the Montreal Expos. With a single sentence Bart had made a friend for life. Bobby, a fine man, never had a chance.

One day at lunch Bart told me the owners were getting serious and asked if I'd negotiate his contract for him. I said of course. Negotiating contracts was something I had done often as a lawyer. I wanted to help Bart, because he had never paid attention to money. He had been paid relatively little at Yale, had nothing put away, nothing to fall back on. I knew this was a terrific opportunity for him to achieve financial security.

"We will start by asking them for everything," I told Bart. "I'm going to ask for things that are aggressive. If something happens to you, I'll ask that they pay the contract off. Their response may be, 'That's life insurance. If Bart wants life insurance, he should go out and buy some.' Maybe then we'll split the difference. In any event, they want you and I'll bet we do fine." Bart was excited but somewhat concerned about my approach. He did not want to appear greedy. By this point, he knew I knew his academician's distaste for money was a piece of skillful acting. He saw the freedom having money could bring. So he let me negotiate the agreement as I wanted.

I knew what Ueberroth was getting and used that as a platform. I asked for $650,000 a year for five years, payable in full even if Bart should die in office. I asked for an apartment in New York, a car and driver, a pension of $150,000 a year for the remainder of Bart's life or, should he die first, his wife's life.

"They'll never go for all that," Bart said.

"We'll see," I said.

I mailed the contract in. I was negotiating with Fred Wilpon of the Mets and Bud Selig of the Brewers. They loved Bart. They moved a few commas, and that was about it.

When Bart died, a friend of mine, John McMullen, the owner of the Houston Astros, called.

"I just read Bart's contract," McMullen said to me. "You should be ashamed of yourself." He loved Bart, but he knew the deal was rich.

"I was just representing my client." On a pro bono basis, of course. I wasn't going to take money from Bart.

"Who represented us?" McMullen wanted to know.

I told him.

"You couldn't have done better if you had a pistol in your hand. Now you know why the players do so well." No one paid attention to the contract until Bart died.

Bart was pleased, pleased to have some money, really, for the first time in his life. A few months later he called me and said, "You won't believe what I've done."

"What have you done."

"Toni and I bought a Mercedes. A roadster."

"Good for you."

"You have a Mercedes, why shouldn't I have a Mercedes? You've made me rich."

"You're not rich and neither am I," I said. "But we're living well."

There was a giddiness, a joyfulness, in him. It wasn't about the material comforts. In fact, Bart and I used to say being rich was having a good book on a good beach on a good day. He used to drive around New Haven in his Yale years in a Volkswagen Bug. It was about doing a thing with a partner and a friend. It was about achievement.

The owners formally elected Bart as commissioner in September 1988, but Ueberroth didn't step down officially until April 1, 1989. That meant there was a half-year period in which Bart was sort of acting commissioner and I was his unpaid adviser. We were having fun; the issues were interesting. There was no discussion of me joining Bart in baseball. Bart would have been hesitant to bring that up, the idea of me working for him. It was contrary to the nature of our friendship. Even in a great friendship, there are times when it makes more sense to be indirect than direct.

One day, I was meeting with Fred Wilpon, working out some of the final details of Bart's contract.

"Have you thought about coming along with Bart as his deputy?" Wilpon asked. "You'd be a great team. You know about business and you could really help us all."

Baseball had never had a deputy commissioner before. Immediately, I could see Bart's handiwork in this conversation, right down to the title. The suggestion was that I had strengths and experiences in places Bart did not.

"I'd have to know it was a real job," I said.

"It'll be a real job," Wilpon said.

In my experience in the business world, a job is real if somebody is paying you a significant sum of money to do it. If there's no salary, you're some sort of decoration. If it's a serious job, you get paid.

"If the salary is $100,000 I would definitely say no," I said. "If it was $200,000 I'd probably say no. If it was $300,000 I'd probably say yes." After that, it came together quickly. The next time I saw Bart he called me "Dep!"

For the rest of his life, that was his nickname for me. (Mine for him was "Angelo.") Bart became the seventh commissioner of baseball, and I became its first dep.

We worked all this out months before Bart officially assumed the office of commissioner. The day he was elected, Bart said he would be looking for a deputy, somebody who had strengths in business areas where he did not. Two days later he said, "I have found the perfect person who matches the criteria, and it is my friend Fay Vincent." Bart knew how to play to an audience. He was good.

We went into baseball to have fun together. That was our high goal. For a brief while, there was the most delightful lightness in everything we did together in baseball. It all seemed a bit unreal to us. Bart was filled with mirth and there was a good humor to our workdays.

There was a time Bart was meeting with leaders of a players' alumni association. A retired pitcher, Jim Brosnan, who was called "The Professor," was carrying on and on about a variety of mundane issues, perhaps a bit nervous in front of Bart. When he was finally done, Bart said, "Jim, you know that's total horseshit."

Our friend Frank Slocum, an executive in the offices of Major League Baseball, was with us. Afterward, Frank said, "You know, Bart, I never had the benefit of higher education. All my life, I wondered what it would be like to be a learned man like you are, Mr. Commissioner, a Ph.D., a former president of Yale, a man famous for his vocabulary. And then I hear you use a word like 'horseshit.' I am stunned."

"Frank," Bart said, taking a long pause for effect, playing up his pseudo-professorial tone, "the test of a good vocabulary is the ability to use precisely the correct word in precisely the proper situation. And in that situation, dear sir, I used precisely the correct word."

Bart loved anything rhetorical and baseball is a talking game. It suited him. I remember a time Bart was giving a speech, going through the motions, which was not usual for him. Then somebody asked a question that caught his interest and he was off, giving a dazzling answer, full of all sorts of literary and classical references. Later I asked Bart how he could change gears so quickly. He said, "Dep, I can play only the melody or I can play up and down the keyboard, with lots of ruffles and flourishes. At that moment, I thought they wanted the full treatment, so I gave them a lot of right hand."

Early in our tenure, we had to decide whether Pete Rose gambled on baseball. Rose was a great and popular figure, and being in a fight with him was a public relations nightmare. At one point, he referred to me as "The Cripple" and nobody challenged him.

"I cannot allow Rose to call my deputy 'The Cripple,' " Bart said.

"Well, Bart, neither of us can walk too well," I said.

"It's uncivilized," Bart said. "Anyway, we are not paid to walk. We are paid to think. We should challenge the other commissioners to a think."

Bart and I were determined not to be consumed with the Rose affair. In the end, that proved impossible. In the beginning, we were more successful at it. Early in the season, we went to a ballgame. It was a beautiful afternoon, the starters pitched into the late innings, the umpires had no problems, it was a perfect day. We were enjoying our jobs, and our friendship. At one point, Bart leaned over and said, "Remember, Dep, this is work. We get paid for this."

	Lineup: BoSox
1.	Bobby Doerr
2.	Johnny Pesky
3.	Dom DiMaggio
4.	Jimmy Piersall
5.	Wade Boggs
6.	Fenway
7.	October 25, 1986
8.	Jean Yawkey
9.	"Smoky" Joe Wood

BoSox

1. BOBBY DOERR

BART GIAMATTI GREW UP with the Red Sox, and he lived and died with the Red Sox, even when he was president of the National League. When he was president of Yale, in the early 1980s, he would spend his summer vacations in a little house in the woods, on the island of Martha's Vineyard, off the coast of his native Massachusetts. A friend who saw him there described for me the scene: On Sunday afternoons, Bart would settle into a beach chair on his little crabgrass front yard, line up his cigarettes and magazines under one arm and a radio under the other, take off his shirt, close his eyes to the sun, and smoke his way through the afternoon, listening to his Sox. He had much love for, but little faith in, his team. "What I expect," he said one day, "is that they will show up this year for all their appointed games." He had a special place in his heart for the Red Sox teams from his South Hadley boyhood, the Boston teams of the late 1940s and early '50s, the teams of Bobby Doerr, Walt Dropo, Johnny Pesky, Dom DiMaggio,

Vern Stephens, Jimmy Piersall, Al Zarilla, Ted Williams. Boston was noticeably short on pitching; the ace was Mel "Dusty" Parnell. The Sox never had it all and they never won it all and that suited Bart's personality. He was a striver, in the best sense.

Bobby Doerr was always Bart's favorite, in boyhood and adulthood both. Doerr was a sure-handed second baseman with a war-interrupted career, a .288 hitter who made it into the Hall of Fame thirty-five years after his final game. A reporter, Jack Craig, once asked Bart, Why Doerr? Why not Doerr's great friend Williams? "I could imagine myself playing second base," Bart said, "but not hitting .400."

When Doerr was inducted into the Hall of Fame in 1986, Bart was there, as president of the wrong league. Three years later, when I spoke at a memorial service at Carnegie Hall for Bart, I fell at the podium and it was Doerr (and Joe DiMaggio) who helped me back to my feet.

It is rare that a grown man gets to know his childhood hero. When he does, he must be prepared for disappointment. Bart had high expectations of Doerr, and as he got to know him, they were exceeded in every way. Bart admired how steady and sturdy Doerr was. He admired his values. He loved talking baseball with Doerr. I was fortunate to be included in some of those conversations, in hotel restaurants and at ballgames and in Cooperstown, and consider myself lucky to count Bobby as a friend. Bart wore his affection for Doerr on his sleeve, all the days of his life. Doerr is a gem. He was Bart's hero, plain and simple.

2. JOHNNY PESKY

JOHNNY PESKY, born John Michael Paveskovich, was the Red Sox shortstop and third baseman from 1942 through 1952, except for the three years he missed, '43, '44, and '45, when he served in World War II. He is one of my favorite people in baseball, and was one of Bart's.

Pesky and Ted Williams have been linked forever. Dom DiMaggio led off for the Sox for years, Pesky hit second, and Williams, batting third, drove them both home. Pesky was a wonderful hitter, with a career .307 average, but all his baseball life he had to take a pitch when he got ahead in the count. His job was to get on base so that Williams could drive him in. "The pitchers knew they could throw underhanded to me on 3–0 or 3–1, and I couldn't swing," Johnny told me one sunny day at Fenway, sitting in my golf cart.

"One day, we're playing the Yankees. I got three balls and a strike on me. Pitcher throws one right down Broadway. Of course, I can't swing at it. My job is to draw the walk, so Ted can hit with a runner on. Now it's a full count. Next pitch is a wicked curve, unhittable. I swing and miss. I'm gone.

"I go to the dugout and I'm hot, really mad. I kicked the ice bucket, I threw the bat, I yelled, I screamed. The manager, Joe McCarthy, just sits there. Finally, when I calm down, he comes down to see me. 'Young man,' he says, 'I'll see you in my office when the game is over.'

"Game ends. I know I'm in trouble. I go in to see him. He says, 'Sit down, young man. Don't open your mouth. Just listen. Your job is to get on base. The big guy does the hitting. As long as I'm here, you're going to take on 3–0 and 3–1. If you want to swing at those pitches, you can do it for St. Louis or some other team. I can have you out of here tomorrow. Or you can stay here and keep your mouth shut and let me manage this club.'

"I got up, walked out of his office, never said a thing. There was nothing to say. I had the take sign on 3–0 and 3–1 for the rest of my career. It pissed me off for forty years, but that's the way it had to be. When I look at my record, I think about what could have been if I could have hit on 3–1. That's the hitter's pitch. But I never could."

Williams, in his career, had 1,839 runs batted in, and a goodly number of them were in the person of Johnny Pesky. He got on base, Williams drove him in, the Sox won. The careers of the two men are inseparable.

When Ted Williams left baseball in 1943 to join the Navy, Pesky went with him. They went to flight training school together and Williams got through it and became a pilot and flight instructor and Pesky did not and became an operations officer. Williams was a fast learner and could memorize things easily. Johnny could not. One night during the school, as Pesky told it to me, Williams came up to Pesky and said, "Johnny, why are you having so much trouble? This should be easy for you. You have a high-school degree and I don't." "Nah, that's not it, Ted," Pesky said. "You have a head for these things and I don't." Still, they served with distinction.

When the two friends came back from the war and returned to the Sox for the '46 season, the Red Sox did something they hadn't done since 1918: They played in the World Series. After six games against the St. Louis Cardinals, the Series was tied. The final game was in St. Louis. With two outs in the bottom of the eighth inning with the score tied, 3–3, speedy Enos Slaughter was on first for the Cardinals and Harry "The Hat" Walker was at bat. Walker hit a soft liner to left-center, where it was fielded by Leon Culberson, filling in for Dom DiMaggio, who was out of the game because he pulled a hamstring muscle while running the bases in the top of the eighth. DiMaggio was possibly the best defensive centerfielder in baseball in 1946, and if he was second it was only to his brother Joe. Culberson was no DiMaggio. He fielded Walker's ball cleanly and made the throw home. Slaughter was running on the pitch. Pesky cut off Culberson's throw, didn't hear his teammates yelling that Slaughter was heading home over the crowd noise, held the ball for a moment, then made the throw home. It was too late. Slaughter scored and the final score was 4–3, Cards. It's all part of the Curse of the Bambino. Ever since the Red Sox dealt Babe Ruth to the New York Yankees following the 1919 season, the Sox have not won a World Series. It is a distinct possibility they never will. The few times they've had a chance, something has conspired against them. (Recently, Ernie Banks helped me understand another view of the Curse. "Commissioner," he said, "the Red Sox tried out Willie Mays when he was a kid. They said he couldn't hit the curveball. That's the real curse.")

Ever since, baseball people have been talking about "Pesky holding the ball," blaming him for the Series loss. When I once asked Ted Williams about it, he said, "I was horseshit. If I'd have hit at all, we would have won." He always defended Johnny and vice versa.

Still, the Slaughter play has been part of Pesky's life since the day the play occurred. He has a sense of humor about it. Following the

World Series, Pesky and his wife headed home, to Oregon. They went to a University of Oregon–Oregon State football game, at Oregon. It was pouring rain and the Oregon backs were having a horrible time holding on to the ball. They fumbled the slippery football four or five times before the half. At halftime, Pesky went to the concession stand to get a hot dog. A man sitting behind Pesky recognized him, stood up and bellowed, "Put in Pesky! At least the son of a bitch will hold on to the ball!"

When he returned, Mrs. Pesky turned to her husband and said, "Did you hear what that man said? That's cruel."

Johnny comforted her as best he could. "Imagine, baby," he said, "what they're saying in Boston right now."

All these years later, they're still saying it. Pesky is a permanent part of Boston's baseball lore. But they love him.

3. DOM DIMAGGIO

DOM DIMAGGIO COMPLETES the foursome of great friends who played for the Red Sox in the mid-twentieth century: Ted Williams, Bobby Doerr, Johnny Pesky, and Dom DiMaggio. At the start of the 2002 baseball season, all four were still alive and still close to one another.[*] They played baseball together, fought in the same war, suffered the same World Series heartbreak, thoroughly enjoyed their times.

Dom DiMaggio, kid brother of Joe, one of the first major leaguers to play ball wearing glasses—he was called "The Little Professor"—has been trying forever to take the blame off Pesky for the 1946 Game Six Slaughter play. DiMaggio told me once that Slaughter told him that had DiMaggio been in center that day, he would never have tried to score, because DiMaggio played a shallow center, got tremendous jumps on anything hit at him, and had a strong and accurate arm. Dom had already thrown out several runners in that Series. But in the top of the eighth in Game Six he pulled a hamstring muscle as he took second on a double. Manager Joe Cronin came out and said, "Williams is coming up. If he hits you can't get home." Dominic was

---

[*] But as this book went to press, Ted died on July 9, 2002.

sorry to come out, but out he came. He did it, of course, for the team. Without the pulled hamstring, DiMaggio told me, he would have prevented Slaughter from scoring on Walker's hit, because he played Walker slightly to left-center, while Culberson played him straight away.

Coming out is difficult for any player to do, and more difficult if your name is DiMaggio. I've gotten to know Dom over the years and am extremely fond of him. The public impression of him is as a modest, quiet man, unassuming, not as lavishly skilled as his brother Joe. He may be some of those things, but he is much more. I've found him to be very much like Joe: filled with passion, supremely confident in his abilities, with an extremely long memory. If you slight him, as some have, you are out for life. If you try to use Dom to get something on Joe, you are out for life. If you defile Joe's memory in any way, you're out. If you don't show the proper respect and the proper manners, you're out. It is the DiMaggio way, the Sicilian way, it's what makes the DiMaggios what they are. Dom would never say in public he believes he should be in the Hall of Fame, but he should be—Pesky should be, too—and he knows it. I very much hope they make it—and soon.

Dom has spent decades leading his own life. He's been married to the same lovely, spirited woman, Emily DiMaggio, for over a half-century. He's raised three wonderful children, two sons and a daughter. He owns a thriving textile plant a son manages today. When strangers talk to Dom, sooner or later they bring up his brother Joe. Part of being Dom DiMaggio is being the kid brother of Joe DiMaggio. Dom learned to accept that fact a long time ago. He'll tell Joe stories to people he trusts, but he prefers to tell the stories of his own life, or better yet, to live his own life. It has been a rich one. At Joe's funeral, Dom's daughter said, "My uncle was a lonesome hero." Those words resonated with Dom. His baseball accomplishments were not in Joe's league. But in the scorecard of life—the one with marks for family and friendships and stability and career—The Little Professor has been on the Dean's List forever. Bart Giamatti—himself a self-made man, devoted to his wife, also the proud father of two sons and a daughter—understood this well. Pride is not always a sin.

4. JIMMY PIERSALL

WHEN DOM DIMAGGIO RETIRED AT the start of the 1953 season, he was re-placed by Jimmy Piersall, whose career I followed with particular interest because he was born in Waterbury, Connecticut, the same town in which I was born, and because he had a particularly interesting career. Piersall played an extremely shallow center field, more so than even Dom, and he played it very well, twice winning Gold Gloves. He was a .272 hitter over a seventeen-year career that ended in 1967. But he was more famous than his career statistics might suggest. Piersall suffered from manic depression and was open about it. He wrote a book about his struggles, later turned into a movie, called *Fear Strikes Out*. He did a great service to the cause of mental health because before that, to my recollection, no prominent athlete had ever been so public about having a mental illness.

There were times when his behavior was bizarre and there were times when crude fans taunted him. He developed an approach to dealing with them: "Give them their money's worth." When he hit his one-hundredth career home run in 1963, then playing for Casey Stengel's abysmal New York Mets, he ran the bases backward.

I met him when I was commissioner. He was still working in base-ball. He held various jobs over the years, in broadcasting or as a coach, but he had a hard time keeping them, because he would do or say some odd thing—a function, perhaps, of his struggles. We shook hands and I said: "Jimmy, I've followed your career closely, because I was born in Waterbury, too."

"Is that right?" he said. "I didn't know that."

We spoke of Waterbury for a few minutes, the people we knew from there, and then he said, "Look, I've got to thank you for something."

"What is that?"

"You helped us get a better pension."

In truth, I had very little to do with it. I encouraged the owners and the players union to improve the pension payments for ballplayers who played before the union became so rich and powerful. In 1990, the new contract finally gave a little help to the older players.

"If you don't mind me asking, what did that mean to you?"

"Well, I was getting thirteen hundred dollars a month, now I'm getting double that. It makes a big difference."

He deserves far more than that. Our society is a long way away from accepting mental illness for what it is, a medical condition. But Jimmy Piersall did a great deal to help bridge the gap between fear and understanding.

5. WADE BOGGS

I LOVED WATCHING WADE BOGGS, the longtime Boston third baseman, hit. He looked like a nineteenth-century ballplayer, with his prominent chin and his bushy mustache and a body that looked made for farm work. Night after night, he sprayed line drives from the left side of the plate all around the outfield and off the Green Monster, and season after season he led the American League in hitting. In 1988, when Bart was the president of the National League, a Boggs sex scandal broke out. Day after day, as sure as Boggs would go two for five there was some new revelation of his longstanding extramarital affair. It was an embarrassing episode for Boggs, old-fashioned in a strange sort of way (it brought to mind Bernard Malamud's book *The Natural*, which we made into a film at Tri-Star Pictures). I was glad that Bart, as president of the other league, didn't have to deal with it. He could do as I could do: sit back and admire the greatness of Boggs's bat. Boggs himself showed no signs of distraction. In 1988 he batted .366.

Even in his eccentricities, there was something about Boggs that was out of another era. He was a slave to ritual in a way few ballplayers have been since the postwar emergence of a world dominated by science and logic. He ate chicken before every game. He ran pregame windsprints at 7:17 P.M. before each 7:35 P.M. start. He made the Hebrew *chai* symbol in the dirt of the batter's box before each at bat.

Whenever he stepped into the batter's box he would look at the second-base umpire and sometimes pat the top of his helmet with the palm of his right hand. This was not another Boggs quirk; it was Boggs employing an ancient baseball signal known to me, umpires, and few outside the game. I knew it only because my father was himself an old-school umpire. Most fans simply never noticed it, and no broadcaster has ever explained it when I've been listening. One day when I was in the ESPN booth with Joe Morgan, I asked him about it. He was working a Red Sox–A's game with Jon Miller at Fenway. Boggs came to the plate, looked at the second-base umpire, and patted his palm twice on the top of his helmet. I asked Morgan if he knew what Boggs's signal meant. It is pretty hard to stump Joe Morgan. He was stumped.

"He's moving the second-base umpire," I said.

"I never knew that," Morgan said.

"He's moving him because the umpire is standing immediately behind the pitcher, a lefthander, and some batters don't want to see the umpire when the pitcher finishes his delivery," I said. The umpire moved to the other side of second base, well out of Boggs's direct line of sight.

Many players are ignorant of umpires' positioning and signals. I don't remember whether Boggs got a hit that particular at bat; chances are better than one in three that he did. The point is, Boggs knew the game in all its particulars. He knew how to manage his environment so that he could be comfortable. Nothing distracted him. If something did, he fixed it.

6. FENWAY

FENWAY PARK, the intimate patch of steel and concrete and green in the Fenway section of Boston, is much beloved. Its urinals are ancient tanks that look like dissected submarines, but no matter, Fenway is much beloved. The seats are small, many of them have obstructed views, the facilities for the handicapped are poor, the aisles are narrow, the parking is a nightmare, but no matter, New Englanders love their Fenway, which the Red Sox have called home since 1912. It is the place where Ted Williams homered in his final at bat in 1960. (We'll forgo the long list of bad things the Bostons have endured there since the Babe's departure in 1919). When a new ownership group emerged in 2002, with many of the principals from out of town, they tried to curry favor with the locals by announcing they were committed to saving Fenway, to fixing it up and keeping it going. All across New England there was rejoicing.

Bart, I'm sure, would have been among the revelers. His romantic attachment to the old park smacked of first love. I was not celebrating. I know Dom DiMaggio was not either. We both feel the same way: It's a great old park. The time has come to tear it down and start over. The ironwork that holds up the stadium is corroding. It will either be razed or come down on its own. I'd much prefer to see the former happen. I am entirely in favor of building a new Fenway, on the site of the old Fenway or maybe across the street. I'd like the new Fenway, on the field, to duplicate the bizarre dimensions of the old Fenway. I'd like the stands of the new Fenway to capture the coziness of the old Fenway. But the new Fenway will have good lighting, be comfortable, have good sight lines and well-engineered concession stands. It will be just like the old Fenway, except that it will be better. It will have no rats.

The old Fenway will live on in our memories. Williams's 521st and last home run in 1960. Carl Yastrzemski's Triple Crown season in 1967, Bernie Carbo's pinch-hit homer in the eighth inning of the sixth game of the 1975 World Series. Winning Game Six, behind Dennis "Oil Can" Boyd, and Game Seven, behind Roger Clemens, to win the American League playoffs over the California Angels in 1986.

I was last there in 1999, for the All-Star game. Ted Williams was on hand, honored as part of an all-century team, and the ovation he received was deafening. There were thirty thousand people and 30 million goosebumps. If that's my last firsthand memory of Fenway, I can happily live with that.

7. OCTOBER 25, 1986

IN OCTOBER 1986, Bart Giamatti found himself in a terrible quandary. The Red Sox, his dear Red Sox, were finally in the World Series again. But Bart was president of the National League, so publicly rooting for his boyhood team was out of the question. I asked Bart how he would handle this obvious conflict. "From the waist up, I'm a Mets fan," he said. "From the waist down, I'm rooting for the Sox. I'll be stamping my feet for the Sox, where no one can see me."

The sixth game of the '86 World Series, on October 25, is among the oddest in World Series history. Boston was leading the Series, three games to two. The nine innings, played at Shea, ended in a 3–3 tie. The Red Sox scored two in the top of the tenth. In the bottom of the tenth, the Red Sox retired the first two hitters, and later came twice within one strike of winning their first World Series since 1918. Three singles, a wild pitch, and a ground ball through first baseman Bill Buckner's legs gave the Mets the win, making a seventh game necessary, which of course the Red Sox lost. They lost the World Series in seven games in '46 and '67 and '75 and now '86. Part of the Curse is that they drag it on and raise the flag of hope. Then they fail.

Bart never blamed Buckner for the Game Six defeat. He always said he had a sinking feeling when John McNamara, the Boston skipper, brought in reliever Bob Stanley with two outs in the tenth. It was Stanley who threw the wild pitch to Mookie Wilson that allowed the game-tying run to score and extended Wilson's at bat. Stanley was still pitching and Mookie was still batting when he hit the fatal grounder that went through Buckner's legs allowing the winning run to score. "I started to get a sinking feeling when Stanley came in," Bart told me. "I felt Steamer Stanley would sink us."

A couple of years later, Bart and I were flying with Frank Cashen, the Mets' bow-tie-wearing general manager, the architect of the '86 team. I asked Cashen to name for me his favorite player.

"Favorite player," Cashen said. "All-time?"

"Of all time."

"Easy," he said. He looked at Bart. "You're going to love this."

"Who is it?" Bart asked.

"Billy Buckner," Cashen said.

"You son of a bitch!" Bart said. "I'm going to kill you, you Irish bastard!" If he could have thrown him off the plane, I think he would have. The wounds were still fresh. For Red Sox fans, the wounds are always fresh, always new.

8. JEAN YAWKEY

WHEN BART AND I WERE IN BASEBALL, the Red Sox were owned by Jean Yawkey, the widow of Tom Yawkey, an old Yalie from a wealthy family who bought the Red Sox in 1933, at the age of thirty, for $1.5 million. He then immediately spent $1.5 million more refurbishing Fenway and millions more buying and keeping baseball talent, from the beginning of the Ted Williams era to nearly the end of the Carl Yastrzemski era. He lived through the joy and anguish of the great '75 World Series, in which Boston lost to the Big Red Machine in seven games. They won Game Six at home in the twelfth inning, courtesy of a Carlton Fisk home run off the left-field foul pole, then lost Game Seven at Fenway, 4–3, despite an early 3–0 lead. The next year, Tom Yawkey died.

Mrs. Yawkey had been a chorus girl in her youth. She remained beautiful all her life and dedicated to her team all her life. Bart and she were a perfect fit: They shared Yale, the theater, Fenway, the Red Sox, the years of suffering, cigarettes. One day, I sat with her at a game and she told stories. It was magical. I got her talking about the early days.

"My husband really loved baseball and he really loved his team," Mrs. Yawkey told us. "Of course, when he first owned the club, the teams still traveled by train. They would go as far west as St. Louis. Tom didn't travel with the team. He took care of things at home.

"On those summer weekends when the team was on the road, Tom and I would come here, to Fenway. Tom was a jock. He'd put on a uniform and I'd sit in the stands and somebody would throw batting practice to him and hit ground balls to him. He enjoyed it thoroughly. When he was done, he'd go in, shower, and then he and I would go out to center field, just beyond second base, put out a blanket, and turn on the radio. We'd lie in the sun and listen to the game. When the game was over, we'd fold up the blanket and go out for dinner."

A perfect day. Every time I go to Fenway I can see them lying in the center-field sun. The Yawkeys had it figured out. They knew how to enjoy what they had. And they had a lot.

9. "SMOKY" JOE WOOD

IF YOU WANT to look up the record of "Smoky" Joe Wood in the indispensable *Baseball Encyclopedia* you have to look in two places. Under the Pitcher Register, you'll see that he pitched for the Red Sox from 1908 through 1915, going 34–5 in 1912, with a 1.91 ERA. Wood had a fastball that rivaled Walter Johnson's and Cy Young's, until a thumb injury slowed him down in 1913. By 1918, he was an outfielder for the Cleveland Indians, for whom he played until 1922. That's why you need to look him up in the Player Register as well. As a hitter, he had a career .283 average over 1,952 at bats. As a pitcher he won 116 games, lost 57, and had a career ERA of 2.03. He had two careers in the majors.

And then he had a third baseball career. After batting .297 in '22 over 142 games, he retired from the game at age thirty-two and took a job as the Yale baseball coach, a job he held for twenty years. For three of those years, my father was his first baseman.

Wood was ninety-five years old when he died in 1985 in the Westville section of New Haven, a few miles from the Yale campus and almost across the street from Yale Field. Bart knew him well, lived in Westville for a while, admired him, and learned a lot of early baseball history from him. In 1979, Wood and Bart and my father separately attended an NCAA playoff game: St. John's University versus Yale at Yale Field. Ron Darling, the future New York Met, pitched for Yale; Frank Viola, the future Cy Young Award winner, pitched for St. John's, Darling no-hit St. John's for eleven innings, but Viola and St. John's won in the twelfth. If there was ever a better college baseball game, I don't know about it.

Joe Wood sat with Roger Angell, the *New Yorker* writer, who immortalized the game in the magazine, using Wood as his primary source. (Nearly a decade later, Roger wrote the definitive magazine profile of Bart.) My father sat with my sister Barbara. I'm not sure who Bart sat with. Maybe he sat by himself. As a lifelong Red Sox fan, he was prepared for the outcome.

Bart was true to Wood, and why wouldn't he be? Wood was a

BoSoxer, Wood was a Yalie, Wood lasted forever. When Bart was Yale president, he gave Wood an honorary degree in a ceremony in the old pitcher's living room in Westville. My father had a wholly different impression of Wood. He remembered a coach who played cards while the team practiced and coached from the stands, as was then the custom, whistling when he wanted a pitching change. He seldom had anything meaningful to say. My father felt Wood was living off his reputation. He said: "He mailed it in." My father knew the man. Bart knew the legend. In baseball, you cannot separate one from the other. Together, they comprise the truth.

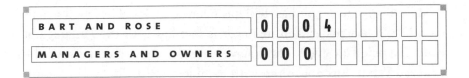

CHAPTER FOUR

Bart and Rose

AS 1988 TURNED INTO 1989, I was hanging around with Bart in the offices of Major League Baseball. It was only a matter of time until Bart became commissioner and I became his deputy, but precisely when that time would come we did not know. Peter Ueberroth was then the commissioner and he was unclear about when he might leave office: If he got a job he liked, he might leave right away, and if he didn't, he would stay on until the end of his term, April 1, 1989. In the end, that's what he did. It's easy to forget how terribly short Bart's term as commissioner was. Five months. He became commissioner on the first of April and died on the first of September. And for those five months, his days were consumed with one issue: Did Pete Rose bet on baseball?

In February 1989, Ueberroth told Bart and me he had received a call from someone at *Sports Illustrated* saying the magazine had information Pete Rose had bet on baseball. An associate of Rose named Paul Janszen had gone to the magazine and offered to tell what he knew about Rose betting on baseball if the magazine would pay him. The call to Ueberroth was a confidential tip.

Since 1919, betting on baseball has been considered baseball's capital crime. Every player and manager is familiar with the language of Rule 21 posted in every clubhouse. In 1919, eight members of the Chicago White Sox conspired with gamblers to fix the World Series, which was won, it so happens, by the Cincinnati Reds, the team Rose was now managing. "Shoeless" Joe Jackson, Chicago's uneducated hitting machine, is the famous symbol of that club, which became known as the "Black Sox." He hit .375 in that series, but he took the gamblers' money. In 1920, when baseball appointed its first commissioner, Kenesaw Mountain Landis, he banished Jackson and the seven others. They were put on the "permanently ineligible" list. Jackson would clearly be a member of the Hall of Fame today, except for his involvement with the gamblers in 1919. Landis, who wrote baseball's Basic Agreement, knew that gambling on baseball by baseball personnel undermined the fan's faith in the game. Landis, correctly in my view, established a policy of zero tolerance for gambling. Because of his forcefulness, he was able to reestablish the credibility of the sport. Fans could watch games and know that the outcome was not predetermined. It is often said that Babe Ruth and Commissioner Landis saved baseball in the 1920s.

Not many fans know about the origins of the title "commissioner." Before Landis, baseball was governed by a three-owner commission. One owner from each league served with a third owner elected by the two. Naturally, the third owner was affiliated with one of the leagues and his impartiality was continually suspect. When Landis was hired, he was offered the job as the third "commissioner." He quickly saw the other two were not needed, and the commission was disbanded as Landis became *the* commissioner, charging himself to act in the best interests of baseball. More than seventy years later, Bart, when he succeeded Ueberroth, was trying to do precisely the same thing.

For Bart and me, the claim about Rose came totally out of the blue. There was no preamble to it. Soon enough, we found out that some years earlier, when Bowie Kuhn was commissioner, allegations had been made against Rose, but we could find no file of a serious investigation. Ueberroth felt it would be best if he could deal with the

Rose matter before he left office, which was decent of him, but unrealistic.

Bart admired Rose. Early in his career, Rose was a second baseman, and Bart always liked second basemen, who are often less physically gifted than their teammates, but overachievers in every other way. Bobby Doerr was Bart's childhood hero. Bart admired the way Rose accepted the thirty-day suspension Bart handed him for bumping Dave Pallone, the umpire. Rose was enough of a baseball man to understand Bart's message in handing down such a severe punishment: *Nobody touches my umpires.* My own initial feelings about Rose were less positive: I remembered well how he needlessly ran over a catcher, Ray Fosse, in the 1970 All-Star game, diminishing Fosse's career for the sake of victory in an exhibition game. I preferred style and grace to Rose's raw hustle and roughness.

I pointed out, and Ueberroth and Bart quickly agreed, that if *SI* published a story about Rose's gambling and we were doing nothing, we would look foolish. I urged that we bring Rose in to see what he said about the allegations. If he denied them, we would have to start our own investigation. I had experience in such investigations, from my job as a special counsel for the Securities and Exchange Commission in the 1970s. Such an investigation can be a tedious process—sorting out fact from fiction often is—but necessary.

Ueberroth handled these early discussions with admirable patience. Peter was one who thought spending a week to reach a decision was an eternity. He didn't like lawyers and was not a slave to process; he believed in intuition and decision and common sense. In most of his life, his approach has clearly served him well—but when he let the owners collude to prevent free agents from signing, his philosophy backfired, costing the owners an ultimate judgment of $280 million and whatever little trust the players had in them. But in the investigation of Rose, he deferred to me and accepted the time frame inherent in such an investigation.

We called in Rose. He was in Florida, getting ready for spring training. He came up to baseball's offices at 350 Park Avenue in Midtown Manhattan with three lawyers, one there just to answer tax questions.

His lead lawyer was Reuven Katz, one of the most prominent lawyers in Cincinnati and a first-rate counselor. He was so good, and so successful on behalf of Rose, I think Rose came to believe Katz could get him out of any mess. And up until then, he had.

Rose was charming, in his own way. He wore a white shirt with a wide tie and a polyester suit, green and shiny and too small for his stocky body. His hair was spiked, standing up on end. He looked like a small-time gangster. He was a legend and he knew it, but he carried himself in a wonderful, ordinary Joe way. I liked him. At that point, I had never been around an important big leaguer before in an intimate setting. There was something exciting about it.

We wanted to treat Rose as a colleague. We didn't have a stenographer at the meeting because we didn't want the atmosphere of a formal hearing. For the first five or ten minutes, you might have thought we were at a cocktail party; Bart was friendly, even gregarious, and so were the others. It was as if we were sitting around a table with a dead dog on it and everyone talked while ignoring the dog. At some point, the question had to be asked. So, finally, in the middle of all the chatter, I said, "Mr. Rose, may I ask you a question?"

The room went silent. Pete swung around to face me—a face unfamiliar to him. Everyone knew what was coming. What we didn't know was how he would respond.

"There are allegations that you have been betting on baseball. I have a very important question to ask you, Mr. Rose, because your answer is critical for you and for us. Have you ever bet on Major League Baseball?"

He answered immediately and forcefully: "No, I'm not that stupid. Look, of course I bet. I bet on everything you can bet on: basketball, football, the horses. I love to bet. But I never bet on baseball."

I said: "Let me tell you why your answer is so important. We are going to accept your answer, but if we find that it is not true, the consequences for you are going to be very serious."

Rose's lawyers jumped in. They said they had looked into the charges themselves and found them to be totally without merit. They described Janszen as a convicted felon who was desperate for money, who had tried to extort money from Rose. They asked us how we or *SI* could believe a convicted felon.

We asked ourselves the same question. I believe all three of us—Ueberroth, Bart, and I—were inclined to believe Rose. He was cool and credible, as were his lawyers. We agreed we would keep the meeting quiet. There was nothing to be gained by being public about it. We knew we would have to continue our investigation, but we all believed the inquiry would quickly exonerate Rose.

As Rose left 350 Park, a reporter was waiting for him. Rose brushed off the reporter and no story appeared. But then a day or two later, Ueberroth got a call from Murray Chass of *The New York Times*. The *Times* covered, and continues to cover, baseball in a very sober, procedural way; it treats baseball as the important quasi-public American institution many of us, myself included, believe it to be. To Chass, Ueberroth confirmed the meeting with Rose and, more seriously, dismissed any gambling allegations as untrue. Peter, I think, assumed Rose was telling the truth and failed to protect against the possibility he was not. Regardless, the story was now out. When such stories are swirling around, fact-finding becomes more difficult. People align themselves with one camp or the other. Accounts become exaggerated. A source's motives have to be more carefully examined. It was only a matter of time before the story became public, but Bart and I would have liked to delay its debut for as long as possible. Now we had to accelerate the pace of our investigation—and we had Ueberroth on record as believing Rose.

Bart very soon became anxious. As the days went by, we started to take hits in the press because it looked like the investigation was dragging while Rose, in full denial of the allegations, twisted in the wind. Bart continually asked: "What the hell are we going to do?" There were no easy answers.

Immediately after the *SI* call, we had brought in a Washington lawyer, John Dowd, who had experience as head of a Justice Department strike force conducting Mafia investigations. Dowd advised us that the baseball investigation would be difficult because, in a private proceeding, baseball does not have the power of subpoena. Still,

Dowd said, there are always ways to get information. Dowd was a pro; a former Marine with a towering physical presence, he had the charm of the Irish and the hard-edged tenacity of a big-time prosecutor. He knew what he was doing and thus had a calming effect on Bart, on all of us.

One of the first people Dowd went to see was Paul Janszen. *SI* still had not published the story. He was not an ideal witness because he was a convicted felon awaiting sentencing, but Dowd felt his report of Rose gambling on baseball was highly credible. In no time, Dowd had turned up eight or ten people—Cincinnati businessmen who had relationships with Rose, or men who worked out at the same Gold's Gym as Rose—who said they were with Rose when he called bookies and placed bets on baseball games. Some had been with him in his car when he used the car phone to bet. Others heard him calling from the gym or other places. These people had no reason to make up stories at that stage, Dowd reported. "It does not look good," he said.

Ueberroth was eager to dispense with the matter before he left office on April 1; he didn't want to leave Bart saddled with it, and he didn't want people saying he had stuck Bart with it. At one point he asked about simply throwing Rose out of baseball, based on the information we had. But there was no way to do that: Baseball had rules governing this sort of thing and Rose was entitled to a hearing before the commissioner. April 1 came, Ueberroth left, and now the investigation belonged to Bart. Part of Bart was excited by the case because he loved detective stories and cops and he enjoyed the discovery of information. He liked John Dowd very much and liked working with him. But the bigger emotion for Bart was disappointment that a baseball hero was so plainly flawed. He knew Rose's problem was now his problem and baseball's problem, and it was a big problem.

As the investigation proceeded, we decided to turn over to Rose and Reuven Katz all the evidence we collected. My guess is that Katz knew or had grave suspicions Rose had been betting on baseball for years, but figured baseball wouldn't want to prove a case against him and therefore would not. After a few months of the investigation, as the evidence started coming in, Katz saw the handwriting on the wall. At one point he called Bart, wanting to meet with him, to talk about making a deal. We knew this was a meeting Bart should not attend, because the commissioner was the person who would ultimately determine Rose's fate, and his involvement in such a discussion could appear to color his judgment. So we decided I would meet with Katz. We wanted to keep the meeting out of the papers, so over a weekend I went to Dayton and Katz and I met at the law offices of one of Rose's other lawyers. (He had several.) It was a fascinating and sad meeting.

Almost at the start, Katz said, "Pete believes he is a national treasure and so do we." I will never forget that phrase, "national treasure." I sat there thinking about Rose's manic levels of betting, and here his lawyer was talking about him as a "national treasure." I knew a settlement was out of the question. Katz talked about Rose paying a fine and doing community service for actions that were "regrettable," but there could be no acknowledgment he had bet on baseball. I told Katz that, as he knew, we had overwhelming evidence Rose had bet on baseball and any deal would have to take into account that evidence. How could we ignore it? We asked for any evidence contradicting what we had. They intimated that they had such evidence, but none was ever offered. (As I write this, no such evidence has ever been put forth, despite many claims it existed.) I told Katz his proposal made no sense to me but I would report it to Bart. I returned to New York and called Bart. His response was classic: "I'll show him who the national treasure is. That's pathetic." Our attitude had changed radically from our meeting with Rose just a few months earlier. It was clear to us we were in the driver's seat. The facts were on our side. We would do the correct thing; we could not and would not back away.

At one point, Dowd took Rose's formal deposition. We put Rose under oath, in front of a court reporter, with lawyers for both sides present, and Dowd took him through the evidence. We wanted to hear what Rose would say when confronted with what Dowd had dug up.

Dowd showed Rose his own handwriting on baseball betting slips and Rose responded by saying, "I couldn't tell you if that's my handwriting."

In the deposition, Rose denied to Dowd he had ever dealt or bet with a bookmaker. Yet he also said, "See, what you have to realize, John, and probably don't, I know you don't. But the majority of bookmakers are crybabies. You know, they could have the biggest weekend in the world and they're always complaining about they lose. In reality, they've got the world by the ass. Because no bookmakers lose." He seemed very familiar with bookies.

Asked about the people testifying against him, testifying that Rose had bet on baseball, Rose said to Dowd, "Those guys could have a quintet in the last three months. Because they're all singing. They're all singing a lot. They have to sing or they'll be in Sing Sing."

We were amazed by Rose's performance. The only reason he showed up at all was that Bart would have suspended him from managing if he had failed to, and Rose needed his job. He was always broke. He had been betting two thousand dollars a game, often betting ten thousand dollars a night. Often losing. Or if he were making money by betting on baseball, he was losing by gambling elsewhere. Over the time we were able to monitor his betting closely, we concluded that Rose made money gambling on baseball, but lost his baseball profits, and much more, betting on the other sports, horses, and dogs. He owed money to lots of people, including Paul Janszen, which was why Janszen went to *SI*. Rose needed his baseball paycheck; much of it was spent before he received it.

Things were getting desperate for Rose. Any juror who heard his testimony would surely have concluded he had bet on baseball. We had Rose making numerous calls to bookies, placing bets on team sports in a time of the year when there's no football, no basketball, no games to bet on other than baseball. We had people who heard Rose make calls to bookies to bet on baseball games. Rose's lawyers must have known they were getting near the end of the line.

And then we handed them a present.

John Dowd was asked to do something for one of our witnesses, a bookie named Ron Peters, who was awaiting sentence on a drug charge. At the request of Peters's lawyer, Dowd drafted a letter from Bart on Peters's behalf to the sentencing federal judge, saying that baseball had found Peters to be "candid, forthright, and truthful" in his testimony to us. Dowd sent the letter to Bart for Bart to sign, as the commissioner of baseball. The letter never went across my desk. I'd like to think that I would have intercepted it, but we'll never know. Bart signed the letter and out it went.

The federal judge was a friend of Katz's. When Katz and Rose's other lawyers saw the letter, they seized on it, on the line in particular where Bart said he found Peters to be "truthful." I am certain they would have challenged Bart anyway, but the letter gave them an opening, and that is why I have never been critical of Dowd—they would have found some other excuse to challenge the process. As it was, they brought suit in a Cincinnati state court, before a low-level elected judge, and argued that the letter proved Bart was prejudiced against Rose and had already determined Rose was guilty before holding the hearing at which Rose could defend himself. They argued Bart had disqualified himself with the letter and they sought an injunction against baseball to stop its investigation of Rose. There was some superficial appeal to their argument. In an internal investigation in baseball, the commissioner is more than just the judge and jury; in a sense, he's also the prosecutor, since he oversees the collection of the evidence and ultimately determines its truth. But throughout the legal system that process exists and has been upheld by the courts. It's no different from the way many administrative bodies function, including various federal agencies, such as the SEC and the Federal Trade Commission. Still, the elected judge in Cincinnati—demonstrating, among other things, a shrewd understanding of how elected judges get reelected—conducted a brief hearing and then issued a temporary restraining order against baseball that briefly shut us down.

It was a painful loss and a very bad time for our team. Some columnists had a field day at Bart's expense. They read the letter Bart signed, in which he said he found the testimony of a convicted drug offender to be "truthful," and some reached the same conclusion the judge did, that Bart should be disqualified. Other commentators saw the court case for what it was—the desperate act of a guilty person to avoid a hearing. It reminded me of the ancient legal maxim: If you can't argue the facts, argue the process. Poor Bart was taking a beating, alone. It wasn't my name in the critical columns against us, and it wasn't Dowd's name. It was Bart's name.

I tried to explain to Bart that it was only a matter of time until we got the suit out of the court of an elected judge in Cincinnati and into a federal court, before a smart federal judge who would understand the historic and legitimate role of the baseball commissioner in adjudicating baseball matters. I tried to tell Bart about similar problems I had had at Columbia Pictures, with untrue charges brought against me, and that ultimately one gets in front of a judge who knows what he's doing and things straighten out. I kept saying to Bart: "The system works. You have to have faith in the system. We will prevail." I had been saying that to him for so long it ultimately became a standing joke between us. Bart would say to Dowd or to anyone who happened to be in the room, "Here is a man who believes in the system, who believes the system will prevail!" Typically, he would say this with mirth. "Can you believe this, a man of Mr. Vincent's abilities who believes in the system!" It was funny. But soon the mirth disappeared and his mood darkened.

In the middle of all this, Bowie Kuhn, Ueberroth's predecessor as commissioner, started lobbying the owners, saying Bart was in trouble and he would be willing to help out: He would take over the Rose case from Bart, dispose of it promptly, then step aside. Bowie has never gotten over being commissioner, the owners knew that, so his overtures were never taken seriously. Still, Bart was growing deeply frustrated.

One night, at the height of this mess—with writers expressing the views of millions of Rose fans every day, that the commissioner was biased against Pete—Bart and Dowd and I went out for dinner. He did what people always do when they're under pressure or they've made a mistake: They look for somebody to blame. At this dinner, Bart blew up. He said, "Goddamn it, the two of you are supposed to be looking out for me! I'm getting killed. All my life I've worked to achieve a reputation and now my reputation is under attack. I'm finished." His voice was loud. He was frightened. It was not a good scene.

I had never seen Bart in so ugly a mood. In that whole period, he was chain-smoking, barely sleeping, eating constantly, getting no exer-

cise, getting pounded in the papers every morning and by the legal system during the rest of the day. But now Bart had turned on me, and I
was hurt. I loved him like a brother. I had gone into baseball with him
as an act of friendship more than anything else, but now the friendship was being tested, in a setting I understood but he found totally
confusing. John and I tried to reason with him, tried to tell him how
this crazy legal process worked, that ultimately things would be put
straight. But Bart was not able to listen to us.

I went home to Greenwich, tired, depressed, upset, and angry. I was
ready to quit. I called an old friend of mine, Vincent Burke, and told
him I was ready to resign, that my friendship with Bart was in jeopardy.
Calmly, Burke, a wise banker and Washington counselor, urged patience. I hung up, and almost immediately the phone rang. It was Bart,
of course. I was becoming accustomed to hearing from him after the
eleven o'clock news. For him, the night was still very young.

"Dep," he said warmly, "how are you? I feel bad. I apologize. I should
have never said those things. I ask you to forgive me and to be tolerant
of me. It was just frustration. You have been a good friend through
this. Where would I be without you?"

I was very touched that he knew he had to call me. "It's a good thing
you called," I said. "I was thinking of quitting."

"Don't even use those words!" Bart said. "I would never let you do
that. We're too close."

I said, "Bart, you have to calm down. You are taking things way too
personally. You're too close to it."

After that, the sky cleared and we were fine. It was the only time we
had sharp words. Bart tried to calm down, which wasn't easy for him.
But he never forgot the underlying reason I was working with him, as
an act of friendship. We had gone into baseball to do some good and to
have fun together. We never anticipated becoming embroiled in the
sort of miserable filth the Rose case had become. Unlike Bart, I have
always enjoyed a good fight when I'm fighting for something I believe
in and the rules are fair. I believed it was important to rid baseball of
any person who gambled on, and therefore jeopardized, the game. But
dealing with Rose certainly wasn't the kind of fun we anticipated.

Moreover, it became clear to me Bart did not have the same stomach for a fight I had. His kind of fight was over the proper interpretation of Dante.

From the day we met at Peter Knipe's house in Princeton, I had viewed Bart as an actor. He was always "on." His wife, Toni, was a talented actress, and they had met at the Yale Drama School. Their two sons, Marcus and Paul, are today accomplished, distinguished professional actors. Bart had a dramatic personality, and every day he was on-stage performing the role of baseball commissioner. Every day the newspapers carried some sort of critique of his performance, and he lived and died by those "reviews." It is not an easy way to go through life, although it is exciting. I believe Toni is much the same. She is a smart woman who reads widely and taught at a private school outside New Haven, Hopkins, including a class in journalism. She has a great ear for language, and when Bart was president of Yale she helped edit his speeches. When Bart was commissioner, she parsed his reviews.

One night, Bart called and said, "Will you talk to Toni? She has all these clippings here, with these Post-Its attached to them, and she says we're getting slammed. Will you explain to her our strategy—what the hell we're doing?"

Toni came on the phone and was frenetic. She started reading to me, sentence by sentence, from one story after another, interrupted only by her saying, "Let me read this to you." She'd read some more and conclude by saying, "What is Bart going to do? How is Bart going to survive this?" Over the course of the summer of 1989, I probably had three or four such conversations with Toni. She was intense and very smart and totally devoted to Bart.

One morning, Bart came in with a fistful of articles by Murray Chass, the senior baseball writer for *The New York Times*. Bart said, "Toni has counted the column inches. She says Chass is on Rose's side. He is devoting more column inches to Rose's position than to mine."

"Bart," I said, "it doesn't go by weight."

"No, sir, Toni is correct." Bart always used "correct" when lesser speakers used "right." If something was really right it was "exactly correct." He said, "Chass is biased against me. I am going to call the *Times*'s sports editor and get this straightened out. I'm going to have lunch with him and you're going to come."

"Not on your life," I said. "You do that and Chass will really go after you. All he's done so far is treat you fairly. He writes every day and you don't. You piss him off and he'll hammer you."

Bart: "We are going to have this out and you're coming."

So we had the lunch, Bart and I and the sports editor, Joe Vecchione, a wise and gentle man who had the good sense to bring Chass along. Bart went through his clippings, as if he were correcting papers. I have to believe Chass and Vecchione had never seen anything like it. Chass made the case that balanced reporting doesn't go by inches, that sometimes a very strong point can be summarized in a very few words. He was thoughtful and unfazed. Vecchione said he'd look into Bart's complaints.

After the lunch, Bart said, "I thought that went very well."

Me: "It was a nonevent. It was absurd."

Bart: "I think we'll get a much fairer shake from Chass now."

"Bart, you're lucky Chass is a nice guy and a fair man, or he'd run you into the ground, day after day." I had watched in Washington when Shirley Povich, the legendary sports columnist for *The Washington Post,* went after the owner of the Redskins, George Preston Marshall, for not having any black players on his football team. He pounded Marshall every day and ran him out of town.

Bart would have none of it. "Next I'm going to bring in Lupica, turn him around." Mike Lupica was an influential columnist then on the *Daily News* in New York. "He's a little guinea who thinks he writes great English sentences." Lupica had been critical of Bart on the Rose case.

"I want to be there for that one," I said.

"Oh, no, that's just going to be Lupica and me, Italian to Italian. I'm going to tell him he's better than the stuff he is writing. He'll love it."

Lupica came in, they had their lunch, and afterward Bart said to me, "I don't think we'll have any more problems with Lupica." I don't know that the meeting had any effect on Lupica, but it certainly made

Bart feel better. I think Bart would have brought in all the big pens if he could have, one by one. His press was very important to him. That he could write circles around them only made the relationships more interesting.

He loved doing little stand-up interviews with the writers and the TV crews as he left his Park Avenue office each evening. They would be lined up, waiting for him, and it was an irresistible temptation for Bart. I waited in the car while Bart answered one question after another, some posed as hypotheticals: If Rose were to do this, what would you do? If the judge were to do this, what would you do? This is an old technique for creating news on slow days. Night after night I warned Bart not to answer hypotheticals. He, of course, ignored me. One day, his response to a hypothetical got him in trouble, nothing significant, nothing even memorable, but he got ripped for the answer.

The next day, somebody posed another hypothetical. Bart said: "It has become my custom not to answer hypothetical questions. It is sound practice, I have found, not to answer such questions as they are not based on fact. Therefore, I will answer hypotheticals no longer."

He folded himself into the car and said, "OK?"

"You're slow," I said. "But you get there."

Finally, we were able to move the injunction case away from the local elected judge in Cincinnati and before a federal judge, John D. Holschuh, in Columbus. Our need and ability to make the move is exactly what the men who constructed our court system—Thomas Jefferson and Alexander Hamilton and James Madison and their brethren—had in mind. They knew if you were from Massachusetts and were sued in Virginia and had to appear before a local state court judge who might well know the person bringing suit, your chances of getting an unprejudiced hearing were diminished. Our aim was to have a judge declare that baseball was within its legal rights to have a hearing at which Bart, as commissioner, would preside, to determine whether Rose had gambled on baseball.

The day Judge Holschuh decided he would retain the case and not return it to the Cincinnati court, Katz knew his client was in deep trouble. Judge Holschuh had not yet ruled on the merits of the injunction, but Katz could see where the case was heading: He knew the judge would quickly rule that Bart was not biased against Rose and that he was legally authorized to conduct the hearing. That would leave Rose with no option but to appear to defend himself, and Katz knew there was no defense. I'm confident Katz told Rose he now had two choices: Go to Bart's hearing in New York, where Rose knew there were no answers to John Dowd's questions and evidence, or cut a deal. Either way, Katz had to know he was cooked. If he made a deal, he could at least avoid the embarrassment of a public finding by the commissioner that Rose had bet on baseball. I know this, because the very day the federal judge made this ruling I received a call from Katz, saying he was ready to discuss a deal. Katz knew exactly what our case looked like because we had given all our evidence to him and ultimately to the public. (People have been saying for years. Why isn't the evidence against Rose public? The evidence *is* public. It's available on the internet at www.dowdreport.com.)

I was exultant, for many reasons. For one thing, I had proven to my friend Bart that one of my underlying life philosophies was correct: The system does work and you can have faith in it. Bart was pleased with the legal victory in Columbus, but I think he still felt damaged by the process. Dowd, of course, felt vindicated and relieved.

We would be negotiating with Katz from real strength. I said to Bart, "We should insist on everything we want. Rose should be banished from baseball for life." It was still in baseball's interest to reach an agreement with Rose, rather than to hold a hearing. The crux of our thinking was that whatever he did, even after a full hearing, Rose would never admit his guilt. In a hearing, Bart could determine that Rose bet on baseball, but Rose would deny it and could fight in the courts to get reinstated; in an agreement, we would prevent Rose from denying he bet on baseball and make Rose promise the agreement would be the final word, so he couldn't appeal it in the courts.

When Katz called me the day Holschuh took jurisdiction of the case, he began, "Do you think we should renew our talks about settling this case." He was very cordial. We both fully understood what had happened and what it meant.

"Sure," I said. "What do you have in mind?"

Katz said: "Pete would now be willing to accept a sanction of significance."

I said, "The only sanction we will talk about is Pete being out of baseball for life. There is no negotiating the sanction. He is out for life." In other words, placed on baseball's permanently ineligible list.

"We might be able to live with that," Katz said, "but Pete will not admit to betting on baseball."

I said, "We might be able to live with that, as long as he won't deny that he bet on baseball."

I went back to Bart. Those terms were acceptable to him. The concept of a "no admission/no denial" agreement was part of my SEC experience. It made sense to all of us, though we had few illusions that Pete Rose would understand all the legal niceties. Still, this was the only way to proceed. I went back to Katz. He now wanted Rose to be able to apply for reinstatement after two or three years. I countered with ten years. Then a Washington lawyer working for baseball—Vincent Burke, Jr., son of my friend Vincent Burke—called me and said, "I've been reading the rules of baseball."

"Good for you," I said. "I'm glad we've got someone on our side reading our own rules."

"The rules say anybody thrown out of baseball may apply for reinstatement after one year," Burke said. Katz and I should have known that, but we did not. In this, as in all of life, details truly matter.

I called Katz with this good news: Rose would be able to apply for reinstatement after one year and no agreement could alter that. But, I said to Katz, he should not take this as any suggestion that after one year he would be coming back.

"That's disappointing," Katz said. "Can I talk to Bart about it?"

The three of us talked. I told Bart before the conversation that he should be clear to Katz on Rose's chances for reinstatement after one year. And Bart was. During the conversation I said, "Pete has to reconfigure his life." Bart jumped on that. "That's a wonderful phrase. Mr. Vincent is exactly correct. Pete must reconfigure his life. We won't tell you what we will do in a year because we do not know. There can be no understanding, no commitment. You have in effect a constitutional right under baseball's rules to apply for readmission but that does not say we will grant it."

Had there been any other kind of understanding, it would have been put into the agreement, in writing. But what is in writing is that Rose acknowledged the commissioner had a basis for throwing Rose out of the game for life, that he admitted to violating baseball's Rule 21, which involves conduct contrary to the best interests of baseball. Rule 21 (d) is the gambling on baseball section. We did not specify what part of Rule 21 Rose violated. That was a concession to Katz. The agreement stipulated that Rose would not challenge the decision in any court.

Katz said, "Pete will admit to betting on other sports and making mistakes but not admit to betting on baseball." We were willing to live with that because we knew Rose would never admit his guilt even after a hearing. We weren't eager to have the matter drag on, to have the game's soiled laundry so prominently on public display. That was not in the best interests of the game. There was much to be gained by ending it all right then. Moreover, we wanted to get the Rose gambling affair out of the courts once and for all. The courts were no place for baseball to sort out its internal problems. Each side had an incentive to settle. I said to Katz, "There will be a paragraph in our agreement in which Pete neither admits nor denies be bet on baseball." I was drawing on my SEC experience where that form of consent decree ends most SEC investigations. It's a sort of *nolo contendere* plea, the no contest plea, which Spiro Agnew as vice president used so famously in his tax evasion charges: I will not deny I did it, but I won't admit it, either.

Katz and I began a discussion about who could say what after we settled. I said I'd need to check with Bart and did; Bart said, "Don't do anything that limits my ability to talk. I have to be able to talk. Talking is what I do best." His humor was returning to him by this point; he knew our ordeal was nearly over. I explained to Bart that whatever he said had to be consistent with the agreement and the agreement precluded Bart from saying that he had made a "finding"—a legal term—that Rose had bet on baseball. Such a finding would have been the outcome of a hearing on the evidence, which was never held. Bart was OK with that. Katz then raised the question: What would Bart say if a reporter asked, Do you believe Rose bet on baseball? That is a different circumstance. Bart actually rehearsed an answer that would be consistent with the agreement: "I have made no formal finding because there has been no hearing. But if you are asking me as an individual, do I believe Mr. Rose bet on baseball, the answer is yes." I told Katz exactly what Bart would say in response to such a question. "We don't like it," he said, "but I guess we have no choice." To this day, I don't believe Katz ever fully explained to Rose how difficult it would be for him to be reinstated or what Bart was going to say at the press conference at which he announced Rose's banishment from the game. I'll explain why a little later, but first allow me to describe the press conference, which was held on Thursday, August 24, 1989, in the ballroom at the Marriott Marquis in midtown Manhattan.

Bart spent the night before in the hotel, writing and rewriting his speech. It would surely be the most important speech of his public life. When he wrote it, he was intensely worried abut getting it just the way he wanted it. He needed it to be perfect. We met for breakfast that morning and went over some of what he was going to say. He consulted intensely with John Dowd. We rehearsed answers to questions we knew we would get. Bart looked awful. There were bags under his eyes, he was perspiring profusely, smoking one cigarette after another, eating one Danish after another. I remember Phil Knecht, my driver, saying to me, "Boss, is the commissioner OK? He's drenched." But by the time the red lights went on, Bart looked terrific, composed and confident. He was back to teaching. He delivered the lecture of his life:

> The banishment for life of Pete Rose from baseball is the sad end of
> a sorry episode. One of the game's greatest players has engaged in a
> variety of acts which have stained the game, and he must now live

with the consequences of those acts. By choosing not to come to a hearing before me, and by choosing not to proffer any testimony or evidence contrary to the evidence and information contained in the report of the special counsel to the commissioner, Mr. Rose has accepted baseball's ultimate sanction, lifetime ineligibility.

This sorry episode began last February when baseball received firm allegations that Mr. Rose bet on baseball games and on the Reds' games. Such grave charges could not be ignored. Accordingly, I engaged and Mr. Ueberroth appointed John Dowd as Special Counsel to investigate these and other allegations that might arise and to pursue the truth wherever it took him. I believed then and believe now that such a process, whereby an experienced professional inquires on behalf of the Commissioner as the Commissioner's agent, is fair and appropriate. To pretend that serious charges of any kind can be responsibly examined by a Commissioner alone fails to recognize the necessity to bring professionalism and fairness to any examination and the complexity a private entity encounters when, without judicial or legal powers, it pursues allegations in the complex, real world.

Baseball has never before undertaken such a process because there had not been such grave allegations since the time of Landis. If one is responsible for protecting the integrity of the game of baseball—that is, the game's authenticity, honesty and coherence—then the process one uses to protect the integrity of baseball must itself embody that integrity. I sought by means of a Special Counsel of proven professionalism and integrity, who was obliged to keep the subject of the investigation and his representatives informed about key information, to create a mechanism whereby the integrity we sought to protect was never violated. Similarly, in writing to Mr. Rose on May 11, I designed, as is my responsibility, a set of procedures for a hearing that would have afforded him every opportunity to present statements or testimony of witnesses or any other evidence he saw fit to answer the information and evidence presented in the Report of the Special Counsel and its accompanying materials.

That Mr. Rose and his counsel chose to pursue a course in the courts rather than appear at hearings scheduled for May 25 and then June 26, and then chose to come forward with a stated desire to settle this matter, is now well known to all. My purpose in recounting the process and the procedures animating the process is to make two points that the American public deserves to know.

First, that the integrity of the game cannot be defended except by a process that itself embodies integrity and fairness.

Second, should any other occasion arise where charges are made or acts are said to be committed that are contrary to the interests of the game or that undermine the integrity of baseball, I fully intend to use such a process and procedure to get to the truth and, if need be, to root out the offending behavior. I intend to use, in short, every lawful and ethical means to defend and protect the game.

I say this so that there may be no doubt about where I stand or why I stand there. I believe baseball is a beautiful and exciting game, loved by millions—I among them—and I believe baseball is an important, enduring American institution. It must assert and aspire to the highest principles, of integrity, of professionalism and performance, of fair play within its rules. It will come as no surprise that like any institution composed of human beings, this institution will not always fulfill its highest aspirations. I know of no earthly institution that does. But this one, because it is so much a part of our history as a people and because it has such a purchase on our national soul, has an obligation to the people for whom it is played—to its fans and well-wishers—to strive for excellence in all things and to promote the highest ideals.

I will be told that I am an idealist. I hope so. I will continue to locate ideals I hold for myself and for my country in the national game as well as in other of our national institutions. And while there will be debate and dissent about this or that or another occurrence on or off the field, and while the game's nobler parts will always be enmeshed in the human frailties of those who, whatever their role, have stewardship of this game, let there be no doubts or dissent about our goals for baseball or our dedication to it. Nor about vigilance and vigor—and patience—in protecting the game from blemish or stain or disgrace.

The matter of Mr. Rose is now closed. It will be debated and discussed. Let no one think that it did not hurt baseball. That hurt will pass, however, as the great glory of the game asserts itself and a resilient institution goes forward. Let it also be clear that no individual is superior to the game.

After the statement was delivered, Bart took questions. Among the earliest was the one we anticipated, the most important one. Bart answered precisely using words that allowed him to talk but in no way violated the terms of our agreement with Rose and Katz: "In the absence of a hearing, and therefore in the absence of evidence to the contrary, I am confronted by the factual record of Mr. Dowd. On the basis of that, yes, I have concluded he bet on baseball." Bart's conclusion was a personal one: it was not a "finding" by the commissioner.

Somebody asked if Bart would consider reinstatement if Rose underwent treatment for a gambling problem. His answer was vintage Bart: "Treatment? Ah, treatment. With all due respect, my friends, I do not practice clinical psychology by remote control. We have not required treatment. It seems to me entirely in Mr. Rose's hands. I'm not here to prescribe, dictate or diagnose. In these matters, I am an agnostic."

Many questions were posed, from all directions, and Bart, naturally, loved it. "Please, please, one at a time, ladies and gentlemen," he said. "All your questions will be answered. We'll stay here all day and into the night, if need be. Please, there are many of you, and only one of me. I'm just a baseball commissioner, wandering, as the poet said, lonely as a cloud."

Of all our moments together, this was my favorite. It was a little wink from Bart to me, a line from the Wordsworth poem "Daffodils," which we both enjoyed:

> I wandered lonely as a cloud
> That floats on high o'er vales and hills,
> When all at once I saw a crowd.
> A host, of golden daffodils;
> Beside the lake, beneath the trees,
> Fluttering and dancing in the breeze.

We had long had a private game in which the opening line of that poem was a signal between us, a way to acknowledge our love for Wordsworth, a private acknowledgment of each other in the most public of settings. To me, it was Bart saying, "Good to be with you, old pal."

Bart talked with the press for about two hours that morning. Immediately after our press conference, Rose had one of his own, in which he denied he had ever bet on baseball. Of course, in so doing he violated his agreement with us. He predicted he'd be back in baseball within a year. He said he had an infant daughter and that he'd be back in baseball before her first birthday party. Bart and I were eating lunch and watched Rose's press conference on TV. We thought he was pathetic, but not surprising. Later that day, he was hawking signed bats and balls on TV, still making money off his name and his status as baseball's all-time hits leader. In Cincinnati, in some of the working-man's bars in the city's river wards, Bart was hung in effigy. But in the rest of the nation, as best we could judge, Bart was praised for being evenhanded but tough, for taking the strong and necessary stance about gambling in the game, the one thing that could undermine baseball in the blink of an eye. People understood, it seemed to us, what we had done and why. We were on a high.

I can only guess why Rose was out peddling his wares and making brash statements while the ink on our agreement was still drying: His lawyer, Reuven Katz, may not have been wholly candid with him. I don't think Rose understood the latitude Bart had to speak about the agreement and how difficult it would be for Rose to be reinstated. I wonder whether Pete ever read the agreement carefully. I imagine that if Katz had laid everything out for Rose, Rose might not have signed the settlement agreement, there would have been a hearing, and the hearing would have damaged Rose's reputation even more. I cannot criticize Katz if in fact he was less than clear with his client. He had made the best of a bad deck of cards.

When I'm asked about Rose, people generally pose one or more of the following five questions. I will answer them here, knowing that I will continue to answer them as long as I walk this baseball-loving earth.

Did Rose bet?

Absolutely. The evidence in the Dowd Report is overwhelming and Rose has never offered any rebuttal to it. For me, there are three convincing elements to the evidence: the calls he made from the clubhouse, the calls he made from home, and the testimony of his former friend, Tommy Gioiosa.

Marge Schott's frugality was costly to her beloved manager. The Reds owner was angry at the number of personal calls being made from the clubhouse phones, calls she had to pay for, so she decided to keep records of all outgoing calls. We got those records. They showed many calls by Rose, just before the start of games. And who was he calling? His bookie, Ron Peters. Rose was asked many times why he would call Peters immediately before game time. He never gave an explanation.

We also got the calling records from his home phone. They showed many calls to his bookie in the middle of summer, when there was no basketball or football to bet on. (Rose bet the horses and dogs at the tracks.) Again, Rose couldn't or wouldn't explain who made the calls if he didn't. Peters confirmed the betting.

Finally, there are baseball betting slips with Rose's handwriting and fingerprints on them. What more evidence, short of a confession, could there be?

After more than a decade, no one has come forward with any factual explanation, defense, or refutation of baseball's conclusions. Rose himself has chosen to ignore the issue. He prefers to attack Dowd or Bart or me, claiming we treated him unfairly. He is like someone who has pled guilty and then attacks the investigation that provided the evidence against him.

What's so bad about betting on your own team?

As far as we could tell, Rose always bet on the Reds to win. But he bet only on select days. A manager who bets on certain days has an inherent corrupt conflict. He might, for instance, save his relievers for days he plans to bet. He might leave a starter in longer, depending on how much he cares about the outcome. More important, a gambling manager might amass large debts, then be unable to pay off those debts without doing special favors for the bookie. The logic behind Rule 21 is sound: Anyone who bets on a game in which he has an interest is banned for life. The punishment for betting on games in which you have no interest is a one-year suspension. Judge Landis knew what he was doing.

Is there any evidence of Rose betting on specific games?

Yes. Ron Peters, Rose's main bookie, recorded Rose's bets. The records show the dates of specific games. We collected corresponding slips noting these specific bets with Pete Rose's name and fingerprints on them. The baseball author Bill James, an expert on statistics who has contributed to our understanding of the game, has tried to poke holes in the Dowd Report, but he does not understand evidence, which is different from definitive proof. Evidence is cumulative; proof is scientific. Evidence must be studied and weighed. We had phone records, the bookie's testimony, and betting slips! As John Dowd said to Bart, "If this were a jury case, we wouldn't order lunch for the jurors." In other words, that's how quickly they'd return a guilty verdict.

Is it troubling that so many of those who testified against Rose are lowlifes, felons, and drug dealers?

Asked that question, the wise old baseball man Frank Slocum once said, "Hey, Rose didn't hang around with priests, lawyers, and college professors. The guys he was close to are the guys who testified. His buddies were lowlifes. Those were the guys he was comfortable with."

Why is betting treated differently than doing illegal drugs, as Steve Howe did?

Two answers. First, there's the baseball constitution, called The Major-League Agreement, drafted by Landis. The agreement specifies that gambling on your own team is the lone capital crime. Second, corruption in baseball is the only serious threat to the game. The 1919 Black Sox scandal nearly killed baseball. Drugs are a serious problem, but they hurt the individual primarily, they don't go to the heart of the game. The Steve Howe case never threatened to undermine the entire institution, but widespread gambling is cancer. The players union has claimed that taking drugs is basically a medical problem, and society accepts it as such. They have not yet taken that view of gambling. Gambling on baseball by those involved in the game is a colossally undisciplined, selfish, and foolish act. Pete Rose, I believe, simply refused to believe anyone would apply the rules to him. He thought he was too big to be challenged. Bart, wisely, proved otherwise.

For years I wondered why Rose didn't come into our office that first day and say, "I've gambled, I've gambled on baseball, I understand you're going to throw me out of the game. What do I have to do to get back in it?" The whole matter might have been handled differently. Rose could have reconfigured his life and worked his way back into the game. But now I think I know why Rose did not do that: His gambling problems were just the tip of the iceberg. Rose had serious tax problems and business associates involved in money laundering and drug dealing. The code among criminals—and Rose, who later served a six-month prison sentence for tax evasion, was a criminal—is to admit to nothing. Admit to something, anything, and you open up yourself to one investigation after another.

I think Rose's ultimate failing as a person was the thing that made him great as a player: his arrogance. A writer for USA *Today*, Hal Bodley, once said to me, "Fay, this is not something I could ever write, because Rose and I were friends, but there's something you should know. You should never feel a moment of guilt about kicking Rose out of the game. He bet on baseball. I know because I was with him when he did. He bet on baseball when he was with the Phillies in 1981. We were in a hotel dining room and he kept running out of the room to talk to someone on the phone and it was clear he was talking to bookies. I said to him, 'Pete, are you betting on baseball?' He said, 'Oh, sure. I've been doing that for a long time.' I said, 'If you don't stop that and they catch you you'll be finished.' Rose said, 'They'll never bother me. I'm too big.' " That's Rose. (Bodley refuses to confirm his statement, I suspect out of loyalty to Pete.)

People often assume that Bart and I are responsible for Rose's failure to get into the Hall of Fame. It so happens that neither Bart nor I felt Rose deserves to be enshrined in Cooperstown, but the fact he's not there was not something we arranged. Of course, on statistics alone, he's a Hall of Famer. He's a first-ballot Hall of Famer. The back of his baseball card is a staggering thing to look at, when you see how consistently he hit for average year after year. But Bart and I believed there should be a significant character component for entry into the Hall of Fame, and Rose failed miserably in that category. Still, the commissioner of baseball does not decide who gets in. Modern-day candidates are voted on by ten-year members of the Baseball Writers Association of America. Until recently, a Veterans Committee decided who among overlooked players and managers from earlier eras should get in, including old Negro Leaguers. During the Rose investigation, Ed Stack, the president of the Hall of Fame, said they were going to institute a change in the voting procedure by which any player on the "permanently ineligible" list could not be a candidate for admission. I was on the board of the Hall of Fame at the time. Right about then, there was a big push to convince the Veterans Committee to have Joe Jackson admitted to the Hall of Fame, even though he was on the permanently ineligible list. Stack, of course, well understood that if there was a rule change that kept Jackson's name off the ballot, it would keep Rose's name off the ballot, too, if he were to be on the permanently ineligible list. In other words, Rose's name would never reach the writers' ballot.

I said to Stack, "This is not an issue I can vote on. It's your idea, not mine. If you want to make that rule change, make it. I'm doubtful the writers would vote him in anyhow. But I don't want to be part of the vote because I don't want it to look like I'm rigging the system against Rose." The Hall made its rule changes. I didn't attend the meeting in which they were discussed. I didn't vote. And almost every fan I've ever talked to about Rose and the Hall of Fame thinks that I'm responsible for keeping him out. In my personal view, a public debate about what role character should play in electing a player to the Hall of Fame would be a healthy thing. Based on statistics, Joe Jackson deserves a Cooperstown plaque even more than Rose; he was a far better hitter. It is my view Jackson should not be in the Hall of Fame, either. He took money from gamblers to fix a World Series. He undermined fans' trust in the game. Yes, he played his heart out in that World Series; yes, he was a simple man who may not have understood what he was agreeing to do. The fact is, he endangered the game and his responsibility was to reveal the gamblers' plot to the authorities. Rose, to me, demonstrates a character with even deeper flaws because of his arrogance and lack of regret. I wouldn't want to see either in the Hall of Fame. But I think debate over the question, as Bart suggested in the final part of his banishment speech, could be interesting—so long as I'm not obliged to participate.

Being placed on the permanently ineligible list is the ultimate deterrent, designed to keep players honest and away from gamblers and gambling. It's critical and it's harsh, as it needs to be. Who can argue with its almost total effectiveness?

In 1999, at the All-Star game at Fenway, baseball honored an all-century team. The living members on that team were invited onto the field. Yogi Berra was there. Ernie Banks, Warren Spahn, Ted Williams, Henry Aaron, Stan Musial, Willie Mays, Sandy Koufax, too, true giants in the game. Bud Selig sadly allowed Pete Rose to participate. I think that was a mistake and I suspect Selig agrees with me—now. The rules state that if you are on the permanently ineligible list you cannot participate in any on-field baseball activity of any sort. You're not even allowed to be a guest of an owner in the stands. You can buy a ticket like an ordinary fan, but that's about as close as you're going to come to being back in baseball. For this one night, Selig made an exception for Rose, who was grilled about his gambling activities in a live interview with Jim Gray, a TV reporter. The way the interview played out, Rose engendered sympathy from the public, sympathy he doesn't deserve. His presence on this great occasion made baseball look hypocritical. Several Hall of Famers, most recently Brooks Robinson, the great third baseman, have told me that if Rose ever gets into Cooperstown without an admission or apology, they would not come back. I don't believe Rose belonged on the same field as Musial, Williams, Berra, Aaron, Spahn, Mays, Koufax, Banks, and Robinson. I certainly don't believe he belongs in baseball's ultimate sanctuary with them.

o   o   o

BART BANISHED ROSE on August 24, 1989, a Wednesday. The next week, on Friday, Bart and I flew to Massachusetts, first to Martha's Vineyard, where Bart had a summer home, and then to Cape Cod, where I had one. We flew in a small prop plane I used to charter, a twin-engine, two-pilot Beechcraft King Air. My sister Joanna, the doctor, was with us, as was Paul Giamatti, Bart's son, now a prominent Hollywood actor.

Bart was in a wonderful mood. The night before, he had had dinner in Princeton with John McPhee, the superb writer, and Bill Bradley, then the United States senator from New Jersey. I don't know what they discussed, but Bradley was being viewed as a possible presidential candidate and I think it's reasonable to assume some of the discussion involved Bill's political future. Maybe Bart dreamed of being Bradley's running mate, or his secretary of education. Those kinds of thoughts can escalate quickly and get heady. Bart was getting high marks from the columnists and from the public for his handling of Rose. (Not, of course, in Cincinnati, but most everywhere else.) The next presidential election was three years away. Bart was a big thinker and a big dreamer; once he dominated a role, as he did at Yale, he was ready to move on. I don't think he would have stayed in baseball much longer. We went into baseball thinking it would be an excellent midlife excursion, our boys' night out. We knew someday we would return to the real world.

On the flight up, Bart was having a good time, bossing all of us around, smoking cigarettes over my objections and acting as if he owned the place. I reminded him that even though he was the commissioner of baseball, the plane was mine and that he was my guest. My argument made no impression on him. My doctor sister was teasing him about his cigarettes. He said: "Joanna, at smoking cigarettes, I am world-class." He used to say that if he had the guts he'd smoke unfiltered Camels.

We were telling silly stories, apropos of nothing. Bart told a story about the time he and his wife, Toni, and his three kids were living in the Yale presidential mansion on Hillhouse Street, on the campus in New Haven. The alarm went off one night at 3:00 A.M. Detective Giamatti quickly determined there was no attempted break-in, no intruders in his house except perhaps some sort of spider that had set off the alarm. While the kids and Toni screamed at Bart to do something, anything, the distinguished Yale president, in his pajamas, grabbed a giant broom and began leaping pathetically in an effort to knock the alarm box, perched above a great stairwell between the second and third floors, from its spot. It was a story about futility, about a man of considerable intellect and power and ability who could not turn off the alarm system in his house, revealing his limitations and his powerlessness to his family. We all laughed.

Bart and I felt the fun was about to start for us. The pennant races, the playoffs, the World Series—now we would start to enjoy the sublime pleasures of our jobs, addressing issues in the game by day, taking in games by night. We agreed we would stop talking about Rose. We had said all there was to say and now we would concentrate on other issues. Getting more black managers and general managers was high on our list of priorities. So were efforts to rebuild interest in baseball among kids and minorities, keeping drugs out of the game, and improving what Bart called "ballpark ambiance." At the top of the list, always, were the myriad economic issues facing baseball.

I told Bart I was all for his moratorium on Rose, but I had a problem: I had agreed to an interview with Rob Duca, a reporter on *The Cape Cod Times*. He was to come to my house in Harwichport that afternoon. Bart said, "That's fine. He's a good paisan. He's local. But then no more."

At about noon, we dropped Bart and Paul off at the Vineyard airport, to a warm embrace from Toni, then my sister and I made the ten-minute flight to Hyannis, on the Cape. Duca arrived around 2:00 P.M. with a photographer, who took pictures of me in sunglasses, with a cigar in my fist, sitting on my deck, looking at the sea, just like a Mafia don. They were both very nice guys and the whole experience was pleasant. Bart's happiness had lifted me, too. The guys from the paper left at about 3:00 P.M. Minutes later I received a call from Dr. Bobby

Brown, the American League president. He said: "Fay, I have bad news. We just got a call from the hospital on Martha's Vineyard. Bart's there. He's had a massive heart attack." Bobby, the former Yankee third baseman, was a cardiologist; the moment he said the word "massive," I thought: "Bart's dead."

Reports of his attack were soon all over the radio and my phone started ringing off the hook. I had only one line: I couldn't get free. Finally, a Massachusetts state police officer broke into a call and asked me to hold for a call from Toni Giamatti. She said: "Fay, Bart's dead." She was crying. I started crying. We were both in shock. She told me the formal announcement would be made shortly. Soon after, a bulletin on the radio announced that Bart had died.

Bart had stepped off the plane and rushed to Edgartown, the old whaling town on the Vineyard where he lived, to buy a wedding present for Wendy Selig, Bud's daughter. When he got into the car to go home he told Toni he felt ill. He said he had pains in his chest and down his left arm. "Bart," she said, "those are classic heart attack signs." But Bart refused to go to the hospital. "I want to go home and lie down," he said, "and have a ginger ale."

When they got to their house in the woods on the outskirts of Edgartown, Bart went to lie down and Toni went to the kitchen to get her husband a ginger ale. He loved ginger ale. By the time she brought it to him, he had had the attack. The EMS ambulance arrived soon after and Bart apparently died on the way to the hospital. An autopsy showed he had previously had a so-called silent heart attack about which he didn't even know. He was pronounced dead at the hospital at 4:32 P.M.

Camera crews soon started arriving at my Cape house. Photographers perched in the driveway and on the beach in front of my house. It was a circus my sister helped manage. The phone rang constantly. One call was from Fred Wilpon, the co-owner of the Mets and a close pal of ours. He said he was going to fly his plane up to the Vineyard to pick up Toni and Paul and bring them back to New Haven. Bart's body would stay at the Martha's Vineyard Hospital, for the autopsy. Fred asked if I would like to be picked up, too, so I flew to New Haven with them. It was a grim, quiet flight. Toni was stunned but calm. Paul looked as if he was in total shock. I was in denial. I couldn't believe Bart was gone, that it was over for us.

Bart's obituaries—his final reviews—were terrific, filled with praise. He would have loved them. President Bush said: "Bart was a close friend of mine for many, many years. He was a great person. He loved the game of baseball and in a short time made a great contribution to the game, striving for the highest possible ethical standards." George Steinbrenner, the man with whom Bart had his last telephone conversation, said, "He was a deep, deep man. Steeped in knowledge. Everybody else pales in comparison. He could have been anything he wanted. He could have been president."

Almost immediately, there were guesses about what killed Bart, or, more specifically, whether the stress from the Rose case contributed to Bart's death. I don't think one can overestimate the pressure the Rose issue put on Bart, but neither can one overlook the fact that he smoked incessantly, ate poorly, barely slept, and never exercised. Even without Rose, he was a heart attack waiting to happen. That he had had an earlier attack shows he was prone. My guess is the Rose debacle accelerated the schedule. If Bart had taken better care of himself he would not have been Bart. No one could affect his conduct—no doctor, no friend, not even Toni. Bart's father had had a heart attack at age fifty-one, the age at which Bart died, then lived for another thirty years. I suspect those extra three decades require life changes Bart could not have made. Bart lived his life skating on thin ice. That's the life he loved.

Several weeks before his death, there was a bizarre story in the *Daily News,* in which that New York tabloid published a picture, a close-up of a hand that reportedly belonged to Bart Giamatti. The story had Dr. Bobby Brown weigh in on the odd fingernail configuration on the hand in question with the opinion that such fingernails generally indicate a serious heart problem. There were only two difficulties with the story. First, the hand wasn't Bart's; it belonged to his beloved security man, Bill Carbone. Second, Bill Carbone had known about the fingernail indications but didn't have any pressing heart problems. Episodes like that didn't inspire Bart's faith in the press or the medical community. The story had him shaken, until we looked closely at the picture and realized the fingers were not his.

When Bart died, New York church officials moved in quickly. An official from the cardinal's office called, offering St. Patrick's Cathedral for a big funeral mass. There was only one problem: Bart wasn't Catholic. He was agnostic. He was interested in religion, especially Judaism, but he was not a man of faith.

Toni arranged a brief graveside service at the ancient Grove Street Cemetery, in the heart of Yale, presided over by a professor named Jarislav Pelikan, a famous Yale historian and theologian and a friend of Bart's, but not a minister. There were very few close friends present and no one from baseball. I did not find the day to be consoling in any way. I was trying to accept Bart's death and as a rationalist I tried to confront the reality. But I felt a deep sadness. Baseball was trying to quickly figure out who should succeed Bart. I wanted to grieve, but I had little chance to do so. I wanted to help Toni, but she seemed self-confident and in no need of my help. I didn't know what to do with myself or my emotions.

When my father died, at age seventy-eight, I didn't shed a tear, even though my love for him was profound. He was riddled with cancer and it would have been selfish of me to wish for anything other than the peaceful death he had. It was time for him to go and he and I had left nothing unsaid about our love for each other.

Death, of course, is part of life. One has to spend one's life prepared for death, even though, as Jesus said, death may come like a thief in the night. But Bart's death changed some of my rationalism. I had lost the brother I never had. I felt pained. I felt lonely. My confidence that I could deal with the death of a close relative or friend was shaken. This loss was immense, totally unanticipated, even if it should have been. For a long while, I couldn't talk about Bart without choking up. I still miss him.

Riding home to Greenwich after the service, I received a call from Carl Pohlad, the owner of the Minnesota Twins. He asked, "Do you want the job?" Unsure though I was of the future, I felt I did; I felt I was in a position to carry out Bart's legacy. But I wouldn't have pursued the job without Toni's blessing. I called her, and she could not have been kinder or more gracious. She said, "You should do it. Bart would have wanted you to continue."

I knew it would not be easy to take over from Bart. It was roughly like taking over center field from Joe DiMaggio. Bart was truly larger than life; I would not be. But I shared Bart's vision for the game, and I knew I could do the job.

I arranged a public memorial service for Bart at Carnegie Hall, where my friend Isaac Stern approved the use of that great hall. Frank Slocum orchestrated it and it was a wonderful event. Claire Smith, then a baseball writer for *The New York Times,* spoke. So did Roger Angell, the *New Yorker* writer, and Bud Selig, who was very close to Bart. Bart's son Marcus also spoke and stole the show with an elegant, funny, moving eulogy. I spoke last. Several Hall of Famers were behind me on the stage, Joe DiMaggio, who flew in from Japan to be there, and Bobby Doerr among them. As I finished and turned around I lost my balance and fell. Everyone assumed I was overcome by emotion. It was not that, just a routine stumble by a man who needs a cane or two. Doerr and DiMaggio jumped to my aid and helped me up. I said, "If you fall in front of hundreds of people and make a fool of yourself, it's nice to be picked up by Hall of Famers."

The Carnegie service was marred a bit by the beginning of troubles with Toni. I had reserved a special room for her off the foyer of the Hall so she could have some space and privacy before the service. She thought I was pushing her aside so the event would be all mine. My only intention was to help her. It was a difficult time for all of us.

Then there was the question of her finances. She was coming into a large sum of money, thanks to the terms of her husband's contract I had negotiated. I asked her if there was anything I could do to make sure she made the best long-term arrangements for her family. Once again, she took offense. She thought I was patronizing to her as a woman. She was angry at Yale and baseball and was taking it out on me. Over the years, I've tried to make my peace with her, unsuccessfully. That makes me very sad. We both loved Bart.

Sometimes, when I'm in New Haven, I visit Bart's gravesite, where his neighbors are other Yale presidents. For a while, there wasn't any stone marking the grave. Toni apparently didn't want one. Maybe erecting a tombstone was an act of finality she was not ready to make. I don't know. Then came a solution. There was an incident in which Lou Piniella, then the manager of the Reds, insulted an umpire, Gary Darling. He claimed Darling missed a fair-foul call out of financial motivation. He said, in effect, Darling was corrupt. The umpires' union and Darling filed a suit against Piniella. It was the kind of mess that came to me far too often. I got Lou to my office to settle the suit. At the suggestion of Richie Phillips, the head of the umpires' union, we agreed Piniella would pay an amount to a charitable trust the umpires had established. The trust, if Toni wanted it, would buy a stone for Bart's grave. He was, after all, the patron saint of the umpires. Toni agreed and the gravesite is now marked.

I still like to read Bart's writings and tell Bart stories and listen to them, too. He led a heroic life, all fifty-one years of it. A few years ago, a good friend wrote a play about my friendship with Bart. It's fitting that Bart should be a character in a play. The final lines are spoken by my character: "They said the heart attack was massive. It must have been. It stopped a massive heart." As Bart would say, that gets it exactly correct.

Lineup: Managers and Owners	
1.	Don Zimmer
2.	Marge Schott
3.	Ted Turner
4.	Tony La Russa
5.	Roger Craig
6.	Casey Stengel
7.	Yogi Berra
8.	Eddie Lopat
9.	Bill Rigney

Managers and Owners

1. DON ZIMMER

WHEN I WAS COMMISSIONER, the manager of the Chicago Cubs was a good pal of mine and one of the great baseball personalities, Don Zimmer. I never expected his name to come up in a conversation with baseball's director of security, Kevin Hallinan, but it did. Hallinan said the FBI had conducted a wiretap of a Florida drug dealer who also happened to be a small-time bookie. Don Zimmer, of all people, had been betting on football and basketball with this guy.

Betting on sports through a bookie in Florida is illegal, and consorting with alleged drug dealers is dangerous, so I could not ignore the information we had received, particularly after our drama with Pete Rose. It saddened me to hear Zimmer's name because he is such a good guy. Still, I put John Dowd on the case. Zimmer told all, and Dowd concluded that Zimmer had been gambling with the Florida bookie, but not on baseball. He also concluded that Zimmer was not

137

involved in drugs in any way and that Zimmer did not know his bookie was also a drug dealer.

Still, betting with illegal bookies is against the law and it's a dangerous activity for baseball personnel. (The FBI wiretap also picked up the names of several umpires betting with this Florida man, and we dealt with them just as we did Zimmer.) That kind of business can lead down a bad road—to debt, to pressure to pay off the debt, and where that leads nobody knows, but it's not good for the individual or the game. I decided on a strategy to deal with the issue: I would scare the bejesus out of Zimmer (and the others) so they would never bet illegally again. The only reason I'm telling this story with Don Zimmer's name in it is that he has told it himself. The others have not.

I called Zimmer to my office to tell him my decision. I wanted the meeting to have a formal air to it. Zimmer never contested the facts, which made things easier. All that remained was for me to tell him the penalty. I had my drivers and security men, Phil Knecht and Bill Carbone, go to the airport to pick up Zimmer. Phil told me later, "Boss, you never saw somebody so frightened in all your life. He was petrified. You would've thought he was going to his execution." Zimmer had spent his whole life in baseball. He often said he never cashed a paycheck from anyone other than a baseball owner. He knew what had happened to Rose, and he did not want that to happen to him. Phil said, "Mr. Zimmer, I've known Mr. Vincent a long time. He's fair. Just tell him the truth and everything will be all right."

Zimmer came in, wearing a suit. He was white as a sheet. He said he was disgusted to learn his bookie was also a drug dealer. I told him baseball could not tolerate any illegal gambling. He said he understood. I also told him I was prepared to put him on probation and to keep the matter quiet, provided he promised to cease all illegal gambling. He was relieved. "Thank you, Commissioner, I won't let you down," Zimmer said. He looked as if he had been granted a stay of execution.

And in a way, maybe he had. Since that meeting, I've seen Zimmer and his wife, Soot, on several occasions, and the conversation is always the same: Zimmer stopped gambling on team sports, and Mrs.

Zimmer has said to me, "It's so nice to be able to watch a football game on a Sunday afternoon without having Don screaming and yelling at the TV because he's got money riding on the game."

I saw Don at my friend Frank Slocum's funeral, and he said, "You changed my life. I enjoy watching sports on TV again now that I don't bet." Don Zimmer is a wonderful guy, and if by enforcing baseball's rules I improved his life, I'm delighted.

2. MARGE SCHOTT

AFTER PETE ROSE LEFT BASEBALL, the owner of the Cincinnati Reds, Marge Schott, hired an excellent baseball man, Lou Piniella, to manage her club. As a player, he was called "Sweet Lou," because of his smooth swing. His temperament was more volatile. As manager of the Reds, some of his blowups at umpires were legendary. His face would turn beet red and start to shake. As commissioner, I disliked seeing such ferocious displays of temper, particularly when they were aimed at my umpires, but in Lou's defense some of the anger had to be displaced aggression: Marge Schott was his owner, and working for her could make any sane person crazy. I only got a little taste of her act and it was more than I could stand.

For the 1990 World Series, Marge, as all owners do, crammed every last paying customer she could into her ballpark, Riverfront Stadium in Cincinnati. Even under the best of circumstances, I was far from beloved in Cincinnati for the role I played in Rose's ouster from the game, but Marge had built a "commissioner's box" for the World Series that would make me no friends. The box was on the field level but was placed in such a way that it blocked the view of the paying customers sitting behind me. As I sat down I heard a fan say, "That shithead commissioner is in our way!"

I found Marge and told her of the problem. She was in the safety of her owners box in the press level. "Oh, don't pay any attention to them," she said. "I never do." So much for my view that fans own the game.

I prevailed upon her to get rid of the box for the second game. For the first game, I was stuck; with my handicap, I can't just plop down anywhere. I sat in the makeshift box, kept my head down, and tried to prevent a riot from breaking out behind me by buying hot dogs and beers for the fans I was obstructing. I told them the box and I would be gone the next night. With that promise, which I kept, they were mollified. Peace reigned.

During the 1990 World Series, the United States was engaged in preparations for the Gulf War and at the last minute Marge decided she wanted to honor the soldiers in the Gulf. She was several sheets to the wind by this point and I told her not to go out onto the field. But off she went, grabbing a microphone right after the National Anthem and making some sort of sodden tribute to the military. I told the CBS producers not to televise anything she did under any circumstances, and they obliged. She came in off the field and somebody pointed out to her she had made a reference to our efforts in the "Far East," not the Middle East. She said, "Oh, Christ, I have to go back out to fix that."

I got word to her quickly directing her not to go back out. I knew she'd only embarrass all of us. It's her ballpark, but the World Series falls under the domain of the commissioner.

Her response to my agent was, "Tell the commissioner to go fuck himself."

When I heard that, my face must have looked like Lou Piniella's when he's going nose to nose with an umpire.

So out she went, again. Again, I told TV to avoid showing her. No one paid much attention to her antics. But I saw vividly how stubborn she could be.

Her famous dog, by the way, was lovable only to Marge. But at least Schottzie was well-behaved and did what Marge asked the dog to do. You could not say the same of Schottzie's owner.

3. TED TURNER

I'VE KNOWN TED TURNER for years and even though we don't see things quite the same way—he is famously brash and I would like to think I am measured—I enjoy his company. Wherever Ted is, something's going on. He is truly outsized. He is *sui generis*.

I remember a World Series at Atlanta where the seating order, from right to left, was me, Steve Greenberg, Jimmy Carter, Rosalynn Carter, Jane Fonda (*never* Mrs. Ted Turner), and finally Ted. Steve was, and remains, famous for eating copious amounts of ice cream, cakes, candies—even giant bags of M&Ms—without ever taking a hit to his trim waistline. On this occasion, he brought a giant bag of Mrs. Field's chocolate chip cookies to the game. He could have easily devoured the entire bag himself, but being the courteous man he is, he passed the heaping bag to his left. The Carters dipped in, husband and wife. Jane might have been good for a half-cookie, maybe a whole. Ted polished off the rest. Steve said, "Where are my cookies?" They were gone.

The next night, the seating arrangement was the same, and Steve bravely brought another heaping bag of Mrs. Field's chocolate chip cookies. "This time," he said, "the bag only goes to the right." I may have dipped my hand in the cookie bag once or twice, and Steve happily ate up the rest.

In 1991, Ted's Braves played the Minnesota Twins in the World Series. The Series opened with two games in Minnesota. Game Three was in Atlanta and Ted invited the former president to throw out the first pitch. This was a breach of both baseball protocol and custom: The protocol is for the commissioner to invite the person who will throw out the first pitch, and the custom, far more important, is for that honoree to be anybody except a politician. Politicians nearly always get booed at baseball games and that's no way to start a World Series game. (President George W. Bush is an exception because he is a known baseball man.)

Ted told me he was in a bind since he had already extended the invitation. I said, on principle, I could not yield. Ted gave up, not something he does easily. Ralph Branca and Bobby Thomson threw out the first pitches. But Carter was on hand for the game, sitting with Ted and me. Carter collected signed baseballs with great vigor. He even had me sign a half-dozen or so. "I give the balls to my family," he said. They made an odd couple, Ted and Jimmy Carter—Carter, who gave the impression of being so genteel and thoughtful, so careful with a dollar, and brash Ted, sitting together. It's an image that lingers in my mind.

Not that Ted and Jane seemed like such a likely couple. My best memory from that Series is of a banner a fan hung from the stands in Minnesota. At one of the previous games, Ted caught up on his sleep during the game and the TV cameras caught him napping with his head on Jane's shoulder. The joke was that he and his new wife weren't getting much sleep. On the night of the next game, a fan hung a sheet from the upper deck that read: "Hey, Jane, if he falls asleep again, call us. We love you."

Some years later, I sat with Jane and Ted at a playoff game at Turner Field. We were in the first row, practically on top of home plate. Ted asked me if I thought we were too close to the action.

"I would have to say yes, Ted," I answered honestly. In our seat, a foul ball could take off your head.

"I guess I could put up one of those plastic screens to protect any-one who sits here," Ted said.

"You could do that," I said.

"No, I could never do that," Ted said.

"No?"

"Nah," he said, then he turned to his wife and said, in a voice loud enough to be heard several rows away, "Jane, the commissioner wants me to put up one of those plastic screens to protect us from the action. Hell, I could never do that—it would be like having sex with a con-dom!"

The bat boys were still giggling a half-inning later. I was left shaking my head. Jane had no response whatsoever.

4. TONY LA RUSSA

COLLEGE ADVISERS LIKE TO SAY that law school is good preparation for anything, and it is true that more U.S. presidents have been lawyers than anything else, but most people who go to law school spend the rest of their lives working as lawyers. This is not always a good thing. I have been lucky in this regard, and so has Tony La Russa, the manager of the St. Louis Cardinals now, the manager of the Oakland A's during my term in baseball. He was a precocious ballplayer and a precocious manager. He appeared in his first big-league game as an eighteen-year-old infielder for the Kansas City Athletics in 1963 and first managed the Chicago White Sox in 1979 as a thirty-four-year-old, a year after he received his law degree from Florida State, which he worked toward while playing minor-league ball. He was the sixth big-league manager with a law degree. The five who came before him—James Henry O'Rourke, John Montgomery Ward, Hughie Jennings, Miller Huggins, and Branch Rickey—are all in the Hall of Fame. Before La Russa is done, he will be there, too.

We became friends during the 1989 World Series, when he was the Oakland manager, facing the San Francisco Giants. He handled everything related to the San Francisco earthquake and the delay of the Series with dignity and heart. Tony understood the positive role he and his club and baseball could play as the city tried to repair itself. He was close to Walter Haas, the Oakland owner, and so was I. That was an important link in our friendship, too. I try to see to it that once a year Tony and I get together, two reformed lawyers, to talk about baseball and the hardships and pleasures of the game.

After the 1995 season, La Russa moved to St. Louis, where he managed his old A's slugger, Mark McGwire. His going to St. Louis was a good move for both Tony and the Cardinals. A manager as smart as La Russa should be managing in the National League, where of course there is no designated-hitter rule, games turn on pitching changes and pinch-hitting, and you have to plan your every move like a chess master. Moreover, the St. Louis fans are some of the most knowledgeable in baseball, informed enough to appreciate (and second-guess) the kind of managing La Russa does. They're accustomed to good managing. For years, the Cards were managed by Whitey Herzog, one of the best managers baseball's ever had.

The ultimate baseball fan might be Bob Costas, the TV broadcaster, who lives in St. Louis. Bob knows as much baseball history as La Russa and understands the nuances of the game about as well as any nonplayer could. Costas and La Russa are longtime friends. Costas is as cerebral an announcer as La Russa is a manager. But one day, courtesy of La Russa, Costas found out that smarts alone will not take you very far in the game as it's played in the field.

While I was commissioner I received a call from Randy Costas, Bob's wife. She was very nice. Bob is turning forty, she said, and as her present she was trying to arrange for her husband to help Tony manage the Athletics during a spring-training game. Did I have any objection?

"Would Bob wear a uniform?" I asked.

"That's the plan."

"Do they have one small enough?"

"They actually do."

"That will be fun," I said. "This is one I want to see."

The game was in Arizona, while I was making the spring-training rounds there. And there was Costas in his Oakland uniform, trying to look like one of the guys. At some point, he boldly went into the batter's box to take batting practice. Not a pretty sight. His feet kept dancing all over the place on every pitch. I could relate, because I had the same problem myself as a schoolboy.

La Russa and his coaches and the players were yelling at him. They were howling. "Hey, Costas!" they said. "Stop those dancing feet!"

It doesn't matter how glib you are, how smart you are, how much you know about baseball: When baseball professionals see your game for what it is, there's no adequate response.

5. ROGER CRAIG

I GOT TO KNOW ROGER CRAIG the same way I got to know Tony La Russa: Roger was the manager of the San Francisco Giants during the '89 World Series. The events of that month—the earthquake and its aftermath—brought a lot of us who lived through it closer together. Roger and I have been friends since then. He did for me once what Tony La Russa did for Bob Costas, except that I didn't get fitted for a uniform. The A's were playing the Giants in a spring-training game and I asked Roger if I could sit beside him in the dugout through the game and see the game unfold through his eyes. He was fine with the plan as long as Tony was OK with it. La Russa said, "You should do that, absolutely, you'll learn a lot. And when we see you sitting there in the other team's dugout, I'll use that as motivation to beat your ass."

Roger and I actually sat not in the dugout but in chairs, in the sun, on the third-base side. Roger said he would give me a running commentary of everything he was thinking. At one point he said, "You know, Fay, in every baseball game I see something I've never seen before."

"Is that right? With all the games you've seen, that's amazing."

"I'm sure there will be something today I've never seen before."

"If it happens, will you tell me?"

"Sure."

As the game progressed I saw immediately the depth of Roger's baseball mind. His analysis was extraordinary. Every so often he'd say to me, "What do you think? What do you do here?" And I might say, "Send the runner." Or, "Have him bunt." Maybe, "Let him swing here 3–1." My thinking was utterly simplistic compared to what Roger was thinking. I was marveling at the refined science of managing at the major-league level when Craig said, "You see our runner on first? I'd like to hit-and-run now, but I can't. Half the time, he misses the signal. Let's see what happens here."

Craig put on the hit-and-run. His baserunner missed the sign. "That's awful," he said.

"What will you do about it?"

"You do what you can. You put your coaches on it. Tomorrow, I'll bring him in and tell him he has to shape up. But the fact is, he's going to miss half the signs. He's made it this far, he's not likely to learn how to read signs now. You've got to know your personnel."

It was a lesson: A manager's science will take you only so far. The players have to be able to execute, both physically and mentally, for the lab experiment to work.

There was never a break in the action, never a gap in Craig's analysis, and then came a nudge.

"What?" I asked. "What do you see?"

"Terry Steinbach," Roger said, referring to the Oakland catcher.

"What?"

"There just was an intentional walk and Steinbach didn't wear his mask. In all my years, I've never seen that."

As I thought about it, I hadn't either. But the point is, Roger Craig noticed it.

"It's really not very smart," the San Francisco manager said. "Every once in a while a batter tries to swing at an intentional ball. If he fouls one off, Steinbach could lose a bunch of teeth. I don't know why he's doing it but he's doing it and I've never seen it done before."

An old baseball saying goes, If you watch the game long enough, you'll see something new. Maybe it should be, If you watch the game *closely* enough, you'll always find something new.

6. CASEY STENGEL

WHEN I BECAME baseball commissioner in 1989, Casey Stengel had already been dead for fourteen years, but by the way his name came up almost daily you'd have thought he was still managing. Frank Slocum knew Casey well and used to cite one of his favorite Casey lines: "The secret of managing is to keep the five guys who hate you away from the five who are undecided." Casey is often made out to be a genius, but I'm sure the legend of the man has contributed to the depth we attribute to him. Warren Spahn pitched for Casey early in his career, on the Boston Braves, and late in his career, for the New York Mets. In between those two stints, Casey had his Yankee years: Stengel managed the Yanks from 1949 through 1960. Only twice in those years did they not win the American League pennant. In his six years with the Braves, Stengel never finished better than fifth; in his four years with the Mets, Stengel never finished better than tenth. Spahn said: "I played for Casey before and after he was a genius."

But here is a story from when he *was* a genius. Stengel was the first manager to almost religiously platoon players, to stock his lineup with righthanded batters against lefthanded pitchers and with lefthanded batters against righthanded pitchers. When a reliever came in who pitched the opposite way, Casey would routinely counteract by putting up a pinch-hitter who batted from the other side. Lefthanded batters

FRANCIS T. VINCENT, SR., captain of the Yale University
baseball team, in the school's traditional mock-pastoral
photograph. (Courtesy of the author)

MY FATHER, DRESSED IN HIS NFL OFFICIAL'S UNIFORM, trustingly holds the ball and looks away, apparently certain that my kick won't threaten his finger. (Courtesy of the author)

THE WILLIAMS COLLEGE FRESHMAN FOOTBALL TEAM OF 1956. I'm the uncommonly large fellow in the front row, second from the right. (Courtesy of the author)

BART GIAMATTI AND I TAKE IN A BALLGAME. There was far too little of this for us in Bart's tragically brief tenure as commissioner. (Ronald C. Modra/*Sports Illustrated*)

COMMISSIONER GIAMATTI ANNOUNCES PETE ROSE'S lifetime suspension from baseball. Bart's countenance attests to the ordeal the case had proved to be. (Chuck Solomon/*Sports Illustrated*)

A NICE LITTLE MEETING AT THE WHITE HOUSE: Barbara Bush chats with
Joe DiMaggio and Ted Williams, with a fortunate onlooker
in the background. (Courtesy of the author)

KELLY DOWNS CARRIES HIS SON from the stands in the aftermath
of the earthquake that postponed game three of the 1989
World Series. (John Iacono/*Sports Illustrated*)

PLAYERS, PRESS, AND ISAIAH NELSON'S POLICE CRUISER form an
unsettled gathering on the Candlestick Park field following the
7.1-magnitude quake. (Richard Mackson/*Sports Illustrated*)

ADDRESSING THE PRESS ON THE MORNING AFTER: If I look like I hadn't slept,
there's good reason. George Steinbrenner took me to task for the no-tie
look that was the least of my worries. (V. J. Lovero/*Sports Illustrated*)

GEORGE W. BUSH, GEORGE H. W. BUSH, AND FRANCIS T. VINCENT, JR.,
in the early 1990s; I hope Mr. Steinbrenner notes which of us is
wearing a tie knotted tightly. (Courtesy of the author)

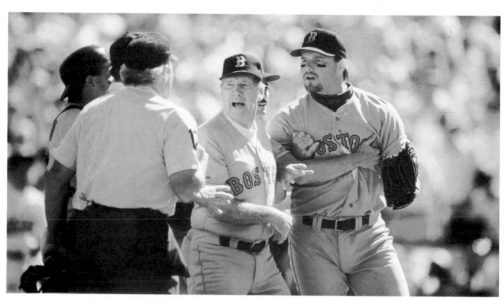

ROGER CLEMENS HAS TO BE SEPARATED from the umpires by manager Joe Morgan,
but he'd already been tossed from this playoff game. I later had to rule on the exact
wording of his deletable expletives. (John Iacono/*Sports Illustrated*)

ALFRED "SLICK" SURATT wore the baggy flannels of the Kansas
City Monarchs on the diamond, and the uniform of the United States
of America in the South Pacific in World War II. His nickname was
well earned, on and off the field. (Courtesy of the author)

AFTER I LEFT BASEBALL, some umpires showed their
displeasure with the circumstances by wearing my name on the
back of their caps—a tribute that warmed the heart of this umpire's
(and football official's) son. (Courtesy of the author)

A LIGHTHEARTED MOMENT with Steve Greenberg, my deputy commissioner;
it's indicative of the sorry state of baseball's executive suites that they let
such a talented man get away. (John Iacono/*Sports Illustrated*)

can see a pitch from a righthanded pitcher better than from a left-handed pitcher and vice versa. A righthander with a .275 average might hit .330 versus lefthanded pitchers and .250 against righthanded pitchers. In most of his Yankee years, Stengel had three true everyday players and an ace: Yogi Berra, catcher; Phil Rizzuto, shortstop; Mickey Mantle, centerfielder; Whitey Ford, ace. Everybody else, to some extent, was a role player, and if he needed to send somebody up to hit for you, he would.

For years, Stengel had two third basemen: Bobby Brown and Billy Johnson. Bobby was a lefthanded hitter who faced righthanded pitching and Johnson was a righthanded hitter who faced lefthanded pitching. Casey never allowed Bobby to face a lefty. He was playing percentages, before the age of the computerized manager.

But in the 1949 World Series, in which the Yankees played the Brooklyn Dodgers, Casey did something out of character: Brown came up in the fifth inning of Game Four of the Series, which the Yankees were leading, two games to one. Brown was due to bat against Joe Hatten, a lefthanded Dodger reliever. "All season long, Casey never let me hit against lefties," Brown told me. "I kept waiting for him to go to Billy, but he didn't. For some reason, he let me hit. I hit a bases-loaded triple. We won, 6–4.

"I had faced Hatten a lot as a kid in San Francisco. I hit him well. But Casey didn't know that. I'm the only one who could have told him that and I never did. And I hadn't faced Hatten in years. Somehow, Casey knew."

In those years, clearly, Casey was a genius. Bobby Brown, by the way, went six for twelve in that Series. Casey was smart enough to keep a hot bat swinging. Casey's career record, with good teams and bad, was 1,905 wins, 1,842 losses. He was able to stay in the managing game for twenty-five years. That takes a certain genius, too.

7. YOGI BERRA

ONE OF CASEY STENGEL's favorite players was his catcher, Yogi Berra. Stengel once said of Berra, "He springs on a bunt like it was another dollar bill." They had much in common, both shortish men with a gift for language. Yogi's specialty was to use the fewest words possible; Casey often answered reporters' questions with long essays for answers. Yogi, who had two stints as the Yankee manager, one with the Mets, and one with the Astros, no doubt learned a great deal about managing from Casey. He won the American League pennant with the Yankees in 1964, as a rookie manager—and was fired the day after the seventh game of the World Series, which the Yankees lost. In 1973, Yogi managed the Mets to a National League title in a season in which they were three games over .500, becoming the second manager to have won pennants in both leagues. When George Steinbrenner fired Yogi sixteen games into the 1985 season, Yogi swore he would never return to Yankee Stadium as long as George Steinbrenner was the Yankees owner. (Many years later, Yogi reversed his position, but only after George made the most effective apology he could: He made a significant contribution to the Yogi Berra Museum in Montclair, New Jersey.) Yogi had seen managing from both sides of the highest perch and the lowest rung of the standings. His career record as a manager is 484–444, with two ties.

I asked him once, "What makes a great manager?"

"Good players," he said.

Even Casey couldn't have answered that question any better. Longer, yes, but not better.

8. EDDIE LOPAT

MY GREAT BUDDY EDDIE LOPAT lasted not quite a season and a third as a manager. The 1963 Kansas City Athletics finished in eighth place under Ed's watchful eye. The '64 A's started with seventeen wins and thirty-five losses and Ed said goodbye to his managerial career. Still, his influence on the game as a manager was considerable.

"When I was managing, I taught my whole pitching staff how to throw the spitter," he told me once. "They were good at it. They threw it and they got away with it. The umpires were winking at it, at least in our league. But after a while they had enough and sent out a letter saying if you got caught throwing a spitter, you're going to be ejected and fined. So I told my pitchers they had to stop.

"The season's going along and we're facing the Yankees. Whitey Ford is pitching for them. I had taught him how to throw the spitter but now the league's clamping down on it. That cheeky little bastard is throwing the spitter at us anyhow.

"I knew what he was doing because I did it myself. He'd bend over and pick up the rosin bag. Everybody's watching the rosin bag. It's sleight of hand. You got to look what the other hand is doing. He was loading up with the glove hand.

"So in between innings, I walk over to him and say, 'Whitey, you're throwing that little horseshit spitter of yours. You got to stop.' He sort of smiled but didn't say anything.

"I said, 'We're not using it and if you don't stop I'm gonna say something.'

"And he said, 'All right then, I'll stop.' And he did."

It was the ultimate sign of respect, from a pupil to his teacher.

9. BILL RIGNEY

MANAGERS ARE THE BEST COLLECTORS of baseball stories because they put in the most time in the game, and therefore have the most opportunity to collect them. Managers routinely show up at the ballpark before noon for 7:35 P.M. games. In spring training, you'll often find managers in their offices or sitting in dugouts by 6:30 A.M. About the best collector of baseball stories I knew was Bill Rigney, who managed in the majors for eighteen years. He was a baseball lifer who played under Leo Durocher on the New York Giants from 1946 through 1953, then managed, then worked many more years as a scout and a TV commentator. When he died on February 19, 2001, I lost a great pal.

One year, Bill and I were invited to join Walter Haas, the owner of the Oakland A's, at his ranch in Montana. Bill and I were roommates in a little wood-frame cottage at an old dude ranch, two bedrooms separated by a kitchen. Every day we'd get up at 6:00 A.M. and he'd fry us bacon and eggs before he headed out to fish. While cooking, he told baseball stories. My favorite concerned Johnny Mize, the Hall of Famer, his teammate on the New York Giants and the pride of Demorest, Georgia.

"Johnny loved his booze," Bill said. "He'd go out on these toots at night, come to the ballpark the next day and say, 'Ah, Jeez, I really did it this time—too much booze last night. I'm gonna have to sweat it out.' He'd go run in the outfield grass in his rubber suit, thinking that he was literally sweating the alcohol out of himself.

"One day we took a bottle of rubbing alcohol and poured the whole bottle under the stool we knew he'd be sitting on when he came in. Finally, he came in and he was drenched. He was pouring out sweat. He sits down on the stool. We say, 'Johnny, that booze is coming right out of you, you're sweating pure liquor! You're gonna have to cut that out!'

"He says, 'Yeah, but I'm in good shape, I put on this rubber suit and sweat it all out.'

" 'Yeah, but you're sweating pure alcohol! Stand up and look at the puddle under you—that can't be good.'

"So Johnny stands up and looks at the puddle. Somebody says, 'Let's throw a match on it and see what happens.' We light it and of course it flares right up.

"Johnny starts jumping around: 'Oh my God, oh my God!' As far as I know, he never figured it out."

C H A P T E R   F I V E

Earthquake

SIX WEEKS AFTER BART'S DEATH, I flew out to San Francisco for the World Series, the Series by the Bay, the San Francisco Giants against the Oakland Athletics—my father's beloved, long-uprooted A's. Major League Baseball had dedicated the Series to Bart's memory, a wonderful and appropriate gesture. It happens that the public transportation system in and around San Francisco is called BART (Bay Area Rapid Transit), so we were reminded of him all the time, all of us. Our mourning continued, and to some degree I felt as if I were holding Bart's coat, as if the show were still his. There had not yet been anything to define me as commissioner.

It was 1989, an odd-numbered year, so the series began in the American League city. Before the first game, the Whiffenpoofs, the legendary Yale singing group, sang the National Anthem in memory of Bart. That was on October 14, a Saturday night, and the A's won, 5–0; Dave Stewart pitched the whole way for the winners, giving up five hits, a brilliant performance. As commissioner, naturally, I betrayed no public rooting interest, but I was secretly pleased, because Walter

Haas, the owner of the A's and of Levi-Strauss, was one of my favorite people in baseball, and I thought Dave Stewart and Tony La Russa, the Oakland manager, were two of the real gentlemen in the game. Early habits die hard, and if you're an American League fan as a boy, as I was as a New Englander, it's hard to change affiliations as an adult: All things being equal, I rooted AL. As it happens, though, I was also fond of the Giants, a team I remembered fondly from when they were in New York. I particularly liked the San Francisco owner, Bob Lurie, his manager, Roger Craig, and the Giant first baseman, Will Clark, with his sweet uppercut lefthanded swing. When you have personal connections to the participants, baseball becomes all the more interesting.

Game Two, on Sunday night in Oakland, was much the same as the first: The A's were dominating and they won, 5–1. There was no game on Monday as the Series moved eleven miles across San Francisco Bay for Game Three, to be held at Candlestick Park on Tuesday night, October 17. The game was scheduled to start at 5:35 P.M. It was a beautiful, soft evening.

Half past five Pacific Time is the fairest time to begin a baseball game for fans of all ages living on the West Coast or really anywhere else in the country—except for those living in the Eastern Time Zone. Young children in the East can catch the first few innings on TV, but by the middle innings the game has usually gone past their bedtime. There is much hand-wringing by Eastern writers over this fact, but the Nielsen ratings tell you precisely the best time to televise a baseball game: The more people who can watch, the better. Period. The goal is to bring the game to as many people as you possibly can. Yes, you lose some kids on the East Coast, and some columnists, with the so-called late starts, but you gain viewers everywhere else. The ratings numbers do not lie; they tell the ultimate truth. I tried to explain that dozens of times during the Series, but the argument never made a dent. In China, they don't have this problem. All of China is on Beijing time. If you live in western China, the sun doesn't come up until 11:00 A.M., and school starts at noon. I think our system is better, although I do feel bad for eleven-year-old baseball fans on the East Coast during the

Series. One hopes those kids will wake up the next morning and read the accounts in their morning paper. If baseball can play a small role in encouraging a new generation of newspaper readers, that would not be the worst thing. Quite the contrary.

By 5:00 P.M. Candlestick was nearly full. There was a wonderful pregame buzz. Willie Mays was hanging around, preparing to throw out the first pitch. The Gatlin Brothers, a four-man singing group from Odessa, Texas—where I had lived with Bucky Bush, brother of one U.S. president and uncle of another, some thirty-three years earlier—were getting ready to sing the National Anthem. The commissioner is in charge of the World Series, so I met with the umpires before the game while the umpire who had the plate was rubbing up sixty baseballs with a special mud from a particular creek in Camden, New Jersey, turning virginal white balls into brownish official game balls. This exercise was old hat to the umpires, part of their ritual, but to me it was fascinating, all of it. We talked about the ground rules, and since it was the first game in the National League park, discussed how strictly the balk rule should be enforced: Throughout the season, the National League umpires had been enforcing the balk rule aggressively, and now we had American and National League umpires working together. We decided we would call only the obvious ones. (When the Series was over, I happily counted up the balk calls: none.) I visited the clubhouses briefly and talked to writers and TV reporters who were milling about behind the backstop. There were scores of them. It was my first World Series and I was in awe that I was a central player, in demand for interviews. The interest was sincere and the questions were respectful. I loved answering them.

I remember bumping into a photographer I had seen during spring training. At one March game, I was hanging around with Bart and Bill White, the incoming National League president, and Bobby Brown, the American League president. We were sitting together in a row of seats and this particular photographer wanted a picture of White and Brown and Bart, the incoming commissioner and his two league presidents. To him, I was a nobody and was ruining his picture, sitting between Bart and Brown. I quickly recognized the photographer's problem, but whenever I'd try to move Bart would say, "No, you stay here, you're part of this." Understandably, the photographer had no idea who I was. In March, I was just some guy messing up his shot. But now, in October, I was the commissioner of baseball and he aimed at me alone. I teased him: "Are you sure you want me?" He was a good sport. I thought, What a difference a half-year makes.

By 5:00 P.M., I was in the commissioner's box, a makeshift seating area built for the World Series, on the field level on the first-base side. I was living out a dream. It was the baseball life Bart and I had envisioned for ourselves, though Bart never made it to a World Series game as commissioner, which is an unspeakably sad thought.

Suddenly, there was a tremendous roar. I looked up. I assumed it was the rumble of Air Force jets on a flyover, as there often is before major sporting events. The roar lasted a few seconds, and then stopped. I was standing, not something I do well, leaning on the flimsy railing of the box. The ground shook and I leaned from side to side, clinging to the railing. I was standing with my then-wife, Valerie, seated behind me. She blurted out: "I think it's an earthquake." She's from Connecticut, just as I am. We don't experience earthquakes, not real ones. How she knew still amazes me. The time was 5:04 P.M.

There was a TV camera next to me pointed at the home-team dugout. I looked into its monitor and saw it had gone black. There was still a lot of sunlight, but the stadium lights were now out. Players soon congregated on the field, somehow instinctively seeking the security of open space, but not panicking in any way. Quickly, reports started to come in, from transistor radios and from the television crews talking to their newsrooms. Somebody said there had been a major earthquake in San Francisco and that power was out across the city. Somebody else said highways had collapsed. Reports trickled in. They grew worse.

And then commander Isaiah Nelson of the San Francisco police department arrived—or, as I did not know the name of the man at that point, a police officer arrived, by squad car, driving over the outfield and stopping in front of my box. He looked like a movie star, like Sidney Poitier, a trim black man in a perfectly fitting uniform and shiny motorcycle boots. (I later learned he loved to ride motorcycles.) He exuded confidence. He looked as if he was in charge. He was forty, but looked much younger while acting much older. He said: "Commissioner Vincent, my name is Commander Isaiah Nelson and I am in charge of the police detail here. We have a serious situation in this city now. There has been an enormous earthquake, and we have decisions to make and we have to make them fast. You are in charge here."

"No, Commander," I said. "You are in charge. Whatever you advise me to do, we will do."

Nelson: "Thank you, sir. The first thing I want you to do is to stay right where you are. If you leave it will cause panic. Please don't go out of sight. If you appear visible and calm, others will see that and remain calm. I'll be back as soon as I have more information. But you should think about canceling the game."

In baseball, there is a significant distinction between canceling a game and postponing a game, but I understood immediately what he meant and the enormity of what had just happened. The reports now were of raging fires and collapsed bridges. There was a great deal of confusion, but no panic; we just sat in our box, stunned, and watched the confusion around us.

Nelson returned in ten minutes—an eternity in that setting—and said: "Things are bad, sir. It's a bad earthquake. We don't know if there will be another one. We don't know what the aftershocks will be like. Chunks of the upper deck have fallen. We have no reports of injuries. But we have no ancillary power source and it's getting dark. We'd like to get people on the move home before dark. I suggest you cancel the game."

I said: "Commander, this game has just been canceled." And that was it. No one else's view could matter.

There were more than fifty thousand people on hand but no public address system. Nelson got in his squad car, turned the volume all the way up on his loudspeakers on top of the car, and said in short, crisp sentences: "May I have your attention. The game has been canceled. There has been a major earthquake in the area. It's important for you to proceed to your car and get on the road as quickly as possible. We want to evacuate the stadium. You are at no risk. Please leave. Walk carefully. Drive carefully. Thank you." He went around and around the stadium. The fans responded magnificently. Everyone behaved perfectly. All were heroes.

Valerie and I stayed for hours and hours, at some point huddling in a hospitality tent behind the center-field wall, drinking coffee with close friends of ours from Washington, D.C., Vincent and Celine Burke. We were nervous, because we knew there would be an aftershock and because everything was so unknown. But we were calmed by the presence of Commander Isaiah Nelson. At about 10:00 P.M. he asked if we wanted to be part of a convoy returning to downtown San Francisco, where our hotel, the St. Francis, was located.

As we drove into the city, along roads that were pitch black, we stopped at every intersection because there were no stop lights. Volunteers were directing traffic. There were fires in a few neighborhoods, but for the most part everything was dark and dim, weird, people out in the streets just milling about. It looked like a scene from a World War II movie, a European war zone. I thought: "This is a major American city, and it is in shock." There was almost no noise, except the wailing of sirens. And no lights. It was an eerie darkness. None of us spoke. We sat with our thoughts.

Finally, we arrived at the St. Francis, a wonderful, ornate old hotel with doormen dressed as Franciscan liverymen in big red suits and enormous hats. The lobby was filled with people sleeping on blankets. The staff was wonderful. You could feel immediately a powerful spirit of cooperation. Most of the hotel was without power but our room, on the thirty-third floor, was in a newer wing that had an emergency generator to run a sole elevator. In the room itself, there was no running water, no electricity, no phone service. Neither was there any sleep to be had. An old friend, Harry Mazadoorian, my roommate from law school, was in San Francisco for the Series; at about 11:00 P.M. he knocked on the door and said, "I have no place to sleep." He had gone to the airport to fly home, but was turned back. We put him on the couch. Suddenly, I had a roommate again. Valerie sat up all night, worried about the aftershock.

Throughout the night, we could hear sounds of breaking glass, as the police went around breaking the jagged, dangerous shards of glass in store windows. At 3:00 A.M. there was a sharp aftershock. The windows shook. So did we. It was a long night.

We had organized a press conference for ten o'clock the next morning, in one of the hotel's meeting rooms. There was no electricity, so candles were lit throughout the room. I thought about Pete Rozelle, the distinguished commissioner of the NFL, and how he later regretted allowing football to be played the Sunday after President Kennedy was assassinated in 1963. I also thought of my hero Winston Churchill, and how he kept the movie houses open during the Blitz in 1940 to encourage his countrymen, Londoners most particularly, to carry on with their lives in the most trying of times. From baseball's point of view, the first consideration had to be safety: Was the stadium safe? Would there be police available to ensure safety at a game? The second concern was as important: appropriateness. How can you return to the playing of a game when a devastated city is mourning the deaths of scores of people?

At a meeting before our press conference, one baseball official, obviously trying to take advantage of my inexperience, said, "I'll handle the press conference. I'll run it. You can just sit there." My friend Vincent Burke was with me at the time; he took me aside and said, "Fay, may I give you some advice?" (Burke was a wise, old friend; his counsel was always welcome. He was a devout Catholic and Bart called him "The Cardinal." He'd say to me, "Ask the Cardinal what we should do now.") The Cardinal was now standing beside me saying, "You run the press conference. You run everything. Show that you're the person in charge. And remind people that baseball knows its place in a time like this." I stole his thought and his line.

Rich Levin, baseball's top public affairs executive, got word of the press conference out to the scattered baseball press corps. The room was crowded, illuminated by candlelight and battery-operated TV lights. I spoke of our sensitivity to people who had lost loved ones and property. I said: "We have to remember we are guests here. Our modest little game is not a top priority." Baseball's annual finale has a grand name—the World Series—but at that moment we knew the true place of our games. There was not much more to say. For some reason, that phrase, "our modest little game," resonated with the public. It was then that I became the commissioner of baseball, in the public's eye. My own, too.

A few little odd and interesting things happened in the period right after the earthquake. The day after the earthquake, the umpires' union—headed by an aggressive lawyer named Richie Phillips, whom Bart used to call Mr. DiFillipo (no Italian name-change got past Bart)—made a formal protest because I had failed to consult with them before postponing Game Three. One American League umpire, Al Clark, was particularly aggrieved, carrying on and on about my ignoring them. I thought their position was preposterous and, to his credit, so did Richie Phillips. For one thing, the umpires knew I was a tremendous supporter of them. They knew of my father's history as an umpire and how much I loved and admired umpires. Second, by baseball's official code, it is the commissioner who makes such decisions in a World Series game, just as the home-team owner makes the decisions about play in his stadium before the start of a regular-season game. (After the first pitch is thrown, the game is the domain of the umpires, and it is up to them, the crew chief in particular, to decide if a game should be postponed or suspended or canceled.) Also, when the earthquake hit, the umpires were in their dressing room, far down the right-field line, at least fifty yards away from where I was sitting; had I gone to meet with them I would have violated the wise counsel of Commander Nelson to stay visible and not to move.

A few days later, when I met with the umpires before resuming play, I said, "Can anyone here tell me what any of you could have said that would have made a difference?" Even Al Clark had nothing to say. (Eventually, we became pals.) So I continued: "If the same thing happens again, if we have another earthquake, I plan to do the same thing I did last time. You guys know how much I respect you, but in a crisis there is no time for talk." They apologized and the issue went away. But it was a powerful reminder of how sensitive any group of people can be—in this case, it was the umpires; in the next case it would be a different group, no doubt—to any perceived slight.

Another complaint was more comical. For the press conference the morning after the earthquake, I did not put on a tie. Neither did I shave or shower, since the hotel was without water. It was not a time for delicate personal hygiene. George Steinbrenner, the Yankees owner, called me right after the press conference and said: "I saw you on TV at that press conference. You weren't wearing a tie. A commissioner should always wear a tie. You looked like a bum." I had on a collared shirt, pressed trousers, a blazer. But no tie. And that is what caught George's eye.

"George, go easy," I said. "You're not here. We're lucky to find a cupful of water to brush our teeth. You're worried about a tie, George? I've got other things to worry about." The fact is, he had a point; at the time, however, last on my list of worries was how I looked. George Steinbrenner is old-school, as am I; ties are part of our culture, as are appearances. But at that moment, there were more fundamental things to worry about.

In the days after the earthquake, there was considerable nervousness among the owners, because there remained a chance the World Series would not be played at all and that would be costly to them in terms of lost television revenues. Some powerful columnists, the eminent Dave Anderson of *The New York Times* most prominently, called for the cancellation of the World Series, out of respect for the dead. If that sentiment had become the prevailing one throughout the country, baseball would have been hard-pressed to ignore it; a World Series, ultimately, exists for the pleasure of its fans and you can't have a Series if people don't want it.

As part of our effort to show that baseball understood its place during the crisis, I thought it was critical for us to make a contribution to the relief effort. Someone told me that the players union was planning to make a significant donation; I thought that was terrific and that baseball should do the same. There were at that time twenty-six baseball teams, and I decided, checking with nobody, that baseball would contribute $1 million to the American Red Cross to help in their disaster relief work. Baseball had a central fund, generated by national licensing and television revenues and managed by the commissioner. I didn't think of it as the owners' money; I thought of it as money belonging to baseball, to be used in the best interests of the game. And clearly, I believed I was acting in the owners' interests.

Within a day I received a call from Peter O'Malley, the owner of the Dodgers and one of the few remaining members of baseball's old guard. His father, Walter O'Malley, had moved the Dodgers from Brooklyn to Los Angeles and is properly considered a baseball visionary. Peter is a decent man. "I am very upset with you," he said. "How can you commit that kind of money without consulting with the Executive Council first?" I didn't think the gift was that significant, and I had the impression that had I checked with the owners' Executive Council first, the answer would have been "Yes." Still, I received his message loud and clear: Process is always important.

The message from George W. Bush, then the president of the Texas Rangers, was more measured. He said: "You did the right thing. We should make a donation in that situation, a significant one, but you should have called around first. I'm totally supportive, but next time, why not call around and save yourself some grief?" It was very sound advice and it may have been the first time I realized the depth of the future president's diplomatic and personal skills.

The response from Eli Jacobs, the owner of the Baltimore Orioles and my very dear friend, was the shrewdest of all. He called and said, "Let me make sure I understand what you've done here. If the donation from baseball helps us get permission from the mayor and others to resume play, then I get my share of the World Series television revenue money?"

"That's correct."

"And you spent about fifty thousand dollars of my money to try to make that happen?"

"Yes."

"And my share of the television revenues for the World Series is worth about a half-million dollars?"

"That's correct."

"Fay, you can make that deal for me every day of the week."

I thought, Here is a man of commerce.

These were my first significant dealings with the owners as commissioner. In a sense, these early conversations served as a predictor of my future relationships with them for the rest of my tenure. As they say, you only have one chance to make a first impression; there were some bumps along the way, but I thought I was doing OK. And for a while, I was.

During that period of uncertainty about the future of the Series, I spoke to someone from the players union—either its head, Donald Fehr, or his brilliant deputy, Gene Orza—every day. It seemed to me wise to keep them fully apprised of the problems and to get their advice as well. From the outset, I believed it was vital for baseball to develop a level of trust between the owners and the players. As commissioner, that was my highest priority and my biggest challenge. It proved to be my ultimate failure.

When a new person comes into a position of authority, those already there try to challenge him, to see what the man is made of. I had seen this in my other jobs and now I was seeing it in baseball in dramatic ways. Sandy Alderson, then the general manager of the A's, came to me a few days after the earthquake, when there was still no word on when or whether the Series would resume. The A's had been working out locally but with many distractions. He was unhappy. He said, "I want to take our club to Mexico and practice there."

I did not like that idea. It would represent baseball fleeing a city in crisis and put the game ahead of the civic help some players were providing. It was not the right message.

"Sandy, I'm not sure you should do that," I said.

"Will you block us if we do it?" He was a former Marine and aggressive. That was his best and worst attribute, and still is. He is now baseball's director of operations, the third-highest-ranking position in baseball.

"I don't have to tell you what I'm going to do. If you do it I may well take some action. But why are you so eager to go to Mexico?"

"Because we want to win the Series."

"Aren't there some more important things going on here?" Some of the A's—most particularly Dave Stewart, who grew up in Oakland—were highly visible in the clean-up effort. "And what do I do if you go to Mexico and then the Giants decide they want to go, too?"

"I don't think the Giants will want to go to Mexico," Sandy said.

"Which is why you do," I said. "The longer we talk, Sandy, the more I realize this is not a good idea."

"I guess we're not going then."

"I'm glad we both agree it's not a good idea," I said.

"No, *you* think that. I think it's a good idea but I'm afraid of what you'll do if we go."

In business, in life, and in baseball—which is a bit of both—some people will only respond to intimidation. I think that's unfortunate. I would always rather come to a meeting of minds based on reason. The real world doesn't always allow for that.

I was reminded of that again when I met with Art Agnos, the mayor of San Francisco, to discuss the resumption of the Series.

Mayor Agnos was not having a great month even before the earthquake. It is traditional for the mayors of the two competing World Series cities to make a public wager about the outcome, offering some delicacy or touristic experience indigenous to each mayor's city. When Agnos was asked what he would want from Oakland if the Giants won, he said, "There's nothing in Oakland I'd want." It was, as they say, a bulletin board quote. When Dave Stewart was helping to restore order in his home city after the earthquake. He said. "When Agnos said that, he spit directly in my face. And my parents' faces."

As the days after the earthquake passed, we were receiving excellent engineering reports about Candlestick Park. The chunks that had fallen from the upper deck were designed to fall, as a way to relieve stress on the stadium. The structural integrity of the ballpark had not been compromised in any way and the engineers cleared us to play. Candlestick was built to withstand earthquakes and it had done so admirably (with the exception that it did not have backup electrical generators). My new friend Commander Isaiah Nelson, our police liaison, was telling me that the police were available to work Games Three and Four (and Five, if needed). Transportation was still very difficult, but the spirit of the city was soaring. I was struck by our resilience—we, the human race—and our ability to come back from disasters.

One night in the hotel elevator I ran into a young couple. The husband said, "Mr. Vincent, I just want you to know you're doing a good job. We live here and we really appreciate what you're doing."

"Thank you," I said. "May I ask you a question? If you had the power to decide, would you have us play ball again if the stadium is OK?"

"Absolutely," the woman said. "You'd be sending out a powerful message that this city is coming back. As soon as they say you can play, you should play."

For whatever reason, I found that short conversation empowering. It validated everything I was thinking. And it made sense.

But Candlestick was owned by the city and I had to convince the mayor to let us play, and that looked difficult. He was busy and not eager to meet with me. Finally, he agreed to see me on a Sunday, five days after the quake. He and I met at the San Francisco apartment of Al Rosen, the former ballplayer and then the general manager of the Giants. Bob Lurie, the owner of the Giants, came, as did several other baseball officials and several associates of the mayor. Before the meeting, I warned Lurie, "Look, Bob. This may be a tense meeting. We may have to play a little poker. No matter what I say, no matter how stupid and outrageous you think I'm being, I want you to say nothing." He agreed. He didn't have to, but he did. He was also frightened, I think. The World Series in his home city hung in the balance. And who knew when it would come that way again?

The mayor opened the meeting: "We're pretty busy in this city right now, Commissioner. We love baseball, but we think it may take another month to six weeks before we're going to be able to have you play again. There won't be available police until then."

"Mr. Mayor, I have reports the police can be ready next week."

"Where did you get that report?"

It was from Isaiah Nelson, of course, but I could not say that. I ignored his question.

"Mr. Mayor, we cannot wait a month or more to resume the World Series. It's not practical for many reasons. I think the city is ready for us in every way. Moreover, I think you're missing one important point. If we play baseball, we are a symbol that San Francisco is back. There must be convention planners all over the world who are thinking about canceling their plans. What would be a better symbol of San Francisco's health than holding the World Series? The players are here. The umpires. The press. We're all ready."

The mayor said something in response, something contrary.

"Mr. Mayor," I said. "I don't think I'm getting anywhere here. Let me be blunt with you. I have to make a decision within the next few days. We have clearance to play the rest of the Series in Anaheim. The mayor of Oakland is happy to have us play the remaining games, including your home games, in his city. We will resume this Series someplace and we will do it soon. At some point you will run for reelection. How will it look to your constituents if you let the Series leave San Francisco?"

There was a pause.

The mayor spoke: "Commissioner, do you play poker?"

"No, Mr. Mayor, I don't play cards at all."

"Well, you'd be a hell of a poker player. I don't know if you're bluffing, but we can't afford the risk."

Five days later we played Game Three of the 1989 World Series, and the next night Game Four.

When we left, Lurie said to me, "Jesus Christ—Oakland? I almost died in there. The mayor's right. I wouldn't play poker with you."

"Bob, did we get what we wanted?" It would have been devastating for the Giants to play their home games in southern California, and worse yet in Oakland. "Look, we had to get the mayor's attention."

"We got it all right. You nearly killed me along the way."

Game Three was played on October 27, ten days after it was first scheduled to be played. At 5:04 P.M., we had a moment of silence to remember the victims of the earthquake. We arranged for a group of people who had made great contributions to the relief effort to throw out a ceremonial first pitch, and they stood for the tens of thousands of others who volunteered their time to help their neighbors in distress. There was a certain sadness, for the lives that had been lost and for the destruction, but more than anything there was a feeling of resilience. I received a powerful lesson in that fortnight about the strength of our collective human heart. I think we all did.

Dave Stewart was a big hero, in every way. He was the starting pitcher for Oakland in Game Three, which the A's won, 13–7. The A's completed their sweep by winning the next night, 9–6, and the longest four-game series in the history of baseball—two weeks to play four games—was over.

Those of us who lived through the peril of that earthquake have a special bond that has not faded over the years. Mark McGwire, Dave Stewart, Walt Weiss, along with many of the other A's, often recall that Series when I see them. So does Tony La Russa. I feel it, too, with the staff at the St. Francis and the writers at that candlelit press conference. Even Art Agnos and Al Clark and Sandy Alderson, though we were at odds during that half-month, shared a bonding experience with me. I sense that most particularly with the Giants. I feel for them. The earthquake was in their city, so they lost two ways. My heart will always go out to Bob Lurie and Will Clark and Roger Craig for what they endured over those two weeks.

To me, the great hero of the 1989 World Series is Isaiah Nelson. The following April, he was at a Giants game, doing his job; on his way home, riding one of his beloved motorcycles, he had a horrifying accident. He crashed into a cement road barrier on Interstate 280 near Twenty-Fifth Street, placed there to divert traffic from an unnavigable spot on a road that had collapsed during the earthquake. Apparently, he had jammed on the brakes but lost control and the motorcycle skidded out from under him. He hit the barrier and was killed. I was devastated when I heard the news. He had seemed indestructible.

Later, I met his wife. Mrs. Nelson told me more about her husband and about their young children. She was a lovely woman, beautiful in every way. I wrote a tribute to him in *The Washington Post,* and I paid my respects as best I could, but I fear my words were inadequate. I have no doubt Isaiah Nelson saved lives with the calm decisiveness with which he handled a crowd of fifty thousand people on the night of a devastating earthquake.

People in the Bay Area tell me Isaiah Nelson would have someday become police chief in San Francisco, maybe even mayor. I don't doubt that for a moment. He was a star and a hero; a father, a husband, a son, and a brother, too. And a friend.

	Lineup: Moderns
1.	Will Clark
2.	Nolan Ryan
3.	Minnie Minoso
4.	Roger Clemens
5.	Lenny Dykstra
6.	Tim Belcher
7.	Steve Howe
8.	Barry Bonds
9.	Ken Griffey, Jr.

Moderns

1. WILL CLARK

I ADMIRED WILL CLARK, the San Francisco Giants first baseman, before I went into baseball. He had a smooth, flowing, lefthanded swing. People called him The Natural and Will the Thrill. In his early years, I thought he would someday land in the Hall of Fame. I thought the same of Mark Grace, the longtime Chicago Cubs first baseman. They both have had very fine careers, long and productive. They haven't, though, had Hall of Fame careers. After the third game of the '89 World Series was delayed by earthquake, time slowed down. The players were doing a lot of hanging around, as was I, and it was a good opportunity to get to know some of them. Will Clark made a particular impression on me. I knew him to be intense in the batter's box, but off-field he was friendly and gracious. We were comfortable with each other, and I wasn't surprised to learn he was born in New Orleans: He was the Big Easy personified. During the long gap between Game Two and Game Three, I would see Clark, the most visible of the Giants, here and there, and we'd have little chats about this and that.

And then there was a binding episode between us. It was just a little thing, but it was memorable, at least to me. It came during the delayed Game Three when I nearly interfered, albeit unintentionally, with Will's professional life. I was sitting in the commissioner's box on the first-base side with, among others, my then-wife Valerie, my son Bill, and Willie Mays. Suddenly, a high foul pop was headed our way. For a moment, I had the chance to get that most prized of baseball souvenirs, a batted game ball. I thought, *I got this one!* This was not the commissioner thinking. At that moment, I was twelve.

And then the professionals took over, the way professionals do. Unseen by me, Will Clark came charging toward our box, his mitt wide open, his nose pointed straight into the sky, his knees right up against the flimsy wall that separated our box from the field. Bending at the waist, he reached as far into the box as he possibly could, raising his mitt right above my poised hands. As this was happening, Willie Mays was getting himself into position, too. As he explained to me later, he realized that as soon as Clark caught the ball, Clark's feet would leave the ground and the first baseman's six-foot, two-inch, 190-pound body would come flipping over the railing and into our box. When that happens, a ballplayer is like a freshly caught fish on the deck of a boat, flopping out of control. The player's spikes can swing around and do some real harm. Willie saw all this about to happen.

Clark caught the ball. Mays caught Clark, grabbing his legs with a bear hug so Clark wouldn't hurt himself or any of us. (What instincts.) Clark ended up sprawled at my feet. Heinz Kluetmeier, a legendary *Sports Illustrated* photographer, caught the moment in a picture, which I have hanging on a wall in my den, signed by Will, who wrote, "Great time, great people."

From that moment on, our friendship has blossomed. Well, maybe it would be more accurate to say Will's friendship with Valerie blossomed. From then on, whenever he saw her he would give her a hug and say, "How are you? That husband of yours treating you OK?" He has a nice sense of humor, and a serious side, too. When I left baseball, Will spoke right up. He said, "A good man got railroaded." I remain grateful.

2. NOLAN RYAN

SIGNING BASEBALLS AND collecting signed baseballs have been part of the game forever. Players sometimes complain about signing baseballs, but that act is a thread in the fabric of the game. Every day when a player goes into his clubhouse there is a box with two dozen brand-new balls in it that each player is expected to sign. There's a clipboard with a team roster attached to it next to the box, and the player runs a line through his name after he has signed. These signed team balls are then given to season ticket holders and advertisers and sick kids. If you have one from the '27 Yankees or the '69 Mets or the star-crossed '86 Red Sox, you have something of value. I don't mean that monetarily, although those balls are certainly worth money; I mean you own something interesting. You have a congregation of signatures representing a group of men who came together for a season to achieve something. Part of the magic is in this idea: *Their hands touched this ball.* Part of the fun is studying the signatures, to examine the lovely penmanship of Charlie Gehringer or the way Ted Williams wrote "Ted."

When Bart became commissioner I was amazed at how many people wanted him to sign baseballs. At first I thought it was because of Bart's charismatic and unique personality. But when I succeeded him and I was asked to sign baseballs, too, I realized what it was all about. A commissioner—for better or for worse, in a major way or in an insignificant way—is part of baseball history, and people who care about such things want the commissioner's name, in ink, on the "sweet spot," on the ultimate symbol of the game.

That, of course, is the baseball.

Players with a sense for their game's history feel the same way.

In 1991, before a game in Arlington, Texas, a little boy in a Texas Rangers uniform came walking up to me. He had a thick south Texas accent and impeccable manners. He might have been ten.

"Commissioner, sir?" the boy said.

"Yes, young man."

"My daddy is Nolan Ryan, sir."

"Your daddy is Nolan Ryan?"

"Yes, sir, he is. And I got a question my daddy asked me to ask you."

"And what, young man, is that?"

"Would you sign two baseballs for him?"

"Sign two baseballs for your daddy whose name is Nolan Ryan?"

"Yes, sir." I thought the kid was going to die.

"You tell your daddy I would sign ten baseballs for him, but I would like one signed by him in return."

"That will be fine, sir," the boy said.

"No, no, you run over to your father and ask him." The great Nolan Ryan was sitting nearby, in a dugout, watching. His son ran over to him. I saw the father laugh, sign a ball, and hand it to his son, who came running back with a signed ball in hand.

"Here it is, sir," the boy said.

"Well thank you very much, young man," I said. "Now how many balls would your father like signed?"

"He says just the two would be fine."

I signed the two balls with pleasure. "You tell your daddy he made a bad deal. One of his is worth more than ten of mine."

"Yes, sir," the boy said with a hint of a smile, running off to his father, the great Nolan Ryan, autograph collector.

3. MINNIE MINOSO

MINNIE MINOSO, the wonderful Cuban-born righthanded hitter, played nine games for the Cleveland Indians in 1949. That is to say, he began his major-league career in the forties. The heart of his career came in the 1950s, during which he played in 1,343 games, most of them for the Chicago White Sox. He retired in 1964, having played another 484 games in the sixties. In 1976, as a stunt, he played in three games at the age of fifty-three, and went one for eight; in 1980, another stunt: two hitless pinch-hit at bats. (In both cases, Bill Veeck was the owner responsible for sending Minoso up to the plate.) These appearances made him the only man to play in five decades in the twentieth century. I always liked Minnie, but given that he qualified for two of the decades with a silly stunt and had a mere nine games in the first decade, it isn't a record that generates the kind of awe that, say, Hack Wilson's 190-RBI season in 1930 does.

Then in 1992, Jerry Reinsdorf, the owner of the White Sox, had what he thought was a brilliant marketing idea: trot out Minoso again for another at bat, so that he could appear in six decades. I told Reinsdorf not to do it, that such a stunt would demean the game. He complained that I wasn't interested in helping owners make money and understood nothing about the value of publicity; I asked if he would next hire a stripper to play center field or a nun to play shortstop. He didn't laugh. The dispute turned into a real donnybrook, but I held my ground. Can you imagine what would have happened if Minoso was struck by a Randy Johnson fastball going one hundred miles an hour? And Johnson was set to pitch the game Minnie was supposed to "play."

Naturally, my decision was not popular in the Minoso house, in the Reinsdorf house, or anywhere in Chicago, as far as I knew. I was the killjoy. Then came a quiet voice of sanity and support from an unlikely source, from one of Reinsdorf's employees. "I have to tell you, I really support your decision on Minoso," the White Sox manager, Jeff Torborg, told me one day in a quiet voice. "Randy Johnson was to pitch that day. If Minnie had been hit, if something went wrong, we would have all felt terrible."

I was glad I could, through the power of my office, prevent Torborg from having to send a player to the plate he felt had no business being there. I'm sure that incident contributed to my very poor relationship with Jerry Reinsdorf, but I know I did the right thing. Later, after I left baseball, Reinsdorf tried again but this time the players union blocked him. They threatened a grievance if Minoso took a "real" player's place on the roster for even one day. Every day on a roster can be extremely valuable for a player trying to earn a pension. Once again, the union proved more sensible than an owner.

4. ROGER CLEMENS

IN 1990, THE BOSTON RED SOX and the Oakland A's were playing in the American League Championship Series. The Sox lost the first two games at home and the third one, in Oakland. In the fourth game, in Oakland, Roger Clemens was the Boston starter. An umpire named Terry Cooney was working the plate. Richie Garcia was the third-base umpire. Jim Evans was the first-base umpire. These are the characters in the story I am about to tell. Those who are sensitive to profanity should take this opportunity to skip along now to a more innocent subject.

Roger Clemens, of course, is one of the great pitchers of the modern era. He is a violent competitor, fierce in every way. In the second inning of the fourth game, a game the Sox had to win, Cooney, out of the blue, ejected Clemens after the briefest of confrontations. It was the biggest start of the year for Clemens and he did not complete two innings. There was a big hubbub just off the mound, attended by Evans, who was the crew chief, Cooney, the managers, and many players. In the stands, none of us could believe what we were seeing.

I was sitting in the commissioner's box on the third-base side. I motioned Garcia over and asked, "What happened?" He went to check and came back.

"You won't believe it," he said. "Clemens went after Cooney. He thought Cooney was missing pitches. He said, 'You motherfucker.' "

You followed by anything profane gets you thrown out. *You* is one of the magic words. Clemens was gone.

The Sox, of course, lost Game Four, and their season was over. Bobby Brown, the American League president, suspended Clemens for three games at the start of the 1991 season for his outburst. Clemens, through the players union, appealed the suspension, and that's when the issue came to me. Clemens maintained he never used the magic words. Cooney claimed he did. I had to decide the following technical and legal issue: Did the great righthander use those two words in that order? For this, all my legal background—three years of law school and practicing law for fifteen years—was brought to bear.

The hearing was held in my office. Roger's wife, a lovely woman named Debbie, was there. Gene Orza, the deputy head of the players union, was there, as the pitcher's defense counsel. Roger, of course, was there. There were many others, including lawyers from my office.

Finally, there was a professional lip-reader there, a slim, elegant deaf woman named Deborah Copeland who taught lip-reading. Orza had hired her.

We played the videotape of the confrontation, taken from the TV network camera situated immediately behind home plate. You could see Roger's mouth during the confrontation and you could also see Cooney's mouth for part of it. Roger made a pitch, and when it was called a ball Roger screamed, "What the fuck!" That, of course, is fine. Then he said, "You better umpire." Cooney came out to the mound and they got in each other's face. Cooney threw Clemens out, but Clemens was correct: The tape proved he had never used the words that get you ejected. Maybe that's why he went ballistic. When Evans came rushing to the mound, Clemens, now out of control, shoved Evans away and screamed, "I'll get that motherfucker in the off-season. I'll kill him!"

I was in a tough spot. I knew Cooney was wrong. By baseball's un-written rules, there was no cause to throw Clemens out. By another unwritten rule, it was difficult for me to overturn a league president's suspension. That would have undercut my relationship with Bobby Brown. I knew Clemens had to be disciplined for threatening one um-pire and bumping another, even if he was, in a sense, baited.

(Sometime later I said to Roger, "If a state trooper pulls you over for speeding, can you say to him, 'I'm going to kill you in the off-season,' even if you weren't speeding?"

"No," Roger said.

"What would happen to you if you did say that?"

"You'd go to jail."

He understood.)

Roger got his three-day suspension. He had challenged it solely to prove the umpire was wrong and that he hadn't started the fight.

I wrote two versions of my opinion, one using the language as it was actually used, the other an expurgated version. Clemens felt vindi-cated because I agreed with him. I concluded Clemens never said, "You motherfucker." Cooney and the umpires and Bobby Brown were vindicated because Clemens's suspension was upheld.

In a wry moment, I sent my ruling to my old friend, Guido Calabresi, the dean of the Yale Law School. I wrote him, "This is how a graduate of your fine school spends his time—warn your students." He thought the episode was *théâtre de l'absurd*.

It wasn't for the big righthander, though. Clemens, the fiercely competitive Clemens, had made his point. Rocket had won again in his eyes.

5. LENNY DYKSTRA

SOMETIMES PEOPLE MISS the central point of the Pete Rose episode. They say, Why did you have to throw Rose out of the game? The answer, simple though it is, is lost on many: because a lifetime banishment from the game is the ultimate deterrent to gambling. A ballplayer may be tempted to gamble on baseball. Then he asks himself: Is this something I should do? He answers himself: No, it's not. Pete Rose got thrown out of baseball for betting on it.

Lenny Dykstra, who came up with the Mets as a centerfielder called Nails and later made himself one of the best leadoff hitters in baseball with the Phillies, understood the deterrent well.

In 1990, we got wind that Dykstra was running up major gambling debts in off-season poker games in Mississippi. (He had played as a minor leaguer in Jackson, Mississippi, and met his wife there.) I had John Dowd investigate. He concluded: "There's good news and bad news. The good news is he's not involved in betting on baseball. The bad news is he's running up some big poker debts." Dykstra was betting large sums.

I knew Lenny a little; his rough-and-tumble game resembled Rose's. Dykstra was a blunt man, but also very straight, and I felt I could talk to him one on one and get more accomplished than in a formal hearing in my office. So when Dykstra was in Clearwater, Florida, for spring training, I went down to see him.

Whenever the commissioner meets with a ballplayer to talk about a situation that may involve disciplinary measures, the players union is involved. I said to Lenny over the phone before I came down, "I don't want to make a big deal about this. Can we meet and talk at the ballpark before a game?"

"Whatever you want," he said.

I arrived at the ballpark. Lenny was there. I said, "Lenny, is there a little room somewhere we could meet privately?"

Lenny said, "Yeah, there's a men's room here that's good."

I had never conducted a meeting in a men's room before.

I asked Lenny if he wanted a union lawyer present.

"I don't need anybody with me," Lenny said. "I'm happy to talk to you alone."

"Are you sure?"

"I don't need the union involved. This has nothing do to with them."

So we went into the latrine. It was not state of the art, but it served its purpose. It was small but empty.

"Lenny, look, I know you've been making big-time poker bets and losing. You haven't violated any baseball rule, but what you're doing is not smart and I'm worried about you."

"I'm worried about you, too," Lenny said.

"Why me?"

"I saw what you did to Rose. You threw him out of baseball. I'm scared because I do *not* want to be thrown out of baseball."

And that's when I realized the deterrent works.

"The reason I don't want the union here is because I'll tell you anything you want to know," Lenny said. "I want to cooperate."

"All you have to do is stop running up poker debts, because you can see the risks there."

"You won't have any problems with me," he said. "I'll do just what you say. Nothing is going to get in the way of me playing ball."

"Fine. I'll put you on probation for a year. I'm going to have the security people check on you. If they find you're doing something you're not supposed to be doing, you and I will have a much different conversation." That conversation would not be in a men's room.

"They can check on me three times a day," Dykstra said. "They're not going to find anything." And they didn't. Lenny had made his point to me. I had made mine to him. We both learned.

6. TIM BELCHER

THE MODERN PLAYER is often mocked for carrying a briefcase in one hand and a cellphone in the other. I think that's unfair. The fact is, many more players today have college degrees than did years ago. They can make enough money in even a five-year career so that, if they invest the money properly, they will never have to work again. They would be foolish not to take a professional approach to their careers.

Many of the players are smart, some on instinct alone, others in a more analytical way. For a period during the spring of 1990, during an owners' lockout that shut down spring training, a group of eight or so players would congregate in my office every morning to try to settle the labor situation. They came to my office as a courtesy to me, in deference to my handicap, and I was grateful. I was impressed with the players, with the depth of their understanding of complex issues. I was also impressed by them as people. Orel Hershiser, the Dodger pitcher, used to come in every morning bringing a box of doughnuts. "This is to prove we don't all hate you," he said. Charm, humor, thoughtfulness, call it whatever you want, his doughnuts and what they represented contributed to a good working relationship (and my expanding waistline).

Tim Belcher, another Dodger pitcher, was particularly impressive during those meetings on a number of levels. When we were getting near the end, Belcher said, "When we get this thing done, we don't want the announcement that it's settled to come first from our side." That was smart, because it wasn't the players who had stopped spring training and caused the delay in the opening of the season; if the players announced the deal, it would appear that they were responsible for the delay. But there was more to Belcher's thinking than that. "We want you to announce it because if it hadn't been for you we'd still be fighting." It was a nice compliment and it made a deep impression on me. In fact, the real hero of that deal was my deputy, Steve Greenberg, who had a long, positive history with Donald Fehr, the players union chief.

The thing that made the deepest impression on me was what

Belcher had in his hands all through the negotiations. It wasn't a cell-phone or a briefcase. It was a baseball, wedged as deeply between the index finger and second finger on his right hand as he could possibly get it.

"What are you doing that for?" I asked once out of curiosity.

"Stretching my fingers," he said. "The deeper you can get the ball into your fingers, the better your splitter." All during our talks, Tim obviously knew he would someday be pitching. He wanted to be ready.

7. STEVE HOWE

STEVE HOWE WAS AN EXCELLENT lefthanded relief pitcher for the Dodgers in the early 1980s. He also had a very bad cocaine problem. He had already violated baseball's drug policies seven times when I found myself sitting in my office one day in 1989, hearing players union lawyers make the case that Steve Howe deserved another chance. The baseball rule on how many violations of the drug policy would result in lifetime suspension was unclear, and Howe kept finding ways to get one more chance.

Steve was likable. He just happened to be addicted to cocaine. Baseball was not doing him any favors by allowing him to return to the game again and again. But this time Howe had a new approach: "You see, Commissioner, I'm a born-again Christian now," Steve said, looking for another "last" chance. "I'm born to Christ. I can stay clean this time." His wife supported his claims. They said the pressure of major-league baseball had made him try cocaine, but now that he had found God he had other ways to relieve the stress. It is easy to be cynical about such things, but it is impossible to see into another man's heart. I had to acknowledge the possibility that what I was hearing was true. Perhaps I was being foolish or naive, but I decided to give him another chance.

"If you're willing to pitch in the minor leagues somewhere for the entire next season, and to submit to our testing, and if you can stay clean for the year, I will let you try to find a major-league job for the following year."

He did that. We tested him and he was clean for his year in the minors. I did not know then what I do now, that urine tests are incredibly flawed for many reasons, one of which is that people being tested often hide clean samples of urine on their bodies and pass them off as their own.

In 1991, Howe pitched for the Yankees. For the year, he had three saves, a 3–1 record, and a 1.68 ERA. Until a midseason elbow injury, he was very difficult to hit. After the 1991 season, he went home to Montana and during the winter he bought an ounce of cocaine in a glassine container from a federal undercover drug agent. When he knew he was going to be arrested he dropped the glassine container in the mud by his truck. That arrest prompted another hearing before me. Several Yankee officials attended, plus Howe and his wife, plus a union official or two. They argued all sorts of nonsense. They said adults, like Howe, who had untreated attention deficit disorder (ADD) as children were more likely to develop cocaine addiction. They said I was taking away Howe's livelihood. I was disgusted, because they were not arguing principle, and they weren't arguing what was best for the human being before them who so obviously had a huge drug problem. The Yankees still thought Howe had good stuff; that was the only reason they wanted him back.

Howe himself argued that because the drugs dropped in the mud he never actually used them. Baseball countered with testimony from a drug addiction specialist from Cornell who said in the long history of drug abuse "there has never been a drug addict who dropped an ounce of cocaine in a glassine container in the mud without using it. It goes right in the microwave and then is snorted."

As the Cornell doctor spoke, I saw a thin smile cross Howe's face. Finally, something truthful! At the close of the hearing, I threw him out of baseball for life. It was his eighth violation. Of course the players union appealed and a baseball arbitrator later overruled my decision. Howe was soon back in baseball again. The arbitrator, George Nicolau, ruled that eight violations was not enough to warrant a lifetime ban, especially in light of the new theory of causation, the ADD theory, that had never led to Howe being treated properly as a child. One more chance, the ruling said. To which I responded, What about the next new theory of causation? Why won't that give him a tenth chance? It was a joke.

Howe pitched in the major leagues for parts of four more seasons, finally being released by the Yankees in 1996. Shortly after that, he was arrested for trying to board a flight with a loaded .45; this time, nobody came running to his defense. The tragedy in all this is that nobody was worried about Steve Howe in any way; it was all about his arm, not about his head. I fear we will read about him again.

8. BARRY BONDS

I KNEW BARRY BONDS best a decade or more before he became the holder of the single-season record for home runs. I knew his father, too, Bobby Bonds, one of the outstanding players of the 1970s. Barry came to me in 1990, when he was a young player for a very good Pittsburgh Pirates team managed by Jim Leyland. He said, "May I ask you something? I'm doing terribly with the media. I'm a better person than the way I'm being treated. What should I do?" The writers were presenting him as a peerless talent but with an ego to match.

I was flattered to have been asked. I wish I had had better advice to offer him. I said, "If you treat the writers with respect, I think you'll see things turn around." That was easier to say than to do. I had heard Bonds in press conferences. His answers were often terse, sometimes dismissive. He seemed to resent the writers' role in the game. He's very smart, and sometimes very smart people see more in reporters' questions than is really there. "Just try to answer their questions," I said.

"I try to do that, but these guys wear me out," he said. "I hustle, I put out, I put in a good day's work, but I don't seem to get any credit."

It was a genuine problem without an easy solution. It has haunted him throughout his career. As a result, he has never really received the attention and adulation he has deserved. He's a very important baseball player, but never became a national figure the way Mark McGwire and even Sammy Sosa did, even after Bonds socked seventy-three homers in the 2001 season. By coming to me with his problem, he showed a vulnerability and a sensitivity the rest of the world did not get to see. I wish it could.

9. KEN GRIFFEY, JR.

I HAD A GOOD RAPPORT with both Ken Griffey and his son, Ken Griffey, Jr., and I was at the game in Seattle on August 31, 1990, when they made baseball history by being the first father and son to appear in the same starting lineup. (They both scored in the first inning.) The father played left and the son played center, and it was joy to watch them before and during the game because they so clearly had a great deal of affection for each other. The father was a superb player and he had taught the son how to play. The son has become perhaps the best position player of his generation, so there is much to be proud of. Junior takes after his mother, Alberta. I traveled in Japan with her; she is a wonderful, decent person, and so is her Junior.

There was a moment in that historic game that I'm sure made for some family drama later. A routine fly ball was hit into left-center, but more left than center, and it was clearly the father's ball. At the last possible second, Junior darted in front of the old man and snapped the ball away and into his glove with a real flourish. He then looked at his father as if to say, How about *that*? They jogged to their dugout but there was not a hint of a smile on the father's face. His kid had showed him up and he didn't like it.

As they passed me on the way to the dugout I waved an admonishing finger at Junior and he smiled sheepishly. He understood what he had done and he knew there would be consequences. After the game, I asked the father what he was going to do about his son's disregard for baseball protocol. I had traveled through Japan with the father, and I knew him to be a forthright person. "I haven't decided yet," Ken Griffey said to me. This was said sternly. The implication was, When I do decide, Junior's not going to like it.

But in the main, Junior was taught beautiful manners by his parents. Many years later, long after I was out of baseball, I was at an All-Star game in Boston, sitting in the Fenway stands several rows back. Junior saw me, came over, and had the security people open the front-row gate so he could come up and say hello. Suddenly my status in my row went up immeasurably: Ken Griffey, Jr., was saying hello to me.

"How you doing?" he said. "They taking care of you?"

"I'm fine," I said. "How are you doing?"

"I'm doing too much," he said. "They're driving me crazy."

"Hey, you're not doing too bad," I said.

"I'm trying."

That was it, just a little hello, barely even a catch-up. But I realized that everybody in our vicinity was hanging on every word Junior said. I recognized him then for what he is: one of the game's true stars. I realized then there must be fans who feel about Ken Griffey, Jr., as I once did about Joe DiMaggio. Always, the game reinvents itself.

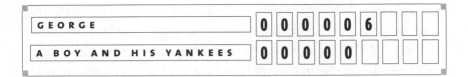

| GEORGE | 0 | 0 | 0 | 0 | 0 | 6 | | | |
| A BOY AND HIS YANKEES | 0 | 0 | 0 | 0 | 0 | | | | |

C H A P T E R   S I X

George

IN THE BEGINNING, I liked George. Sure, I knew all the stories about him—the whole sports-following world did. Red Smith, in his column in the *Times,* used to call him King George III; everybody else called him The Boss. From the time he bought the Yankees in 1973, George M. Steinbrenner III provided the New York baseball writers and sports columnists with captivating fodder. His ongoing battles with Reggie Jackson and Billy Martin made for a madcap sports-section soap opera. For a period, Yankee baseball was called "The Bronx Zoo." Always, George was presented as a loudmouthed buffoon who orchestrated seventeen managerial changes in his first seventeen years as owner. That was the George I knew from the papers. The George I first got to know in the late 1970s was a wholly different man. He wasn't a buffoon; he was impressive.

George went to Williams College, class of '52, eight years ahead of me. He played football for Len Watters, the man who convinced me to attend Williams. By the late 1970s, Watters was an elderly man, not well, and George was quietly and generously raising money to help him and his wife, Amy. They were in Florida, in need of round-the-clock nursing, for which the costs were considerable. I was then chairman of Columbia Pictures Industries and George, bless him, called me, though we had never met, asking me to make a donation to help Coach and Mrs. Watters. I had no idea they were hurting and I was delighted to help. George knew I was close to Herbert Allen, the chairman of Allen & Co., Williams '62, so George asked if I'd be willing to solicit Herbert. I was honored to do so, and Herbert, who loved Watters, readily pitched in.

Thereafter, George called once a year.

"It's time to help Len and Amy again, Fay. Can I count on you?"

"Of course."

"Will you call Herb Allen?"

"Certainly."

"I really appreciate it."

"I appreciate what you're doing, George."

George was doing a good thing for a couple I cared about. I was impressed. It was the only contact I had with George before I came into baseball.

When I was named Bart's deputy commissioner, George's first comment to me was nothing short of sweet. We were at a Player Relations Committee meeting and George arrived late. As he passed my seat he said: "Hello, Fay. Welcome to baseball." He could not have been more gracious. I was encouraged.

George admired and was very fond of Bart, even though Bart was unsure about George. When Bart was starting out as commissioner, he said to me, "Look, we have to specialize. I'm putting you in charge of two owners: John McMullen and George Steinbrenner. An Irishman and a Williams man. They'll be easy for you." It was a joke: Both men were legendary for being difficult and autocratic. McMullen, the owner of the Houston Astros, had the greatest line about George. He had once owned a small piece of the Yankees, and when asked about the experience he said: "There is nothing so limited as being a limited partner of George Steinbrenner." No one ever doubted who was in charge of the Yankees. George barely acknowledged the existence of his partners.

In the early days, George often made life easier for Bart and me. He was helpful and supportive. He heard useful stuff. During the Rose investigation, it was George who tipped us off to the fact that Bowie Kuhn was working against us, calling the owners, trying to get back into baseball by inserting himself into the case in a prominent way. You have to know who your enemies are in this world—and who your friends are. In those days, George was far closer to friend than enemy.

Of course we knew George was no angel, to say the least. I was on the board at Williams and saw some of his behavior from that perspective. At one point, one of George's sons was running track at Williams; there was a meet in which the son jumped the gun several times and was disqualified from his race. George had run at Williams and he loves track and field, from the schoolboy level right through the Olympic level. George, who was at the meet when the son was disqualified, totally misbehaved: He complained about the incompetence of the starter and ended up screaming something like, "I will not give one cent to Williams again if that man ever works another race!" He had to be calmed down. It wasn't easy to do. And, of course, the tirade was soon known all over campus. His own son was naturally mortified.

We didn't conduct ourselves the same way, to say the least. George and Bart talked on the phone the day Bart died, and George later took pride in saying he was the last person to talk to Bart, which could not have been literally true—but it was close to the truth, and for George that was enough. He was infamous for screaming at his employees, or threatening to fire them, or firing them. Then there was our little sartorial conversation after the earthquake in San Francisco, when George told me I looked like a bum because I wasn't wearing a tie at a press conference the day after a major earthquake. Maybe he was trying to tell me he was The Boss. George was certainly the boss of a fair number of people. But he was certainly *not*, as the kids say, the boss of me. I think he knew that. He knew I was independent.

Still, for a long while, we were on good terms. When I first became commissioner, Williams arranged for a joint press conference for George and me after the "big" Amherst football game in 1989. George said, "The new commissioner is a gem. We couldn't do any better than Fay." I thought to myself, maybe it will be possible to deal with him. Bart had demonstrated George would take no for an answer: At one point, George had told Bart he was thinking about bringing Billy Martin back as the Yankees manager, a job from which he had already fired Martin five times. Bart said, "You can't do that, George. You and Billy are catalytic. He has issues with alcohol. You have issues with patience. You will kill each other and bring disrepute to baseball. I forbid you to rehire Billy Martin as Yankees manager." And George accepted this. In doing so, he demonstrated he was capable of being reasonable.

During spring training in 1990, my first spring training as commissioner, baseball was having its usual labor problems. This time around, the owners shut down spring training in an effort to show their resolve against the players union. The biggest owners, Steinbrenner chief among them, were against the lockout. He called me and said, "Make a deal, Commissioner. Use the power of your office. I can live with anything." George and I were in the same camp. We both knew the lockout was futile.

The players union had never been stronger. The players had just come off a successful arbitration in which they won $280 million in damages by proving the owners had colluded against them in the mid-1980s, agreeing not to sign any free agents. Bud Selig, the owner of the Milwaukee Brewers, and Jerry Reinsdorf, the owner of the Chicago White Sox, were the two ringleaders of collusion among the owners; Steinbrenner went along, I believe, mostly because of peer pressure. You might not think of Steinbrenner as susceptible to peer pressure, but an owner can be a maverick only to a certain point. You have to go along to get along, and Steinbrenner knew he might someday need votes from the other owners, particularly if he ever wanted to move his club out of Yankee Stadium. (My feeling about that particular threat is that if George wants to move his team to New Jersey, he should go ahead—and then baseball should move another team into Yankee Stadium and call them the Yankees!) The spectacular payout to settle collusion made George view Selig and Reinsdorf skeptically. George and I had a bond: We both felt Selig and Reinsdorf were handling baseball's labor issues about as poorly as they could be handled.

So George took to calling me daily, often at home. He'd call and say, "Fay, I have evidence that two umpires were drinking in a bar in Boston last night."

"Do you, George?"

"Drinking in a bar in Boston where other patrons were using illegal drugs."

"Send in your evidence, George. I'll deal with it."

I thought he was a poor listener. He would talk endlessly about some issue but hear little of what I or anyone else had to say about it. But his behavior so far was fine.

We settled with the players on March 18, a Sunday, ending the lockout. The same morning, the New York *Daily News* ran the following headline: "The Boss's Secret: Why Did George Pay This Gambler $40,000?" The *News* had an exclusive. Steinbrenner had been paying off a small-time New York gambler-hustler, Howard Spira, to get information on one of his star players, Dave Winfield. Here we go again, I thought.

There truly is no rest for the weary. I got John Dowd on the phone. "Let's do it again," I said. We both knew what that meant: Let's investigate, find out if the allegations were true, take the necessary action if they were.

In 1981, Winfield had signed a ten-year contract with Steinbrenner that was out of the ordinary not only for its length but because it had a protector against inflation in it. It practically assured that Winfield would always be among the highest-paid players in the game. (Over the course of the contract, Winfield was paid about $23 million, a vast sum then.) Moreover, the contract required Steinbrenner to donate three hundred thousand dollars a year to the David M. Winfield Foundation, a charitable organization for children. Over the years, Winfield put up wonderful numbers—Hall of Fame numbers, it turned out—but the Yankees were not winning World Series with Winfield in a Yankee uniform, and Steinbrenner was regularly ridiculed by fans and writers for his folly in tying up so much money with one player when the team's pitching and infield fielding needs were so obvious.

What made matters worse for Steinbrenner was that Winfield was immensely popular in New York, a tall, lean, handsome, rich man who was welcome in any club or restaurant in the city. He was leading an elegant life, made possible because of his many talents, and because of the millions Steinbrenner paid for them. If Steinbrenner overpaid for them, that was not Winfield's fault, but Steinbrenner didn't see it that way. His wars with Winfield were well-known in New York baseball circles.

Howard Spira, a sad little man who had worked low-level jobs for Winfield, somehow found his way to Steinbrenner's ear and began whispering to him irresponsible allegations about Winfield. Essentially, Spira claimed he could prove that Winfield was using his foundation's money for personal purposes, that he was cheating the foundation. The moment Steinbrenner heard these charges, if he believed them to be legitimate, he should have turned the matter over to my office. That's why baseball has a security operation, to investigate such allegations, as we did in the Rose case and in many other instances that have never become public. It is not appropriate for owners to take the investigatory role upon themselves, especially when a player is involved.

But Steinbrenner didn't call me. He took things into his own hands. He paid forty thousand dollars to Spira for his so-called information. He continually refused to make the contributions he owed the Winfield Foundation. He planted negative stories about Winfield in the press, most notably through Howard Cosell. (Because of this incident, I could never regard Cosell as the paragon of truth-telling he always claimed to be. He did anything but tell it like it is. He took Steinbrenner's information, originally from Howard Spira, made no effort to verify it, and ran with it. His stories about Winfield, obviously intended to curry favor with George, were lie-filled diatribes.) I was seeing Steinbrenner at his worst, the side I had hoped I would never see as commissioner. My hope was proving delusional.

Why Steinbrenner paid money to Spira, why he didn't come to us, I will never understand. I've asked George that question several times, in formal and informal settings, and the only answer I've received is, "I made a bad decision." Maybe Steinbrenner realized our investigation would be dispassionate and thorough and fair, and that didn't interest him. For an owner to start an investigation of one of his own players defies logic and decency. For some reason, Steinbrenner was crazed on the subject of Winfield and lost all sense of balance. Winfield had out-maneuvered him on the contract—a ballplayer had outmaneuvered an owner—and now Steinbrenner was trying to destroy him. He paid Spira forty thousand dollars for lousy information. Then he started planting erroneous stories in the press about his own star player. Then he sent one of his cohorts, Bill Fugazy, to the Manhattan district at-torney, Robert Morgenthau, in an attempt to convince him to begin a criminal investigation into Winfield and his relationship with his foundation. (To its shame, Morganthau's office began a file on Win-field, but soon closed it for want of substance.) One of the claims was that Winfield had used foundation money to pay for his limousine ex-penses; with that, Steinbrenner tried to convince the IRS to start its own investigation into Winfield, hopeful the agency would find tax fraud. This was the system at its worst, the rich and the powerful tak-ing advantage of governmental relationships for their own selfish pur-poses. All the while, Steinbrenner was not paying the money he was contractually obligated to pay Winfield's foundation. Naturally, Win-field sued him. This was all in the papers, day after day—another black eye for baseball.

Spira knew he had a good gig. He went back to Steinbrenner and said he wanted more money for new information.

This time, Steinbrenner did something smart. He refused to pay. He must have known, I believe, that Spira's information was worthless, that he was about the least reliable source you could imagine.

Spira added a threat: Pay me or I'm going to the newspapers.

That sounds like extortion and extortion is illegal. But Steinbrenner had put himself in this position. If you pay a guy like Spira once, you'll be paying him for the rest of his life. He'll come back every six months and say the same thing: Pay me money or I'm going to talk. As usual, Churchill said it best: "If you continue to appease a crocodile, eventually it will eat you."

Steinbrenner refused to pay Spira, Spira went to the paper, the paper ran the story, and suddenly baseball was launching another investigation.

This investigation was straightforward for an investigator of Dowd's skill. The case against Steinbrenner was overwhelming: He had violated Rule 21 again and again, taking actions that were not in the game's best interests. We had a hearing. Steinbrenner brought in three lawyers. I hired Harold "Ace" Tyler, a retired federal court judge, to manage the process. I wanted an independent person at the hearing who could respond to any claim of unfairness by Steinbrenner (this was prescient, not paranoid). The accused in a baseball hearing doesn't have much in the way of civil rights. It's a private proceeding, no different from a private men's eating club kicking out a member for chewing gum in the dining room. You may argue all you like about the unfairness of the process or the punishment, but there's not much you can do—few constitutional rights extend into private affairs. Tyler, although he was hired by me, was there as a sort of ombudsman. His role was to make sure everything I did, intentional or inadvertent, was beyond reproach. (Later, in my fight with the owners, they claimed I had been unfair to George and set up a committee of the owners to look into the claim. Bill Bartholomay of Atlanta and Jerry Reinsdorf, to no one's surprise, concluded I had been unfair. As I look back, that was one of the most shameful actions taken by any owner.)

Steinbrenner and his lawyers offered no real defense. He acknowledged he should have come to me much earlier, and that his dealings with Spira and Winfield were not in baseball's best interests. It was clear what Steinbrenner had done and why he had done it. It was clear he had done things that were stupid and wrong. The question became: What do I do with him? None of Steinbrenner's actions went to the heart of baseball, the game as it is played on the field, as gambling does, as Rose's misdeeds did. I wrestled with the proper sanction.

Some owners and others were saying, "Throw him out for life. You'll be doing baseball a service." He was already a convicted felon because of the illegal campaign contributions he had made to Richard Nixon in his Watergate-marred 1972 reelection campaign. For that, Bowie Kuhn had suspended him and placed him on probation. (He was later pardoned.) You could make the case he was a recidivist. Still, I believed throwing him out for life would be overkill. It would have been like giving him the electric chair for a speeding ticket. Steinbrenner, though, didn't know my feelings, which was to my advantage.

Even though the discussions were serious, there were moments of comedy. There always are with Steinbrenner, inadvertent though they may be. I think that's why the New York writers had such fun with him. At one point during our hearing, my Yale-educated deputy, Steve Greenberg, said to him, "George, isn't what you've done here really very Machiavellian?" He was referring, of course, to Niccolo Machiavelli, the sixteenth-century Italian political theorist who dismissed the role of morality in politics. Steve assumed his Yale education and Steinbrenner's Williams education must have covered pretty much the same ground.

"You Yalies," Steinbrenner said. "I don't know what Machiavellian means."

That's when I said to Steve, "You defend Ron Darling, I'll defend George." Darling, who had a successful pitching career, mostly for the Mets, had attended Yale. Darling once referred to a $5,000 check from the players union to each ballplayer during the 1990 lockout as "dog-track money." That's the kind of tin-ear line one might normally expect to hear from a Steinbrenner.

Naturally, Steinbrenner worried what punishment I planned. It didn't help that, as far as I could tell, his lawyers were fighting among themselves and failing to do their homework. I try to impose order in any situation I manage, but Steinbrenner's chaos was almost impenetrable. Still, he knew the bottom line. When the hearing was over and the dust had settled, he knew he would be thrown out of baseball for some period of time. But for how long? That was the question.

One weekend after the hearing, Greenberg, Dowd, Tyler, and I met at my summer house on Cape Cod, trying to decide on the proper sanction. The range was pretty much one year to five years. My own feeling was two years was about right, with the possibility that the sentence could be shortened for good behavior. Then I said, "Is it possible George will come in and say, 'I want out; I'm fed up with baseball'?" I was thinking, in part, of Rose, who tried to leave on what he felt were his own terms rather than on somebody else's. Steve said, "I think it is possible, and I think we should prepare ourselves for it." We all concurred we should have the language of an agreement in place in case George came into our next meeting and said he wanted out. As good lawyers, we had to be prepared for all eventualities; if he asked out, we wanted to be ready to act. We weren't eager to have another sordid baseball saga taking up valuable space in the nation's sports sections and on TV sports reports, not after Rose and the earthquake and the continuing labor problems. The best thing for baseball is for fans to focus on the game.

We called Steinbrenner in for sentencing. He came in with two lawyers, one to play good cop, the other bad. I said: "George, what you've done is a serious violation of baseball's rules. You ran a program of terror against one of your own players. You had him investigated. You bought information from a bad source. You used governmental agencies inappropriately to intimidate one of your players. You opened yourself to extortion and you brought an embarrassing episode to baseball at a time when we need all the good news we can get. You've been involved in a lousy business, George. I'm going to suspend you for two years. No involvement with the team of any sort for two years."

"A suspension is terrible, Fay," he said. "That's the worst thing that can happen to me. I'm about to become a member of the U.S. Olympic Committee. If you suspend me, I'll lose my position on the committee. That's the most important thing to me in my life right now. I'd rather leave the game than have a two-year suspension. In fact, that's what I want to do. I want out of baseball. I'm sick and tired of it. I hate what's happening in the game. I've got two sons, one of them might someday be interested in running the team. What would you think of me just agreeing to leave baseball?"

Even though I had prepared myself for this possibility, I was still stunned. I said, "Wait a minute, George. You understand that if you leave baseball, there's no guarantee you'll ever come back."

He said, "I understand that. Don't patronize me."

I said, "If you leave baseball, you'll be on the permanently ineligible list."

Steinbrenner said, "I don't know what that is."

I found that hard to believe. That phrase came up every time the Rose penalty was discussed. "Why don't you talk to your lawyers," I said. Steve quickly produced our draft of an agreement, the one by which Steinbrenner voluntarily agreed to leave baseball for life and to be put on the permanently ineligible list, and gave it to Steinbrenner's lawyers.

This was around noon on Monday, July 30, 1990. Earlier in the day, we had called for a press conference at 2:00 P.M. to announce the suspension. In New York, Steinbrenner's future with the Yankees was a story of nearly epic importance. But Steinbrenner's lawyers were arguing with each other about what to do, and we kept having to postpone the press conference. We moved it to 4:00 P.M., then 6:00 P.M., then 8:00 P.M. One of the lawyers argued that it was a good deal, and that George should take it. The other urged George to take baseball to court.

As the day wore on, I grew more frustrated. Late in the day, near 6:00 P.M., I joined the three of them and said, "George, you've got to pick your poison. Either it's the two-year suspension or you agree to leave baseball and are put on the permanently ineligible list. You tell me you can't be suspended because it will hurt your standing in the USOC. That is what it is. If you take us to court, I believe your chances of winning are very, very slim. You are fortunate I am giving you options. But you have to decide."

George said: "I want out. I don't want to be suspended. One of my sons will come along eventually and he can run the team."

"Fine," I said. "Then sign the agreement."

Another two hours passed. George and the lawyers argued among themselves and George had still not signed the agreement. Finally, I'd had it. I said, "George, I'm fed up with you and your lawyers. I'm going over to the press conference. I'm going to tell them you're suspended for two years. If you want to do something else, we can discuss it tomorrow."

"No," George said, "you can't do that."

"Enough is enough, George." I picked up my briefcase and started to the elevators with Steve Greenberg and my colleagues. We were headed to the press conference.

As we passed him, Steinbrenner's hawk lawyer said, as if in a movie, "We'll see you in court, Commissioner."

"Just tell me where and when," I said. I didn't say, Counselor.

I'm a slow walker, because of my handicap. It took me a while to get to the elevator. Finally I did, the doors opened, and I stepped in. As the elevator doors were closing, the dove lawyer dashed up, stuck his hand between them, and said, "He's going to sign. Could you come back? We don't want you to do what you're about to do. Come back inside, please. He'll sign." And so he did.

We had our press conference. I remember Dave Anderson, the lead sports columnist on *The New York Times*, looking up at me and shaking his head, as if to say, "How did you get George to go for that one?" Of course, I didn't. My preference was for the two-year suspension, but I let George have the more severe penalty because that's what he wanted.

I have been told of a conversation between George and Jerry Reinsdorf, the White Sox owner, that took place from George's car right after he left my office. It went about like this:

Jerry: "What happened?"

George: "I just made myself a great deal. I took Fay's jockstrap."

Jerry: "Oh yeah? What did you do?"

George: "He was going to suspend me for two years, but I agreed to leave baseball on my own."

Jerry: "George, they killed you. You have no idea. You made a terrible deal."

This was a misreading by Reinsdorf: I didn't kill George, and his crime was not a capital one, not in baseball terms. Whatever George did he did to himself, both the crime and the penalty. But the public was interpreting the situation differently. The *Daily News* headline the next day read: "Fay Faytal to George."

In the years since, when I talk to baseball groups about my baseball years, I'm sometimes asked my views on the Steinbrenner-Spira-Winfield episode. I describe how George made a series of bad decisions, but that his ultimate failing was in choosing his legal counsel. George later told me his choice of lawyers was awful. The two guys George brought in that day did not serve him well. I saw no indication that they understood how baseball operates, that they had studied the Rose case, or that they understood what it means to be on the permanently ineligible list. They simply seemed unprepared. And more than anything, they didn't appear to have their eye on their client's ultimate goal. George's objective was to keep his position on the USOC and to stay in baseball. They should have worked out something with the USOC before they saw me. The two lawyers eventually heard about my being publicly critical of their work and wrote me a threatening letter. I didn't feel the slightest bit bad about what I'd been saying because I knew it to be true and because I wasn't saying anything I wouldn't have said directly to them. In their letter to me they said if I didn't stop talking about them they would sue me. I can think of few things funnier than being sued and then using George Steinbrenner as my main witness. (He had told me many times how poorly he had been represented and how Steve and I were too good for his lawyers.) They would have been killed in a court case. I never heard from them again.

Almost immediately George arranged to have two suits filed against baseball and me, even though in our agreement he had expressly agreed not to sue. Naturally, he used different lawyers this time. First, one of his limited partners in Cleveland sued baseball, and then on the heels of that, Steinbrenner's accountant, Leonard Kleinman, sued me as well. The first suit claimed it was illegal for baseball to remove the club's general partner, claiming it was devastating to the team. For his part, Kleinman claimed I had wrongly blocked him from running the team in George's absence. I am certain George was behind both these suits. Of course, they wouldn't have even been necessary had George accepted his two-year suspension.

Those lawsuits refuted George's realization that he needed to get back in the game. Once gone, he learned how much he missed being a public personality. He needed the attention, he needed to be a big man in New York. During his exile, he could have nothing to do with baseball; the only way he could enter Yankee Stadium was if he bought a ticket. I know how much he missed baseball because he called me several times to tell me about his life out of baseball and how empty it was and how much he wanted to get back in. He made some sense, but I was hardly sympathetic. He had caused me too much grief.

I said: "George, I shouldn't even be talking to you. The only reason I am is that I have always believed the two-year suspension made more sense. Your problem with the USOC never added up. I can't believe they would care so much about a suspension from baseball." I was thinking to myself: They didn't care that you were a convicted felon in the context of a presidential campaign, so why should they care about a suspension in baseball centered on your involvement with a pathetic small-time hustler? I said, "If you want to have a conversation with me, you must make those two lawsuits go away."

"I can't control Kleinman," George said. "We've had a big fight and now he's turned on me."

"Make the suits go away, George," I said.

A few weeks later, George called me back. "You know what Kleinman wants?" he said. "A million dollars!" Kleinman claimed Steinbrenner wanted him to be the general partner in his absence and that I was wrong to block him. Kleinman was correct in that I knew he was incapable of acting independently of George. Instead, Bob Nederlander, a member of the famous Broadway family, served as the acting general partner; he proved to be a solid citizen who performed nobly in trying circumstances and we remain good friends.

"George, I'm sorry, but Kleinman is your man. Now you know what he is," I said, "But I'm not talking to you until those suits are withdrawn."

George kept calling me, always at home, often at night, and I kept saying he had to get rid of the suits. Eventually he did, and then we met, George and—not surprisingly—a new lawyer and Steve Greenberg and I. At this point, I have to acknowledge, my feelings for Steinbrenner were now purely negative. He had wasted a considerable amount of my time and had sullied baseball and Winfield and his team with his stupid behavior and pointless lawsuits. I had lost whole days to depositions when I should have been working on issues important to baseball. With my ambulatory struggles, it was difficult for me to go to the various offices for these depositions. The lawyers for Kleinman were miserable people and Steinbrenner didn't care. And now he was in front of me, appealing to me, trying to get back into baseball. On a personal level, I was inclined not to let him back. There was little about him I admired or respected. Then his lawyer began the meeting by suggesting the agreement George had signed could be challenged in court. That did it. I lost it.

"If you threaten me, this meeting is over," I said. "There is no chance this agreement will be overturned by a court and you know it. George had two lawyers and signed of his own free will. The only way George is getting back in is out of the goodness of my heart. Mercy is the only thing you have going for you. If you ask me to let you back in I might do it. *Might.* Not because I want you back in baseball. I don't. But because it's not right for you to get life for a speeding ticket. I can't live with that. That is not fair."

Eventually I let him back in, on the two-year anniversary of his original departure from baseball. He served the two-year suspension I felt he should have served from the beginning. He came back, ironically, just as I was leaving baseball in the fall of 1992. Shortly before his official reinstatement, his stand-in at the Yankees voted against me in the pivotal owners' meeting.

Yogi Berra, a friend of mine, was upset I let George back in. Yogi had been fired by George in 1985 as Yankee manager and he swore he would never enter Yankee Stadium again as long as Steinbrenner owned the team. Whenever he saw me he'd say, "Commissioner, you really gave in. You should never have let him back." Much later,

George and Yogi made up; George made a donation to the Yogi Berra Museum in Montclair, New Jersey, and Yogi returned the favor by coming to Yankee Stadium to throw out the first pitch of the home opener in 1999. They say time heals all wounds. Maybe.

People still say to me, "You kicked George out of baseball and then you let him back in." That really is not correct. I never suspended him; he made an agreement to leave. Moreover, he served his time. People ask me if the game is better with or without Steinbrenner in it. I don't think there's much difference. John McMullen used to say that any new owner who comes into baseball, no matter how depraved, can only elevate the level of ownership. One of the biggest problems within the ownership group in my time as commissioner was drinking; more than a few of the owners were alcoholics. Others were stupid. Some were venal. Others were egomaniacs. Others had poor advisers. Quite a few were decent and capable. For a long time, George picked one bad adviser after another. In my time, he continually hired people who were afraid of him. He surrounded himself with "yes" men, people and lawyers who knew they were just one wrong remark away from being fired. They were scared, unable to tell him when he was wrong. In any organization, the emperor must be told when he is naked—and when he is wrong.

Since George's return to baseball, his behavior has been improved, bordering on exemplary, and his team's success has been magnificent in every sense. He started hiring good advisers and that's made all the difference. He's had two excellent general managers, Bob Watson and Brian Cashman, and, since 1996, a rock-solid field manager, Joe Torre. He has spent his money wisely and bought some of the best talent available, and done well to keep an eye on how the talent would mesh. It has been a breathtaking run, and George deserves some of the credit. Meanwhile, his investment has soared. He bought the Yankees from CBS for $10 million in 1973. Thirty years later, they were worth more than $700 million. One really good business decision can outweigh two dozen poor ones. Of course, one really good business decision does not make you a cultivated, educated person, even if you went to Williams. Still, George looks like a genius today.

I've only seen him once since I left baseball, and that was at Joe DiMaggio's memorial service in 1999, held at St. Patrick's Cathedral in New York. He initiated a hello and I initiated a handshake and said, "Does this remind you of the Williams chapel?"

"I wouldn't know," George said. "I was never in the Williams chapel."

I think he was trying to be funny, although with George you never know.

I was with my old friend Ralph Branca, the former Dodger pitcher. Ralph said, "You're a better man than I am. I wouldn't have shaken his hand, after all he put you through. That's the difference between us." As a younger man, I felt as Ralph still does; as an older man, I've come to believe there comes a time when you must let bygones be bygones. You have to make your peace. Yogi made his peace. I made mine. Yes, George drove me crazy and wasted my time, did dumb things, hurt and annoyed me. Along the way, he hurt himself the most. Anyway, we both survived it. As Camus wrote, that which does not kill you makes you stronger.

When I think of George, I try to remember the good things he did. He raised money for a lovely old Williams coach and his wonderful wife in their time of need. He showed he had heart. I cannot forget that when evaluating the man.

Howard Spira went to jail and is long forgotten, barely a baseball footnote.

Dave Winfield has prospered. When he was inducted into the Hall of Fame in 2001, there was some question which cap he would wear on his bust, a Yankees cap or the cap of the team he came up with, the San Diego Padres. He chose the Padres.

I understand.

Lineup: A Boy and His Yankees	
1.	George Stirnweiss
2.	Spec Shea
3.	Yogi Berra
4.	Lou Gehrig
5.	Phil Rizzuto
6.	Tommy Henrich
7.	Whitey Ford
8.	Roger Maris
9.	Eddie Lopat

A Boy and His Yankees

1. GEORGE STIRNWEISS

I THINK MANY BASEBALL FANS grow up with this: You know somebody who knows somebody who *played in the bigs.* These words are said in a hushed tone. He may have had a whole career, or just a cup of coffee, or there may be a mistake in the telling of the story: in actual fact, the guy peaked at Double A ball, but somewhere along the line the facts got blurred. Tangential links can become outsized. *My cousin's neighbor used to be the bullpen coach for . . .* whomever. It really doesn't matter. It connects you to big-league baseball. It tears down the wall between the spectator and the player, for even the bullpen pitching coach is on a first-name basis with all manner of regulars, All-Stars, maybe even a future Hall of Famer.

In my house growing up, I had a link to George "Snuffy" Stirnweiss, the New York Yankee second baseman from 1943 through 1950. I came of baseball age in 1947, when I was nine and my Yankees defeated the Brooklyn Dodgers in seven games in the World Series. Only one player got more at bats than Snuffy in the '47 Series: Tommy Henrich, who became my ultimate hero. (Thirty-one ABs for Tommy; 27 for Snuffy, same as Jackie Robinson.)

Snuffy was born in New York, but had ties to the Naugatuck River Valley—or as they say in the area, "to the Valley." My father was born in that valley and knew Snuffy, although he called him George. He followed his career as George graduated high school and left to play football—he was a halfback—at the University of North Carolina. My father got to know Snuffy at some point, admired him and knew all about the ulcers and hay fever that kept George out of the service during World War II. He knew all about the scoring controversy that gave George the American League batting title in 1945. (Many of the big-name players were in the service and batting titles were going to lesser players.) Going into the last day of the season, George was batting .305 and Tony Cuccinello of the Chicago White Sox was at .308. The final White Sox game was rained out and never rescheduled. In the Yankees' final game, played at home, George went two for three—until the official scorer changed an error into a hit. This three-for-three day raised George's average to .3085, which rounded up to .309, and the title was his. I picked up my father's interest in Snuffy, and when he was traded to the St. Louis Browns in an eight-man deal early in the 1950 season, I was twelve and learned for the first time the cold realities of the business of baseball. My father consoled me with the first of many admonitions to keep the game in perspective. To him, my grades in school were truly important; who played second for the Yankees surely was not.

One September day in 1958, we got sad news: George, out of baseball for five years, was coming home by train to northern New Jersey from Washington, D.C. when the train jumped its track, fell into the river, and George Stirnweiss was killed. It was big news across the valley and in the gin mills where the shopworkers had a beer on the way home. We all felt we knew him, even if we didn't.

2. SPEC SHEA

IN MY FIRST YEAR as a Yankee fan, 1947, there was a rookie pitcher in the rotation named Frank Joseph O'Shea who pitched under the name

Spec Shea, because of his Irish freckles. Another Valley boy, he was from Naugatuck, just down the road from Torrington, Connecticut, and Mel Allen, the Yankee broadcaster, called him the "Naugatuck Nugget." He came up in midseason and went 14–5 that year, won two games in the World Series and would have been the American League Rookie of the Year easily, except that only one Rookie of the Year was named that year and the next, and the award went to Jackie Robinson. All through the season, Spec Shea earned banner headlines in *The New Haven Register,* and my father spoke of him as he spoke of George Stirnweiss: He was one of us. My father knew him because they had both played in Waterbury before the war. Spec spent most of 1942 through 1946 in the military. After the war, he was again pitching for a Waterbury team that played an exhibition game against the Yankees. Spec pitched, won 1–0, and was invited to a Yankee spring-training camp. He eventually made the team, turned twenty-seven the day after he pitched the World Series opener, then pitched a four-hitter in Game Five a few days later. He was the local boy who made good.

In the winter of 1957, a few weeks after I fell off the ledge of my dormitory building at Williams, I met Spec Shea. I was in Waterbury Hospital, recuperating. Spec Shea, after eight years in the majors, was out of baseball. My father arranged for the visit through a local sportswriter. I don't remember a thing about it, except that it happened, and that I told everybody it happened, and since then I've been telling anybody who will listen. That day in the hospital, out of it though I was, I met my first big-league hero. I met the Yankee Spec Shea. He played with DiMaggio, and that was more than enough.

3. YOGI BERRA

I'VE KNOWN YOGI—who else can travel the world on just their nickname?—for years, I've admired him since boyhood, and I've never known him to be out of character. He is like Jack Benny, who never wavered from his brilliant act as a parsimonious cheapskate. Yogi was always modest, never oversold himself, never pretended to be something he is not. But I'm on to him. A few years ago I said to him: "Yogi, you've been doing a con job on the world for years, haven't you?"

"Ah, Commissioner, c'mon."

Another one of his ploys, to answer questions with shrugs. Very effective.

"You've done a brilliant job of persuading everyone you're this simple little Italian kid from the Hill. But I'm on to you. You're probably the smartest player of your generation."

"Ah, Commissioner, c'mon," he said, shrugging.

"Come on, Yog, who else in baseball can use just their first name and sell books, write movie reviews, appear in all sorts of ads, make money?"

He will admit to nothing, not even to the fact that he has the first nickel he ever made, which I am certain is true. For that, he gives all the credit to his wife, Carmen, without ever acknowledging its truth.

Yogi is well-known for being witty, and unlike some people with that reputation, he actually *is* witty. He's more than witty; he has a gift for language. He can't help himself. He was playing in a pro-am golf tournament a few years ago. It was a quiet thing. A friend of mine happened to be there. The course superintendent, fishing for a compliment, approached Yogi and asked him how he liked his fairways. They were perfect emerald carpets. Yogi, without pausing: "They're too narrow."

A while back, I visited Yogi at his museum in Montclair, New Jersey. We were talking about his Navy service during World War II, before he joined the Yankees. He talked about D-Day, June 6, 1944. "I was in the Navy. We were off the coast of Normandy in a little rocket launcher. We would go up under the cliffs and fire rockets at the Germans. We'd fire them all, then go back and get more. We were there six days."

I asked, "What was it like on D-Day that morning? The world is blowing up, the sky is exploding, what was it like?"

"It was just like the Fourth of July!" Yogi said.

"The Fourth of July? I don't think so, Yog."

"Yeah, it was like the Fourth of July, everything going off."

Who else but Yogi would say it that way?

(He shrugs.)

4. LOU GEHRIG

I GREW UP WITH THE LEGEND of Lou Gehrig—everybody my age did—and when I went to Williams, his legend only grew for me. Gehrig played college baseball at Columbia, and at one point, his Columbia team came to Williams for a game. The ballfield at Williams has a football grandstand well back of left field. Gehrig, of course, was a left-handed hitter. He hit a tremendous shot over the grandstand from the left side of the plate—an opposite-field homer that had to be on the order of five hundred feet. No visiting player to Weston Field leaves without hearing the story of Gehrig's colossal home run. Less well-known is that Gehrig once struck out seventeen Williams batters in a game, but lost.

Later, when I got to know Joe DiMaggio, I asked him about Gehrig. Gehrig wore 4, DiMaggio wore 5, their lockers were next to each other for three seasons and part of a fourth. I asked Joe how Gehrig led.

"By example," DiMaggio said. "He never said anything. He hustled on everything, every swing, every foul ball. He ran out everything. He was a big, strong player and he really put out. He did everything hard. He swung hard. He hit the ball right on the nose. He hit line drives. If he swung up on it just a little, like Ted or me, he would have hit a lot more home runs.

"After a bad game, especially if he went o for 4, I'd watch him. He'd come in, all sweaty, and just sit on his stool in front of his locker. He'd be drenching wet and he'd just sit there, smoking one cigarette, then another. He wouldn't say anything to anybody and nobody would say anything to him. You could tell he was upset. He'd stay there for maybe fifteen minutes. Then he'd get up, go in the shower. He'd come out and sit there again, having another smoke. Then he'd get dressed and, if we were on the road, go out for dinner with Dickey."

Bill Dickey was the Yankee catcher. He was having a Hall of Fame career, too.

"Did he ever say anything when he sat on his stool?" I asked.

"Nothing."

"And did you ever say anything to him?"

"Oh, no. I wouldn't do that."

I asked DiMaggio about the 1939 season, Gehrig's last. On May 2, while batting just .143 and fielding poorly, he took himself out of the lineup after playing in 2,130 consecutive games. He never played again. Soon after, he was diagnosed with a rare, incurable, deadly disease: amyotrophic lateral sclerosis, or ALS, now commonly known as Lou Gehrig's Disease. (Curt Schilling, the big righthander for the Arizona Diamondbacks' 2001 World Series–winning team, works tirelessly as an ALS fundraiser and has a son named Gehrig.) On July 4, 1939, the Yankees held a day to honor Gehrig. Babe Ruth, in his fourth year of retirement, was on the field in street clothes. DiMaggio, of course, was in Yankee pinstripes. Everybody knew Gehrig had a rare disease and everybody knew the disease was a death sentence. That's what made the day so poignant.

"In the clubhouse before the ceremony, Gehrig said he wasn't going to say anything. He had nothing planned," DiMaggio told me. "Then just before we went out, he changed his mind. I heard him give that little talk. I was standing right behind him. It was all off the cuff." That was the speech in which Gehrig said the immortal words, "Today, I consider myself the luckiest man on the face of the earth." Two years later he was dead.

"The Babe was right there," DiMaggio said. "People said he and Gehrig were not close but that was not true. It was the wives who didn't get along. If it wasn't for the women, they would've been great friends. When Gehrig finished, the Babe came right up and hugged him. I could see tears streaming down his face. He was crying like a baby. That was some day."

5. PHIL RIZZUTO

THERE WAS A PERIOD, when the Veterans Committee of the Hall of Fame was passing on Phil Rizzuto year after year, that people said the legendary Yankee shortstop was overrated. There were people saying that his main genius was to have a career with the Yankees that exactly coincided with their most dominant era. The Scooter played for thirteen seasons—missing three for war service—and played in nine

World Series. Here's my view: You can't get to the World Series year after year unless you have a very capable shortstop. A good catcher, a good shortstop, a good centerfielder, and an ace who can stop any losing streak—no team wins without those four centerpieces. Rizzuto was a good hitter, a superb bunter, and an excellent fielder who played the hitters well and put just enough mustard on his throws to first to get runners by a half-step. His arm was not his best asset but he got the job done. His game was smart. He was the first guy I ever saw go deep in the hole between short and third, field the ball cleanly, and flip it to the third baseman, Billy Johnson, who had a real gun for an arm; he would fire the ball to first for the out. I used to marvel at Rizzuto when I saw him practicing short-hopping little humpback liners so he could turn one out into two. He finally got into the Hall of Fame in 1994, but only after the death of Charlie Gehringer, the superb Tiger infielder who had been on the Veterans Committee and who was opposed to Rizzuto. My feeling is if Pee Wee Reese, the Brooklyn Dodger shortstop of the same period, deserves to be in, Rizzuto belongs, too. They both are there, and properly so.

Rizzuto's long career as a broadcaster is another matter. I never had a problem with his constant use of "holy cow," but his long discussions of the perfect cannoli and his niece's list of bridesmaids for her upcoming wedding I could have done without. Bill White, the National League president, worked with Rizzuto for years in the broadcast booth. I asked him once what that experience was like.

"Rizzuto kept a scorecard with all sorts of cryptic notations on it," Bill told me. "I noticed in a lot of the boxes were the letters 'WW.' I asked him once what that meant. He said, 'Wasn't watching.' "

We, of course, were. It was the Yankees, our Yankees.

6. TOMMY HENRICH

I FELT ABOUT TOMMY HENRICH as Bart Giamatti felt about Bobby Doerr. Henrich was the Yankee rightfielder in my youth and was my hero. He was solid in everything he did. Henrich was a very visible Catholic, the Yankee star who went to church every Sunday, and as I had the same habit I took pride in claiming Henrich as one of our own. As an adult I was able to meet him and get to know him, and he exceeded my expectations in every way. Mel Allen, the longtime Yankee broadcaster, used to call Henrich "Old Reliable," because you could count on him to come up with the clutch hit or the spectacular play. He was "Old Reliable" in his off-field life, showing up when he was supposed to, saying the correct thing, embodying what the old-timers call Yankee class. He has a value system I respect. He has become a good friend.

I know his true age. *The Baseball Encyclopedia* lists his birthdate as February 20, 1913; in actual fact, he's three years older than that. "When I signed," he said, "I took three years off my age. It was better to be eighteen than twenty-one." Which means when he played his final game in 1950, he was forty. I followed the last four seasons of his career as a boy, and have been catching up on the rest of his career and life ever since. It was Henrich who taught Rizzuto about trapping those soft liners to try to double up a baserunner. Henrich used to do the same thing in shallow right. He'd wave off the backpedaling second baseman, let the ball drop, and turn two. They later changed the infield fly rule to apply to an outfielder because of Henrich's maneuver. He was a great fastball hitter; even Bob Feller couldn't throw it by him. He batted third, right in front of DiMaggio, and he got pitches in the strike zone because nobody wanted to walk Henrich and face DiMaggio with a runner on.

I once asked DiMaggio who was the smartest player he ever played with. He answered immediately: Henrich. I told Henrich what DiMaggio had said and I asked him if he knew why DiMaggio considered him to be so smart.

"It's because of something I did during The Streak," Henrich said, using the shorthand, as all old Yankees do, for DiMaggio's record-breaking fifty-six-game hitting streak in 1941. "In game thirty-eight, DiMaggio didn't have a hit going into the bottom of the eighth. We were ahead by two runs. DiMaggio is due up fourth that inning. If somebody doesn't get on, he's not getting another swing. I'm batting third. I don't want to make the last out. Johnny Sturm makes an out and Red Rolfe draws a walk. If I hit into a double play, the inning is over and The Streak is over.

"I go over to Joe McCarthy and I ask, 'What would you think about a bunt here?' I never bunted, but the manager is smart. He knows the worst-case scenario: I make an out. I'm not going to bunt into a double play. The manager looks at me for a moment and says, 'That'll be fine, young man.'

"So I bunt. Nobody was expecting it and I beat it out. Now DiMaggio's got two on and two out. The first pitch, DiMaggio hit a liner to right. The Streak's alive. So if he thinks I'm smart, maybe that's why."

That's why, Tommy.

7. WHITEY FORD

I CAME UP AS A FAN AS Whitey Ford came up as a pitcher. In his rookie year, 1950, when he went 9–1 for the Yankees, I was twelve. That fall, the Yankees swept the Phillies in the World Series. The Yankee starters were Raschi, Reynolds, Lopat, and Ford. (Beat that!) By the fall of 1955, when I was a senior at Hotchkiss, Ford had emerged as the team ace. He went 18–7 that year and won twice in the World Series. By 1960, when I graduated from Williams, Ford was the so-called Chairman of the Board. He had none of the eccentricities one associates with lefthanders. He was the consummate pro. In 1963, when I graduated from law school and, in a sense, from the Yankees, he had his second and last twenty-win season: 24–7, with a 2.74 ERA.

Ford and Mickey Mantle were regularly in the headlines, for their on-field heroics and their off-field ventures through New York's nightlife. For a kid like me who played things straight, that life was foreign, but the idea of going through life with a buddy was appealing. Ballplayers and soldiers seem to excel at that. Ford played from 1950 through 1967, missing two years after his rookie year for military service. Mantle played from 1951 through 1968. I think the nightlife was easier on Ford than Mantle. Mantle, the world learned late in his life, was an alcoholic. Ford was just having a good time. I asked Ford once about how he dealt with those nights. He said, "My old man had a bar in Queens. Liquor was just part of my everyday life. I grew up knowing how to handle liquor. Besides, I only worked every fourth day."

Whenever he pitched, he was ready. He pitched nothing like Bob

Feller or Warren Spahn; his stuff was good but not overwhelming. But he was smart. He had the best pickoff move I've ever seen, and a bulging quiver of pitches to choose from: fastball, curveball, change-up, slider (developed in midcareer), spitter, scuffball. Everybody knew about the last two and nobody could catch him. He was too smart. He was charming, too. When he heard I admired his pickoff move, he sent me a picture with the inscription: "I could never have picked you off—you were too quick." For someone who walks on canes, those were nice words to hear.

I value consistency in life and I marvel at Ford's. He never had an ERA higher than 3.24. Even in his final two seasons, at the ages of thirty-nine and forty, working sparingly as a spot starter and reliever, his ERAs were 2.47 and 1.64. I once asked Yogi, who caught Ford for years, to explain it to me: How could Ford be so good, year after year after year?

"Commissioner," Yogi said, "he could throw a curveball at 3–0. He could throw any pitch at any time for a strike. He always figured whatever the count, he'd get you."

Ford exuded confidence every time he went to the mound, just as an excellent business leader exudes confidence every time he comes to a meeting. Ford was aptly nicknamed; he truly was the Chairman of the Board. If I were a manager, Ford would be my ultimate big-game pitcher. (Although Bob Gibson makes that choice very close.) Nothing intimidated him. Watching him as a kid growing up, I picked up on that. I think he helped me, and thousands of others along with me, on the road to adulthood. In any tough spot, you could ask yourself: What would the Chairman do?

8. ROGER MARIS

IN THE 1927 SEASON, Babe Ruth hit 60 home runs for the New York Yankees. In the 1961 season, Roger Maris hit 61 home runs for the New York Yankees. These are facts. In 1927, Ruth broke his own record; he had hit 59 in 1921. In 1961, Maris broke Ruth's record. If you lived through that summer of '61, you can't help but remember it. Mickey Mantle and Roger Maris were swatting homers at the same pace, a pace fast enough to pass Ruth, all season long, and everybody was rooting for one guy or the other. Most were rooting for Mantle; I was rooting for either or both. Then in 1998, Mark McGwire broke Maris's record, hitting 70 home runs for the St. Louis Cardinals. In 2001, Barry Bonds broke McGwire's record, hitting 73 home runs for the San Francisco Giants. These are not complicated issues. Since 1921, the single-season home run record has gone from 59 to 60 to 61 to 70 to 73.

Ford Frick, the commissioner of baseball in 1961, had a blind spot to Maris's accomplishment. He had begun his professional life as a midwestern sportswriter, and as a young man was Babe Ruth's ghostwriter. Evidently, he could not bear to see the Babe's legend diminished in any way. He decided that Maris would have to top Ruth in the first 154 games (the length of Ruth's season) of 1961 to be recognized as a record holder; otherwise, there would be two single-season records for home runs: one for the 154-game season, and a second for the 162-game season. This might seem logical, except that no other single-season baseball record is treated this way, given separate but equal treatment. The record is home runs, single season, period—just as it is for steals, triples, ejections, whatever. But Maris and his family and his friends had to endure the indignity of what came to be called "the asterisk," the mythical notation attached to his record that made it less than whole. In actual fact, there was no asterisk—just two lines where there should have been one.

In 1991, Steve Greenberg, the deputy commissioner, came into my office and said, "Fay, did you read this?" It was a column, written by Roger Angell, the esteemed writer and editor at *The New Yorker*, making the case that the time had come to undo Frick, to remove the so-called asterisk and make Maris the single-season home-run champ. I had the power to do it and I agreed with Steve that we ought to fix the error, so we did. I convened a meeting of baseball's committee on records and statistics; I, conveniently, was its chairman. No one disagreed. We eliminated one line from the record book. We corrected a wrong done to a good man.

I was totally unprepared for the response—not from the public, which applauded the move, but from the Maris family. Roger had died in 1985, at the age of fifty-one, from cancer. The record, even its shared state, was their ultimate family legacy, but it was tied up, so to say, in probate. Giving Roger Maris the full credit he was due made the family feel complete. They wrote me gracious letters of appreciation. I feel I did nothing; the credit goes to Roger Angell and to Steve Greenberg. Ultimately, the credit goes to Maris. (And the boo to Frick.)

In 2000, Billy Crystal, the actor and Yankee fan, produced and directed a movie for HBO called 61*, about the summer of '61 when Maris, batting third in the Yankee lineup, hit 61 homers and Mantle, batting fourth, hit 54. Mantle was beloved and fans everywhere were pulling for him to break Ruth's record. Maris was reserved and undemonstrative and spent the summer of '61 battling writers and losing his hair. Crystal did an excellent job with the movie. Near its end, you hear the voice of Bob Sheppard, the Yankees public address announcer since 1951, saying that in 1991 I removed the asterisk. I said to Crystal, "I get in this movie late." Crystal said, "But you get in big." He was being nice, but accurate, too: Deleting the extra line turned out to be a big deal. In 1998, when McGwire homered 70 times, nobody talked about him breaking two records, just the one, and that was plenty.

9. EDDIE LOPAT

EDDIE LOPAT—born Edmund Lopatynski in New York City in 1918—came to the Yankees in 1948 from the Chicago White Sox. In other words, he came to the Yankees almost the same year I did. He spent his life in baseball, as a player, scout, coach, manager, and general manager, and was still in baseball when I became the commissioner. We became friends. In 1991, I went into the hospital for surgery. I had my spleen taken out, and there was an infection. It was serious. Jerry Reinsdorf, the White Sox owner, complained that I was away from the office too much. Maybe I should have had my doctor write him a note: *Patient nearly died*. Whatever. But some good came out of the hospital stay. I got a visit from Eddie Lopat.

He was very ill at the time, too. He came into my room and said, "Fay, you're sick, I'm sick. You don't want to hear about my problems, I don't want to hear about yours. Let's talk baseball." And that's what we did, for three hours. It was one of the best times of my life.

As a pitcher, Lopat threw nothing but junk. "Lopat throws tissue paper," Casey Stengel once said. He had every pitch but the fastball. He had no fastball. All of baseball knew that. That day, sitting in my room at Greenwich Hospital, Eddie told me the story of the day he struck out Al Rosen, the terrific fastball-hitting third baseman for the Cleveland Indians, on nothing but fastballs. He called Rosen—later the president of the Yankees and the general manager of the San Francisco Giants—by his nickname, Flip. They were good friends and competitive.

"I said to him one day during spring training, 'Flip, you can't hit my fastball.'

" 'What fastball?'

" 'I'm telling ya, I'll bet I could strike you out on three fastballs.'

" 'Not in a million years,' Flip said, with reason on his side.

" 'You wanna bet?' So we bet two hundred dollars that at some point in the season I could strike him out on three fastballs.

"Later in the season we're at the Stadium, playing Cleveland in a Sunday doubleheader. During batting practice I say to him, 'Flip, today's the day. I'm pitching the second game. I'm gonna get you on three fastballs.'

"The first time up, he doesn't see anything like a fastball and he makes an out. Second time up I yell at him. 'This is it. Here it comes!' I throw him a curveball first pitch. He lets it go. It's ball one. Then I say, 'Here comes another one!' It's a fastball, right down the middle. He's frozen. He's never seen my fastball before. It's slow and it's straight. Count's 1–1. I say, 'Here comes another one!' It's another curve, misses for a ball. Now it's two balls and a strike. 'Here comes another one.' Fastball for a strike. Even count. Again: 'Here comes another one.' Miss with a screwball. Full count. Payoff pitch: 'Here comes another.' He knows I can't throw my fastball full count. It's a batting-practice fastball. He'll kill it. He's looking for anything but the fastball. I throw him my fastball. He's frozen. Called third strike. He called me very bad Polish names!"

Sometime later, we were both healthy enough to go to Yankee Stadium and watch a game together. Eddie studied the pitchers. He was not happy with what he saw. "This kid is not a pitcher," he said. "He just isn't being smart. You don't throw in the same location at the same speed two pitches in a row. Watch this. Look at this. He should have never thrown that. He should be going in and out, up and down. Movement and timing. Get the hitter off his timing. Move the batter around. Get him thinking. Think."

He could go on for hours about the game and he did, and I could go on listening to him for hours and I did. All our conversation was ultimately about a shared deep love for the game and the bond felt by those who share the game.

Soon after, he was dead. A lot of the old great Yankees, the Yankees of my youth, attended his funeral. Tommy Henrich, of course, was there. Henrich showed up for funerals, even if it meant flying across the country to do so. That's what the old-school gents do. He's still Old Reliable. George Steinbrenner was there. Yogi was there. I was there. I was a reader. I read from St. Paul's first letter to the Corinthians. All about love.

Later, my old friend Frank Slocum said, "It took Eddie Lopat to get Yogi, Steinbrenner, and Fay into the same church at the same time." Slocum had it right. Eddie could get anybody together. His enthusiasm was infectious. I miss him.

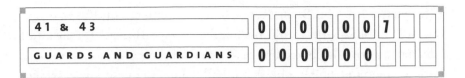

CHAPTER   SEVEN

41 & 43

TO BART, number 41 represented his pitching hero, Tom Seaver, who wore that number on his back when he pitched for the New York Mets with such grace and skill. The number 43 is most noteworthy for how seldom it is used. (I believe no team has retired it.) But to me, those numbers represent two presidents of the United States: George H. W. Bush, the forty-first president of the United States, who was in the first year of his presidency when I became the commissioner of base-ball, and George W. Bush, who was the president of the Texas Rangers when I was commissioner and who subsequently became the forty-third president. I met both of them one hot dusty summer a long time ago, in 1956, in Midland, Texas. I found my way there through my friendship with George H. W.'s kid brother, Bucky.

I first met Bucky in the fall of 1952, in my first year at Hotchkiss. One day a very large boy filled the frame of my door. He was friendly from the start: "Hi, I'm Buck Bush." He was six-five, 280 pounds. He dwarfed even me.

In formal references, he was William Henry Trotter Bush, son of

U.S. senator Prescott Bush, Republican of Connecticut. But to everyone at Hotchkiss, and within his family, he was "Bucky." Bucky and I became fast friends, linked by our size and our love of sports—we were both linemen for the Hotchkiss football team, of course. I was six feet two inches and weighed 230 pounds. Of course we were linemen. How could we not be?

In the summer of 1956, after we graduated from Hotchkiss and before we went off to college, we decided to put our size to good use. Come September, Bucky would be enrolling at Yale, which his family had been attending for generations, and I would be off to Williams. Bucky, like his older brother George, had an adventurous streak in him. That summer, Bucky went to work for his brother George in the west Texas oilfields. He invited me to come along with him, and my parents agreed I could go.

We drove to Texas from Connecticut in a tiny Renault, a rare car in the United States in those days, unheard of in Texas. George had bought the car—a tin can on four wheels—in New York and asked us to drive it to Midland. It was a memorable trip. We couldn't both fit in the front seat, so when one of us drove, the other sat sideways in the rear. Bucky loved popular music and had a good voice. He sang the entire score to *Oklahoma* as we crossed Mickey Mantle's home state. He sang it so many times it remains lodged in my head to this day. In the early morning he'd sing, "Oh! What a Beautiful Morning." We were young, excited by the adventure ahead. We were having fun.

On the drive west, we developed a little comedy routine. We would pull into a service station and Bucky would yell out something like, "Hey, Fay, is there something stuck under one of the front wheels?" (The engine was in the rear.) I'd go to the front and lift the lilliputian Renault. Then Bucky would join me and we'd have the front end waist high without a grunt. I remember an old mechanic in a roadside filling station staring at us and saying, "Gee-sus, look at that—and they're damn Yankees, too!"

We made it to Texas in one piece, more or less. Our first stop was at George and Barbara Bush's house, driving the little Renault to the front door on the sidewalk, as if it were a golf cart. George, often called

"Poppy," was thirty-two and starting out as a west Texas oilman. He had no cowboy boots, no twang, and now he had this little French car, but he was serious about making a mark of his own and he was determined to do it in the oil business. He and a friend, Hugh Liedtke, had formed a small oil company called Zapata Petroleum, and they were starting to make some headway. George and Barbara had a lovely, spacious home in Midland, with a big den. It had an intercom system. I had never seen one before; that was something in 1956. They needed it to keep track of the four young boys in the house: George W., Jeb, Neil, and Marvin. Robin, their only daughter, had died a year earlier; they later had another daughter, Dorothy.

There was a modest backyard that led down a hill and to a Little League field. Bucky and I would go down there from time to time with George and Barbara to watch their oldest son, nine-year-old George, play baseball. On one occasion, Bucky was pressed into duty as the home-plate umpire. His nephew came to bat. Quickly the count went to two strikes and then came the inevitable: "Strike three!" And Bucky quickly added, in the gentle way of the Bush family, "I'm sorry, George."

George's father was worried about us working in the oilfields as roughnecks. We were young and inexperienced. Drilling for oil involves taking steel pipes, each thirty feet in length, linking them together, and driving them over a mile straight down into the ground. You drill a pipe thirty feet into the earth, you put a new one on top of that, then drill in that one. When the bit gets dull, as it invariably does, you pull all the pipe out, change the bit, then put the pipe back in. This work goes on twenty-four hours a day. The men who work these jobs are called roughnecks. It was a prized job, though it was dangerous work; in the oil fields, a man with ten fingers was rare. We worked fifty-six hours a week, the first forty at straight time, the last sixteen at time and a half. I made over two hundred dollars a week, a fortune. We impressed the other roughnecks with one thing: our size. They called Bucky "Heavy-Heavy." They called me "Big 'Un." We told nobody that Bucky's brother was the boss or that we would soon be off to college, but I don't think we were fooling anybody; when I'd drive the crew out to the rig, I'd find a radio station that was playing some popular standard and the reaction was immediate: "Turn that crap off. Find some good ole music." Johnny Cash's "I Walk the Line" was popular that summer. If I heard that mournful tune once, I heard it a thousand times. I tried to learn their ways. They were simple, rough men. I learned to drink their beer, Pearl.

My indoctrination was only partially successful. For lunch, I'd bring four bologna sandwiches with me to work. The crew would howl: "You eatin' that Texas round steak again?" These guys could smell a Yankee.

At night, in our first weeks there, Bucky and I went back to George and Barbara's to swim in the pool and have a good meal. We were a mess. They'd say, "Don't worry, boys. When you're done, we'll just skim the grease right off the top." We bought ourselves a beat-up 1950 Ford for one hundred dollars. We rented a one-bedroom apartment—overrun with cockroaches—on Main Street in Odessa. (In those days, the bosses lived in Midland and the crews lived in Odessa.) We slept and worked in shifts. Bucky worked the "graveyard tour," from 11:00 P.M. to 7:00 A.M., and slept during the day. I worked the "evening tour," from 3:00 P.M. to 11:00 P.M., and slept at night. We never overlapped, so we needed just the one bed. We were so filthy all the time we slept on a piece of plastic on top of the bed. Barbara Bush visited us there only once; she stood at the foot of the stairwell and called for us to come down. She knew what she would find.

Our old Ford, we soon discovered, did not come with brakes. The guys who sold it to us had gummed up the master cylinder for the sale. After we bought it, we discovered brake fluid leaking from that master cylinder. Every morning we had to put brake fluid in the master cylinder, but one morning I forgot. I went out to get breakfast, and as I pulled into a Texaco station for gas I realized I had no brakes. The old Ford was probably going twenty miles an hour when I directed it into a Coke machine stationed between the two bays of the garage. What choice did I have? The Coke exploded in a geyser of water shooting fifty feet in the air. The owner came bursting out of his office. I got about two words of apology out when he shouted, "You're a goddamn Yankee!" Not a good scene. I called up Bucky—the car was in his name—and he got out of bed and trudged the mile or so to the Texaco station. By the time Bucky arrived, the owner was talking about having me arrested.

Buck was magnificent. "Hi, I'm Buck Bush," he said. "There's no need to panic, no need to be talking about arrest. We'll get this whole thing straightened out, don't you worry." The owner was a lot of things, but worried wasn't one of them. We finally got him to let us leave. He kept the car, not worth much but worth more than his old Coke machine. We left on foot and never looked back.

That hundred-dollar Ford turned out to be an expensive mistake as I tried to put away money for college, but the summer was a gratifying one in every way. I saved about five hundred dollars, which paid one-quarter of my freshman year tuition. (My father paid another five hundred dollars and a thousand-dollar scholarship from Williams took care of the balance.) George Bush knew I didn't have any money and at the end of the summer, as a present—or maybe to get rid of me—he treated me to an overnight train ticket from Midland to Dallas, in a sleeper car. In Dallas, he had arranged for me to fly north with his close friend Neil Mallon, then CEO of Dresser Industries. (George and Barbara named a son for Neil Mallon.) Mr. Mallon was flying to New York on business in his corporate plane, and we made three or four stops on the way. It was my first time on a plane I boarded my large self, my little suitcase, and my great memories on that plane. I think everyone has a summer where they take a leap toward adulthood; that happened for me in the summer of '56. I said goodbye to my boyhood and started to become a man. The most gratifying thing about the summer of '56, the most lasting thing, was getting to know the Bushes.

When I became commissioner, George W. Bush of the Texas Rangers was one of my ardent supporters. The feeling was mutual. The day my election was announced, I received a call from President Bush. He said, "If I had known this was going to happen, Fay, I'd have been a lot nicer to you in Texas." My response was in the same vein: "Mr. President, if I had known you were someday going to become president of the United States, I'd have been a lot nicer to you." One of the most endearing traits of all members of the Bush family is their sense of humor. In the family, the trading of good jokes is common, and teasing one another a high art.

George and Barbara Bush were wonderful to me. I have admired and loved them ever since. I feel lucky to have known them before most Americans ever heard of them. To me, they were Poppy and Bar.

o   o   o

AS COMMISSIONER, I attended a game in Baltimore one day where I sat a few rows behind President Bush, who was sitting with the queen of England. She had asked to attend a baseball game. My seat was perfect because I could watch both the game and the queen's response to it. She seemed utterly bored. Baseball, of course, to the uninitiated is a slow, complicated game. The president, bless him, was exceedingly courteous and polite and he tried again and again to engage her in conversation. Every so often, there would be a little flicker of conversation, and then it would die out. At some point, the president gave up. His brother Jonathan was sitting behind him and the president turned around and the two brothers chatted. The queen sat quietly.

After the game, I said, "Mr. President, that seemed like tough duty today."

"Oh, no, Fay, I enjoyed myself," he said.

"Mr. President, I saw you. You tried and you tried. But at some point you had to give up."

"She was very tired, Fay," the president said. He was (and is) such a gentleman. He would never concede I was correct.

Joe DiMaggio was then on the Orioles board of directors and, out of the blue, he heard the queen was coming and asked for the queen's autograph on a baseball. Larry Lucchino, the president of the Orioles, was saddled with the difficult job of securing the signature. Long before the game he went through the necessary channels and received permission to present a ball to the queen, explaining the custom of signing baseballs and who Joe DiMaggio was. Again, I was watching carefully, fascinated. I suspect the same was true for President Bush. Finally, the ball made it into the gloved hands of the queen. She rolled it around in her fingers for a moment or two, examined it as if it were contaminated. She said nothing. Finally, she handed the ball back, unsigned. We learned she does not sign baseballs, for Joe DiMaggio or anybody else. It turns out she does not give autographs. She signs formal documents and decrees, but almost nothing else. It was probably one of the few times in his life DiMaggio wanted something and didn't get it. It took the queen of England to stymie him.

It was ironic for DiMaggio to be in that position, since he could be churlish about giving autographs himself. I know of only one person who was able to convince Joe to sign and be gracious about it: Barbara Bush. This was in 1991, when DiMaggio and Ted Williams and I were flying on *Air Force One* to attend the All-Star game in Toronto. The White House press corps was flying on the plane and of course many of those reporters are great baseball fans. They knew Williams and DiMaggio were on the plane, sitting up front, in the plush guest quarters. Barbara Bush, with no prompting from anyone, went back to where the reporters were sitting and collected their press credentials, the ones they wear around their necks. She brought the credentials up to DiMaggio and Williams and said, "Would you please sign these? All the reporters would love to have your autograph." She wasn't trying to curry favor with the reporters, who, of course, were often critical of her husband and the job he was doing. She understood their obligations. She also understood they were people, working people with demanding deadlines, people with kids and interests and lives. She was trying to do something nice. It was her nature to be thoughtful.

Had it been anybody else, I'm sure DiMaggio would have looked at the collection of press credentials and said, "This is a lot," just so he would have the deposit in the chit bank he valued so. Of course, he made no protest. He signed as if he enjoyed signing. She has a knack for connecting with people, because she genuinely likes almost everyone. You can see that same quality in George W. It is the essential political asset.

She's also funny. The 1990 A's-Reds World Series opened in Cincinnati. Mrs. Bush and I were sitting high up in the owners box at Riverfront Stadium. The owner was the now infamous Marge Schott, who had inherited the team from her husband. She was not an easy woman to deal with, and I had to deal with her often. At the start of the game, the First Lady said, "Marge, how long have you loved baseball?"

"I hate it," Marge blurted. Her cigarette and her drink could not have been far away.

Mrs. Bush turned to me and said, *sotto voce,* "That's a real show-stopper, Fay." I knew, from experience, that Mrs. Bush's words would prove prophetic.

The Bushes are an exceptionally thoughtful family. President Bush called the day I became commissioner, but he also called the day I resigned. That was not a call he had to make, but he did. When Bart died in 1989, President Bush spoke movingly about him and was not afraid to make a reference to Pete Rose, even though Rose was a beloved figure in baseball and Bart had thrown him out of the game. The president said, "Bart was a close friend of mine for many, many years. He was a great person. He loved the game of baseball and in a short time made a great contribution to the game, striving for the highest possible ethical standards. I told him I'd like, just as a baseball fan, to know the aftermath, know exactly how this matter had been resolved. But all through that I was thinking of the difficulty he had in setting these standards that high and staying with it." Those words were not necessarily politically prudent for President Bush to say; Rose's fans vote and they resented Bart. But in choosing his public words, President Bush chose loyalty to his friend over political expedience.

His son George W. had also shown himself to be a straight shooter on many occasions. In 1991, I raised the issue with the owners whether we should allow foreign ownership (meaning non-American and non-Canadian) of baseball teams, and if so to what degree. I knew the issue was bound to arise and I wanted baseball to have a well-thought-out position. Some owners felt we shouldn't allow any foreign ownership. Eli Jacobs of the Orioles felt you had to permit some international ownership if you wanted to maintain a strong market for the teams. My own view was that baseball should allow foreign investment up to 50 percent; if the majority ownership was held overseas you'd run the risk of having to involve foreign courts to resolve baseball disputes.

But my opinion wasn't determinative; I wasn't an owner and this was an issue I wanted the owners to decide. They established a good committee, studied the issues, considered various positions, and ultimately voted to block all foreign ownership. Of course, my views were not then public.

Soon after, the Seattle team came up for sale, and a major Japanese company became interested. As I was leaving for a week's vacation in Jamaica, I went on the *Today Show* and was asked if baseball would permit foreign ownership. I stated the owners' position. When I arrived in Jamaica, messages from Steve Greenberg, my deputy commissioner, were piling up. He told me I was getting killed in newspaper columns all across the country for being an isolationist. Some of the owners were attacking me despite the formal vote they had taken.

Within baseball, George W. Bush spoke up, saying, "Wait a minute. Why are we letting Fay get killed for this? We took the vote. It's our decision and not his. We should speak up. This has nothing to do with Fay."

George W.'s straightforward honesty was unfortunately not common in baseball. But the Bush family values loyalty deeply, and they foster loyalty, within their family and in their friendships. In 1983, when I was at Columbia Pictures, Jonathan Bush, the older brother of Bucky and younger brother of George H. W., paid me a visit with his nephew, George W., who was starting a drilling fund and looking for investors. Oil is a very risky investment and always has been. If one is lucky, of course, the returns can be spectacular. I was doing well. I was not looking for oil investments, but I was happy to invest in George's fund out of loyalty to the Bushes. I invested, as I recall, twenty-five thousand dollars. In the ensuing years, I got some of it back. It has never upset me. I understood the risk. Moreover, over the years it has been considered a badge of honor to have been one of George's early investors. Since then, George W.—President Bush—has shown the same loyalty to me I feel toward his uncle Bucky and his father.

I underestimated George W. in one sense: I was always concerned for him, believing it is not easy to have a great man for a father. I feel my own father was a great man. It's not easy to follow in the footsteps of a celebrated father. Of course, I underestimated George's ability to carve out a niche for himself. It took me years to realize that George W. has his mother's sensibilities. His father was wonderful at writing personal notes to people, or picking up the phone and making a call; he kept up with hundreds of people that way, kept friendships alive. George W. doesn't do that, but he has his mother's ability to connect with people in the most concrete way. When he asks you, "How are you?" he means it. When I was at Columbia and Coke and in baseball, I had a man working for me named Phil Knecht. He drove for me and, as a former cop, served as a bodyguard. We were as close as brothers. He had an uncanny ability to size people up. One day he saw Walter Mondale up close and concluded, "Mondale's not a real politician. He doesn't pay attention to the little guy." You could bank on Phil's opinion. Phil loved George W. He'd say, "He talks to you." Or, "He's solid. His Secret Service guys love him." That meant that George W. had real political skill in the best sense of the word: the ability to talk to people from all walks of life, to look them in the eye and enjoy them. That's a gift. Bart had it. George W. has it. I know few others who do.

George truly loved baseball. At our baseball meetings, he'd always have Secret Service around, a reminder that he was not just an owner but the son of the president. You'd read in the paper that he was advising his father on this or that, that he played a role in the firing of John Sununu as chief of staff. But he was absolutely captivated by baseball. If you asked him how his club was doing, he'd say, "Oh, our third and fourth starters are really struggling and our catcher has an infected finger." He was a guy's guy, loved being with the players, with his manager, Bobby Valentine, loved being in the clubhouse. Loved to hang out with the fans, take their pulse. He was a good owner. He brought in talent. He convinced the city of Arlington to build a stadium with public money; that takes skill. He took a team that had no future and made it viable. He did the work and was rewarded for it. He made real money in baseball and that is not an easy thing to do.

Some months after I left baseball, I got a call from George W. At this point, Bud Selig was, in effect, the acting commissioner, even though

he was still the owner of the Milwaukee Brewers. He was, in my opinion, a walking conflict of interest, hiding behind his formal title, chairman of the owners' Executive Committee. George said, "Fay, what do
you think about me becoming commissioner?"

"I think it's a great idea," I said.

"Do you think I'd make a good commissioner?"

"Absolutely. You're smart. You love baseball. It is something you
want?"

"Well, I've been thinking about it. Selig tells me that he would love
to have me be commissioner and he tells me that he can deliver it."

All my alarms went ringing at once. When I was commissioner, a
labor lawyer for baseball named Chuck O'Connor had warned me to
look out for Selig, that Selig wanted to be commissioner and that he
would try to knock me off. I didn't believe him. Selig was my friend, I
thought. But O'Connor was smart. He said, "Selig thinks being called
commissioner is one of the important titles in American life. He thinks
it would make him a great American, a historic figure. He wants your
job. Watch out for him." O'Connor proved correct. When George
called, I could only imagine that O'Connor's words were now even
more true.

I said, "George, my guess is that Selig wants the job himself."

"He tells me he doesn't want it and that I'm his guy."

"Well, I hope it all works out," I said. But I was skeptical.

In the weeks to come, other names were floated—Mario Cuomo,
the former New York governor, and George Mitchell, the former
Maine senator, among them. I told each of them I thought they'd
never get the job. I'd also talk to George W. from time to time.

"George, I'm worried. I think Selig wants the job for himself."

"He told me that I'm still his man but that it will take some time to
work out."

"George, he can't tell you the truth because the truth is painful and
telling painful truths is not his strength. He has never been able to tell
people what they don't want to hear."

A few weeks passed. By this point, I knew that Selig was delaying any action, buying time, I believe, to solidify his own position. George called and said, "Some people are interested in having me run for governor of Texas. I've got to make a decision pretty soon."

"I'm afraid Selig is bullshitting you," I said. " I don't think you or any of the other names being floated are going to get it." The rest is truly history: On January 17, 1995, George W. Bush began his first term as the governor of Texas. The most significant money he ever made was as an owner of the Texas Rangers; when he sold his piece of the ballclub in January of 1998, he netted well over $10 million. So baseball had proven good for George W., too.

In July 1998, Bud Selig was formally elected as the commissioner of baseball. In a sense, he is my successor. From my resignation in September 1992 until he became commissioner, almost six years had passed. Baseball was not well-served in that period and missed having a true commissioner. I believe the strike of 1994—the year the owners attempted to break the players union, the first time in ninety years that there was no World Series—did serious harm. Bart used to say people grow scared at the end of a millennium, historically speaking. I know from experience he is correct.

Late in George's second term as Texas governor he called me up and asked my opinion of his running for president.

"I'm here trying to decide what to do," he said. "I'm afraid if I run, it will be very disruptive for my daughters. I really haven't made up my mind. What do you think?"

"We've known each other for a long time," I said. "Somehow, a miracle has happened. The stars and the moons have aligned properly and you have a real chance of being the next president of the United States. That is an astonishing development."

"I agree with that," George said.

"If you look ahead, put yourself at eighty-five, at the end of your life, in a rocking chair up at Kennebunkport. Do you want to sit there and wonder: Could I have been president? What kind of president would I have been?"

"You know, Commissioner, I think you're right."

"Don't blame the decision not to run on your daughters. Run. Because it is a miracle you are where you are. Maybe you'll get it. Maybe you won't. That doesn't matter. You very seldom regret the things you try to do. The things in life you regret are the things you didn't try."

"That's very sound advice, Fay," George said.

I don't think I changed his mind in any way. Perhaps I affirmed for him what he was already thinking. But I'm proud to have had that conversation. I voted for him on November 7, 2000, with pride, and I am even prouder he is our president. Loyalty has nothing to with it.

o   o   o

THERE IS A LONG and great tradition of presidents throwing out the first pitch at baseball games. The Bushes, with their abiding interest in baseball, revel in their first-pitch throwing. George H. W. Bush was once, like my father, a first baseman and captain of the Yale baseball team. George W. is a good athlete; he has an arm. I can remember George W. teasing his father, then president, about the quality of some of his first pitches. George W. once said, "I had my father come to Texas to throw out a first pitch at a Rangers game. He bounced it in the dirt. The whole family was embarrassed. I told him, 'Do that again and we're not having you anymore.' " The president blamed his first-pitch woes on his flak jacket. They both have a wonderful sense of humor; they can kid each other.

The flak jacket is a legitimate excuse. When a president goes out in public, he is required to wear one, for protection, underneath his windbreaker or his suit jacket. I lifted the president's flak jacket that day when we were riding on *Air Force One* to Toronto, and it must have weighed twenty or thirty pounds. It is heavy armor.

When people have to throw out a first pitch, I always give them the same advice: Throw from in front of the mound. You can practice all you want in the backyard and throw quite well, but when you stand on a mound, in a major-league park, in front of thousands of fans, you'll feel like you've never thrown a baseball before in your life. But people don't want to throw from in front of the mound, politicians especially, presidents most especially. They want to throw from the hill where the big leaguers toil. Invariably, they bounce the ball in the dirt.

In April 2001, the Milwaukee Brewers opened their new stadium, Miller Park. Commissioner Selig threw out the first pitch. George W., then in the third month of his presidency, threw out the second "first pitch," after Bud. I believe that to be a breach of presidential baseball protocol—the president should always be front and center—but I suppose there's no real guideline for such a thing. In any event, the president followed Bud and reached the catcher from the rubber. His presidency was off to a good start—the baseball part of it, anyhow. I can only imagine the father heard about the son's pitching success while the mitt of the guy catching him was still warm. A half-year later, President Bush was on the mound at Yankee Stadium, before the third game of the 2001 World Series. He toed the rubber and threw a called strike and the crowd stood. Baseball crowds don't stand for politicians. But the president is not a politician.

The Bushes are baseball people, and of course they are much more than that, too. I consider myself lucky that the game we love in common brought me closer to them.

Lineup: Guards and Guardians	
1.	Shirley Povich
2.	Gene Orza
3.	Steve Greenberg
4.	Len Coleman
5.	Claire Smith
6.	Murray Chass
7.	Bill Carbone and Phil Knecht
8.	Mel Allen
9.	Jon Miller

Guards and Guardians

I. SHIRLEY POVICH

TO MANY PEOPLE, the late Shirley Povich is the father of Maury Povich, the television personality, or the father-in-law of Connie Chung. To me, he is an icon of American journalism. (Yes, we share odd first names for men.) Shirley Povich grew up in a rural outpost of Maine where the wealthy had summer homes. He caddied for them as a kid, and one of the men he caddied for was Edward B. McLean, then the publisher of *The Washington Post*. McLean took a liking to his caddie and in 1922 asked him what he planned to do. He said he hoped to go to college. McLean told Povich to come to Washington, that he'd give him a job on the paper; he could attend college at night. Povich was a *wunderkind*; by 1926, at the age of twenty-one, he was the sports editor. In those days, sports editors wrote. Young Shirley covered Babe Ruth, Walter Johnson, and Lou Gehrig as a rookie. He knew every commissioner starting with Judge Landis. He loved baseball. He was a firsthand witness to nearly all of twentieth-century baseball. His memory was astonishing and he wrote like a dream.

I read him religiously when I lived in Washington. He wrote what I consider to be one of the great leads in the history of sportswriting. The Washington Redskins were owned by a man, George Preston Marshall, who dragged his feet on integrating his team. He was a relic. One morning after another Redskins defeat, this time to the Cleveland Browns and their superb black running back Jim Brown, Povich began a column with these words: "Jim Brown, born ineligible to play for the Redskins, integrated their end zone three times yesterday." For that lead alone, he is one of my writing heroes.

Soon after I became commissioner, Povich called me and said, "I've known every commissioner, starting with the first, Judge Landis. I would like to know you. May I come to New York to see you?" He was then in his mid-eighties, but still writing regularly and still writing beautifully, often on the front page of the sports section. Whatever he wrote, the *Post* made it a big deal.

"Mr. Povich, the honor would be mine," I said. "Why don't I get on a plane and come down to Washington?"

"No, no," he said. "I will come to see you." And he did.

In between his questions, I got in as many of my own as I could. I asked him about Walter Johnson.

"Oh, I knew him very well," said Shirley, a trim, elgant man, dressed impeccably, precise in every way. "Johnson lived in Rockville, Maryland. He was a fine person. He was a big man and he threw sidearmed. Nobody focuses on that, but he did: one of the hardest-throwing pitchers of all time and his delivery was closer to sidearm than overhand. I saw him in the '24 World Series. Bucky Harris was the manager. The only time Washington ever won it."

Everything I asked him about, the answers were along those lines: first-person accounts of historic players or historic moments. He had seen it, interpreted it, remembered it. He embodied all the ingredients one needs to be considered, in my book, a guardian of the game. A guardian of the game must have a sense of history, for without it you cannot appreciate the present. He must be discerning, must know what is and is not important, in baseball and in life. And he must be smart. What defines smart I do not know, but when you encounter somebody who is smart you know it. Povich was smart. He was truly a guardian of the game. He loved it, but he also understood its place. That's rare.

When I left baseball, Povich wrote: "What the club owners have done is to fire probably the best commissioner the game has known." Povich, of course, knew all the commissioners. What can one say about such praise from one of one's heroes? I'll take those words to my grave.

2. GENE ORZA

I REGARD GENE ORZA, the number-two man at the players union, as a guardian of the game. His boss, Donald Fehr, is not. Donald is smart, but he is not devoted to baseball. Fortunately for him, his deputy is. It makes an important difference.

At Fordham, taught by the Jesuits, Orza studied Greek and read the great Greek poets, as did I, and during the breaks in our many contentious meetings, he would occasionally cite lines of Greek poetry to me. He was showing off, of course—we both were—but along the way, we were doing something more important: We were establishing a bond between us. Every good working relationship needs that, a deposit of goodwill there when things don't go exactly the way you want. I'm sure he was irritated when he was left out of my men's-room meeting with Lenny Dykstra. He could have held that and numerous other things against me, but he didn't. Good lawyers like to be on the inside as much as possible, and Orza is a very good lawyer. When he hired the deaf lip-reader to defend Roger Clemens, I gave Orza the highest marks. That was some of the most brilliant lawyering I've ever seen.

Donald Fehr once said, by way of threat, that if baseball died the country would not miss it. Gene feels otherwise. He is a devout fan and a baseball labor lawyer of the highest order. (He is to the left of the Trotskyites, politically.) He defends all baseball players with equal vigor, which I see as a fault but he sees as a mark of fairness. There is much on which we disagree. He defended Steve Howe, which I thought was a waste of his time and talent, but to Orza the fight to keep Steve Howe in baseball was important. To Gene, it was an issue of personal liberty, and Gene is a rabid civil libertarian.

The players union is the controlling party in baseball. The owners don't accept that, but the power center of baseball today is in the hands of the players. At the helm of the players union are two highly intelligent and skillful men, one of whom is devoted to our game. They have both done a superb job, but Gene is the true baseball man. He actually *likes* the players. The good owners, the good fans, the good union officials, the good commissioners, they like the players and they understand it's the players who are at the heart of the game. Because Orza likes the players and the game they play, he serves the game well. That's critical. At some point, for everybody who is in the game, baseball should be at least in part a labor of love. When it's not, the game is diminished; when it is, the game is elevated. Gene Orza elevates the game.

3. STEVE GREENBERG

ONE OF THE BIGGEST MISTAKES baseball has ever made—and baseball has made some whoppers—was not to make my deputy, Steve Greenberg, commissioner after I left office. Steve had qualifications like no other person I knew. He was smart, and excelled at Hotchkiss, Yale, and UCLA Law School. He knew baseball. His father was Hank Greenberg. He played baseball for Yale and later for the top farm team of the Washington Senators franchise that became the Texas Rangers. He understood the business of baseball (he represented many players before joining me), and he loved baseball. He was also very wise in business matters. (His maternal grandfather was Bernard Gimbel, the New York department store mogul, and Steve seems to have inherited much of his grandfather's business sense.) He had the trust of many players and many owners and that's what a commissioner needs to be effective. He would have been a superb choice.

When Steve left baseball he was a founder of what eventually became the ESPN Classic Sports Network and much later went to join my friend Herbert Allen at Allen & Company, Inc.

Before getting to know Steve, I didn't know it was possible to be so wildly successful, handsome, and athletic and still be so well-liked. I have never heard a single negative word about Steve from anyone and I am not being hyperbolic.

Shortly before he died, Bart Giamatti wrote Steve a letter, suggesting he join us in baseball. (Steve had been a student of Bart's at Yale.) When Bart died and I became commissioner, I knew who I wanted as my deputy and pursued him immediately. I could not have had a better deputy. He took a substantial salary cut when he came to baseball—he had been a partner in a major Los Angeles law firm—but the lure of our game for him was irresistible.

I know Steve would have loved to have had just one major-league at bat, so he could join his father in *The Baseball Encyclopedia*. But there was, it so happened, another Jewish first baseman on the Senators just ahead of him, Mike Epstein. Ted Williams, when he managed the Senators, used to joke that his club was stockpiling all the best Jewish first basemen. With expansion, he surely would have made it. He was born too early.

Steve's never said this to me, but I suspect it would have meant far more to him to be selected as commissioner than to get a big-league at bat. In both cases, he was close enough to taste it. Had he succeeded me as commissioner, the devastating cancellation of the 1994 season by the owners would never have happened. Steve would have refused to let it happen. His love of the game is too pure to allow something like that to happen on his watch. He would have improved the relationship between the owners and the players, because both groups trusted him. You find a person like that, you make sure you keep him. They're rare. Baseball should rectify its mistake at once!

4. LEN COLEMAN

THERE WAS ONE other person I hired as commissioner whom baseball should have kept forever: Len Coleman. As a boy, Len knew Monte Irvin, the first black player for the New York Giants. He played three sports at Montclair High School, football, basketball, and baseball. Baseball was the game he loved, but football was the game he excelled at. After high school he went to Princeton, expecting to play four years of football there. Historically, right through Len's time there in the late 1960s, Princeton football was virtually all-white, season after season. After his freshman year, Len figured out why: The program was hostile, Len felt, to blacks. He stopped playing after one year. Instead, he became an academic and social success at Princeton, from which he graduated in 1971. Later, he did graduate work at Harvard and Episcopal missionary work for four years in Africa. He is sophisticated, smart, worldly, handsome, athletic. He knows how to work a room, he knows how to solve problems, he knows how to get along. He is a friend of George W. and a committed Republican, but found himself in a genial conversation one day with President Clinton, talking about juiced baseballs. Len could find common ground with anybody. Like Steve Greenberg, he could have been a superb commissioner. The owners let him go.

In Africa, Len listened to World Series games on short-wave radio, and in 1980, when he returned to the United States, Len wrote a letter to another Princeton man, Bowie Kuhn, trying to find a job in the game he loved. Nothing came of it. Eleven years later, I went knocking on his door, hiring him away from Kidder Peabody to be the senior marketing executive for baseball. Kidder Peabody was owned by General Electric, which means that Len's ultimate boss was Jack Welch, the legendary GE chairman. Jack tried to keep him but Jack also loves baseball, so he understood the appeal of working in it. When Bill White resigned as National League president in 1994, the National League owners actually did something smart: They made Len the National League president. Then, in 2000, Bud Selig did away with the league presidencies, putting the league presidents out of the game. He should have kept Len in a senior capacity.

As National League president, Len was committed to keeping baseball alive in the cities, particularly among black children. There are often no Little League programs in black neighborhoods in the nation's biggest cities. Len became very active in a program called RBI, Reviving Baseball in the Inner Cities. (Claire Smith wrote important pieces about the program, helping it get on the map.) In his second month as

National League president, Len agreed one day to meet the Reverend Jesse Jackson for a so-called press event at an inner-city field in Washington, D.C., where they hoped baseball would someday flourish again. Jackson's Rainbow Coalition was active in the RBI program.

A couple of local TV crews showed up to hear Jackson and Len make their comments about how baseball and organized sports can build character in a young man. But near the end, Jesse Jackson realized that the most important "media outlet" in Washington had failed to send a representative to this manufactured news event. Jackson, working himself into a rhetorical tizzy, practically pushed Len into Jackson's limousine. The National League president, for all practical purposes, was now a hostage as Jackson stormed the editorial offices of *The Washington Post*, demanding coverage for RBI, this important joint initiative of MLB and the Rainbow Coalition. This was not Len's way of doing business, but he went along with it; it was a chance to see an important civil-rights leader in action and Len was not going to pass it up. He was always listening and always learning.

Len learned baseball from his father, as I did from mine. He learned about the black experience from his father, which I did not. His father was a baritone and a member of a black choir that used to perform at Princeton. One day, as a payment for their singing, the choir members were given tickets to a Yale-Princeton baseball game. Len's father went with a friend. A man sitting behind them yelled, "Get those niggers out of here." Len's father made a vow to himself that day: If he ever had a son, his son would go to Princeton. He told Len that story on the day Len received his Princeton letter of acceptance. There's a sensibility that comes with knowing that kind of experience that no organization or company can afford to be without, baseball most especially. But Len is gone from baseball and the game has not seen the likes of him since then. Baseball is poorer for it. Len is doing just fine. He's back to being a fan, just like me.

5. CLAIRE SMITH

WHEN BART GIAMATTI was the president of Yale he read *The Hartford Courant* daily, in part because he liked to read the paper's baseball writer, Claire Smith. Bart told me, and many others, that she was the best baseball writer in the country. Later, when I quoted Bart on Claire to Max Frankel, then the executive editor of *The New York Times,* he hired her. From then on, he teasingly called me Claire's agent. She is now a sports columnist at *The Philadelphia Inquirer.* They say a reporter can't become friends with the people she or he is covering, but Claire and I have proved that wrong. She wrote about me for years, very thoroughly, and we have maintained an enriching friendship. It has only helped that we share a social agenda for baseball. To Claire, baseball is truly the national pastime—an important American institution, as Bart would say—and it should reflect the nation in every way. When it doesn't, it fails. I tried to change that, with only partial success. Claire reported on my efforts, brought needed attention to them and the issues at their core.

As a black woman covering baseball in the 1970s, Claire was an anomaly, for there were very few blacks covering baseball then, an even smaller number of women, and no black women except for Claire. She put up with a great deal of abuse. When Claire was in a baseball clubhouse, some of the players would become even more vulgar than their normal selves, which in the case of some players can be amazingly vulgar. They would parade around naked in an effort to embarrass her. Some clubhouses were worse than others, but everywhere she's gone, Claire has, sooner or later, been able to break down the barriers the Neanderthals put up in a pathetic attempt to amuse themselves by making her job more difficult. She has opened doors with the sincerity of her questions and the depth of her knowledge.

Some teams were just impossible. In 1984, she was writing about a very good San Diego Padres team that would go on to play in the World Series, losing to the Detroit Tigers. Some players on the team made her life miserable, demeaning her in ways large and small. They were so bad to her that Claire left the clubhouse one night after a game, crying. She was in a tough spot because she needed postgame quotes for her story, but the players were impossibly rude to her. They were preventing her from doing her job. As she left the clubhouse Steve Garvey followed her out. He had seen everything and was disgusted.

"What do you need?" he said.

"I need quotes," she said.

"You tell me what you need and I'll get it," the first baseman said. For that night, Garvey was Claire's leg man. He ran quotes to her and Claire got the holes in her story filled and filed her story on deadline. Ever since, Garvey has been one of her heroes.

Claire and I have traveled extensively together, doing interviews for an oral history project I'm working on for the Hall of Fame. The old players and especially the old Negro League players love to talk to her. She went through some of the experiences they went through and her empathy comes shining through.

But my favorite thing is to see her with the old-time major leaguers, guys who came up before Jackie Robinson, guys who played the game when baseball was exclusively populated by white men. Many of these players grew up on midwestern farms. Bob Feller was exactly such a man. We interviewed Feller on tape for four hours and Claire's questions were outstanding. She had done her homework, as always. When it was over, Feller said to me, "She really knows her stuff." That's what he said: She knows her stuff. Period. Not, I've never met a black woman who knew so much about baseball. Feller made all his judgments about Claire as a baseball person. Somehow, Claire has made it look easy. For that, for reminding her readers regularly about the importance of Jackie Robinson and Larry Doby and the worthlessness of the designated hitter rule, and for many other things, I am filled with admiration for her. She doesn't cover me anymore so I can write this without fear of embarrassing her: I am proud to call her a friend.

6. MURRAY CHASS

YOU MIGHT WONDER, What would the owners do if nobody were watching? Some of them, certainly, would run wild. They would collude to keep player salaries down. They would reduce roster sizes, increase the lengths of the preseasons and postseasons. They would do whatever they could do to increase revenues and decrease spending. But fortunately for fans, somebody is always watching: Murray Chass, the dogged senior writer on *The New York Times* who writes the history of the modern baseball business almost daily. Bart once tried to prove that Murray was biased against him in the Rose case, but Bart couldn't touch Murray. He is scrupulously fair.

Fearless, too. Nothing intimidates him and nothing prevents him from getting the story he seeks. He's a careful craftsman. He cares deeply about getting every fact in every story correct. We're the same age, we both love classical music, we're both deeply interested in religion. He loved the Pittsburgh Pirates of the 1950s the way I loved the Yankees of that same era. We have a lot to talk about, before we even get to the owners. We both care about proper English grammar—imagine that! (We are both, we have discovered, fallible in that.)

The owners and Bud Selig complain that Murray is prounion in his coverage. Murray's response is, "You would be too, if the owners lied to you routinely. The players union never does." Murray once told me there are four people in the decades he has covered baseball who have never lied to him. They are Donald Fehr, the Mets co-owner Fred Wilpon, former Mets GM Joe McIlvaine, and I. The business of baseball has become a big story over the years and nobody understands it as well as Murray; I'm sure I learned as much from him as he has from me. As with Claire, we proved that writers and sources could be friends. Since I've left baseball, we've become better friends.

After I left baseball, I went to England for a long vacation. I lived it up, rented a big house, hired a chef, had my friends visit. Murray came with his wife, Ellen. I had a superb cook there, Peter Lewis, who prepared a beautiful English roast beef for the Chasses the day of their arrival. Shortly before dinner, I realized we had a problem: Murray is an observant Jew who keeps kosher. Roast beef, properly slaughtered and certified, can of course be kosher, but our meat was not. "No problem," Peter said, "there's a wonderful trout farm ten minutes down the road. I'll get the Chasses trout for dinner." Murray appreciated our awareness of his religious needs. That's one of the bonds of our friendship.

Steve Greenberg used to say to Murray that I was the only commissioner who knew how to use the word *tsuris*, the Yiddish word that combines elements of worry, trouble, headache, heartache, and sorrow into a single word.

"That's probably right," Murray would say. "I can't imagine Bowie Kuhn using the word *tsuris*."

They both tried to take credit for teaching me the word, but they can't; I learned it in the movie business, where I had a lot of *tsuris*. Of course, in baseball I did too. Many of the subjects Murray raised with me brought me *tsuris*, but Murray never did. His motivation was always noble: to sort out the facts and spell them out black and white, and gray when necessary, and publish them without fear or favor. He's always called them as he sees them.

7. BILL CARBONE AND PHIL KNECHT

WHEN I BEGAN WORKING at Columbia Pictures in 1978, I hired a driver and security man named Phil Knecht. When it was first suggested to me I needed such a person, I was dismissive; after about a week with Phil, a former Army officer and New York City policeman, I realized he was invaluable. Not just because of the death threats I received—in Phil's capable hands, I learned to dismiss them—but because he was such a superb sounding board. Phil stayed with me until the day he died in 1999. We were partners.

When Bart became commissioner in 1989, he decided he wanted a driver and security man, too. He hired a wonderful man named Bill Carbone, a former Marine and the resident agent for the New York Mets. Carbone was Italian and a Mets fan and Phil was Irish-German and a Yankees fan. Phil carried his gun under his arm; Carbone carried his in his left sock. They became great friends; their friendship, in many ways, mirrored mine with Bart. Some of my happiest times in baseball came with Bill and Phil in the front seat of the car, while Bart and I rode in the back, listening to their police war stories. Bart loved those stories, but I knew they were forever leaving out the darker parts of police work so as not to destroy Bart's romantic view of how detectives solved cases. Bill and Phil were quite a show. More than anything, they were devoted to us, and we were devoted to them.

We were a foursome. When Bart received death threats during the Rose investigation, he took them very seriously. I don't know if he would have made it through those days and nights if Phil and Bill were not on the scene. For myself, I only recall one death threat in baseball. It came when I was commissioner, and it was very specific: My end was supposed to come in the sixth inning of a game I was attending at Shea. I was sitting in a front-row seat and I was not particularly nervous. I had had many death threats in the movie business without suffering a single fatality. My batting average was good. Bill Carbone said: "Boss, we've got you covered. There are a ton of New York's finest here. We don't think the threat is serious, but we're going to treat it like it is. When the game is over, we're going to whisk you out of here. A group of us is going to pick you up and carry you out of here. Your feet will not hit the ground." My feet did not hit the ground. I survived that sixth inning and many more since then.

In 1989, when Bart was commissioner, Phil and Bill and Bart and I went to Anaheim, California, for the All-Star game. One morning during the All-Star break, Phil and Bill went to Bart's enormous presidential suite. They asked if he needed anything. Yes, Bart said: Could he have a small pot of coffee and a brioche? Sure, Bill said. Right away, Boss, Phil said.

They closed Bart's door, looked at each other in the hallway. Then one said to the other, "Do you know what the a hell a 'brioche' is?"

"No," the other said, "I was hoping you did."

They both wondered if Bart meant Brioschi, what you take for an upset stomach, frequently advertised on New York radio years ago.

They went down to the hotel lobby, hoping to find somebody who knew what a brioche was. They tried to call one of their East Coast culinary sources—my wife—but she was out. They tried the hotel kitchen. Nothing. They tried people in the lobby. Finally, somebody suggested that a brioche was nothing more than a fancy word for a roll and that, in a pinch, a croissant could fill in for a brioche.

A half-hour after they had left, Bill and Phil returned to Bart's suite with his coffee and "brioche." It was now a croissant.

"What took you so long?" Bart asked, apparently satisfied with his bread selections.

"Oh, we had problems," Bill and Phil said. They would never embarrass Bart by telling him their problem was Bart's vocabulary—more specifically, that Bart didn't know how to talk to two cops from Queens. Their purpose was to serve and protect. They did so admirably. Great and lasting friendships were forged along the way.

Only once did they have a slip-up with me. The three of us were flying somewhere together. I entrusted my cigars to Phil and Bill, and they left them on the plane. Bill said, "Oh, Boss, we feel so bad, we'll make it up to you." Phil said. "We'll get you another box of cigars." I told them not to worry about it, but I knew they would.

Later that day, they presented me with two or three cigars. "That's very nice of you," I said. "But what are you doing with the rest of the box?"

"Well," Bill said, "they were much more expensive then we realized." Phil said, "We decided we'd just buy a few at a time." That's what they were like. Their feet were always on the ground.

8. MEL ALLEN

I GREW UP WITH A VOICE. As a boy, a teenager, a college student, a law-school student, as a young lawyer, the voice that accompanied me on a thousand summer days and a thousand summer nights belonged to Mel Allen, the longtime Yankee broadcaster. He was a southerner with a gentle lilt in his voice and perfect grammar. His spoken sentences, written down, read as if they came out of a book. Part of my interest in him came from meeting him as an eight-year-old. My father was officiating a football game at Yankee Stadium and Mel Allen was working the game. This was in 1948 and my father was letting me tag along. Mel had a request for the officials: "Make your signals clear," he said. I can still remember him saying that. This was many years before football officials started wearing microphones. Mel Allen wanted to be able to tell his listeners at home exactly why a play had been called back. To do his job well, he needed help. Mel always made things clear.

My father did not share my high opinion of Allen only because Allen represented Yankee success and my father's rooting interests pointed elsewhere. Mel Allen was the voice of the Yankees, and if you disliked the Yankees his voice was hard to take. I loved him. After home runs he'd say, "How about that?" His voice would be filled with surprise.

When I became commissioner, Mel was long finished with the Yankees; George Steinbrenner had forced him out in the 1970s, saying that Mel represented the voice of the old Yankees. (But somehow Phil Rizzuto could represent the voice of the new Yankees?) There may have been other factors. Mel had a well-known drinking problem, not an uncommon problem in baseball. When you saw him, even when surrounded by a large group of people, there was a lonely quality about him. He was an educated man, a lawyer. He happened to be Jewish. He was never one of the boys. He reveled in his work and when it was done, his drink. As far as I knew, his drinking never affected his work. When I was commissioner, he was still the cheerful and historic voice of the show *This Week in Baseball*.

Near the end of his life, Mel and I were in Cooperstown at the same time for the induction ceremonies. This was in 1990. Phil Knecht was there with me and he was going to drive me home to Greenwich, Connecticut, when it was all over. Mel lived in Greenwich, too, in an apartment with his sister, so we offered him a lift back. He had never married and he lived modestly. He must have made a lot of money in his life, because he worked all the time. He was a valued pitchman for various products, including Ballantine beer, White Owl cigars, and Pompano Harness Track. Wheaties, too. What he did with his money was his business.

The ride was long and memorable. Mel told one story after another after another, about Casey and Yogi and Mickey. My mind went into a pleasant drift.

All the while, he kept calling me "Mr. Commissioner." It is common, I quickly discovered as commissioner, for old-world baseball people to call the commissioner by his title. The same, I noticed, was true for Bart and Peter Ueberroth. But "Mr. Commissioner," that was something else.

"May I ask you something, Mel," I said from the front seat. I thought he would be more comfortable having the backseat to himself.

"Of course, Mr. Commissioner."

"Would you mind calling me Fay?" It seemed odd, having this man, a figure who was larger than life to me in my boyhood, refer to me with such an honorific.

"Oh, no, Mr. Commissioner, I could not do that. Your position is an important one, due respect. I appreciate what you're saying, but I would not be comfortable calling you anything else. It wouldn't show the proper respect."

My father would have understood and appreciated that sentiment very much, as did I. I dropped Mel Allen off at his apartment, bade him a good night, and never saw him again.

9. JON MILLER

JON MILLER, the ESPN and San Francisco Giants baseball play-by-play man, wrote a book called *Confessions of a Baseball Purist.* He was being ironic. Bud Selig labeled Jon a purist, as if it were a bad thing, using the word the way some people use "liberal." Purists, in the view of some owners, are those opposed to the designated hitter rule, interleague play, artificial turf, uniforms not made of heavy flannel, ballpark music recorded after 1960, night games, and fluoridation. Such people should be ignored in the interest of progress. Too bad modern baseball doesn't have more purists, more Jon Millers. He follows in the great tradition of the Mel Allens and the Ernie Harwells and the Vin Scullys, announcers who carry the rhythm of the game in what they say and how they say it. (Have you ever heard Miller's imitation of Scully? He does Scully better than Scully. What an ear he has, and what an eye.)

Jon's a reader, and when he would have me in the booth we'd compare our summer reading lists between innings. Once I was on with Jon and his broadcast partner Joe Morgan, and Miller was giving his sidekick a hard time about an important literary matter. He asked Morgan whether he knew what important literary event was being celebrated that day. Morgan didn't know and turned to me.

"Jon's just showing off," I said to Morgan, out of Jon's earshot. "Today's Bloomsday [June 16], the day James Joyce used in *Ulysses.* Let's see if we can stump him. Ask him if he knows Joyce's wife's name."

Morgan asked him. Miller didn't know. "It's Nora," I said. Morgan was exultant. "We win!" he said.

Miller himself rejects the "purist" label. For reasons unfathomable to me, he favors the DH. He believes players today are better than ever, with a broader range of skills than ever before, and that all the "golden days" nonsense we hear is really about grayhairs trying to reclaim their youth.

In fact, I feel Miller *is* a purist, in the best sense of the word. The purists warned there wasn't enough quality pitching to stock four new teams. The purists predicted that interleague play would make the All-Star Game an irrelevance and diminish the first-meeting excitement of the World Series. The purists howled when baseball introduced the Baseball Network and initiated regional coverage of the first round of the playoffs, meaning out-of-town fans hoping to see their team were out of luck. If only baseball had more purists like Miller.

Jon Miller, like Scully and Harwell and Allen, sees his job as a position of trust. He is there to report on what he sees, and does so with unbiased clarity and honesty. This has not always endeared him to his employers, but it has endeared him to baseball fans, which tells me he's doing something right. He values his credibility, aims to entertain, cares deeply about the written and spoken versions of the game, his booth partners, and the place of baseball in people's lives. What more could you want from a guardian of the game?

| BASEBALL IS SORRY | 0 | 0 | 0 | 0 | 0 | 0 | 0 | 8 | |
| SLICK AND CO. | 0 | 0 | 0 | 0 | 0 | 0 | 0 | | |

CHAPTER EIGHT

———

Baseball Is Sorry

I GREW UP in a segregated world. My block of Orange Street in the New Haven of my boyhood was all white. My church was all white. When Jackie Robinson made his major-league debut in April 1947, it made little impression on me: He played in the other league, and as a boy of nine I didn't care what the National Leaguers did, until they were playing my Yankees in the World Series. When, four months later, Larry Doby became the second black man to play major-league baseball and the first in the American League, that made more of an impression. He played for the Cleveland Indians, and the Yankees had to get past the Indians to get into the World Series, and Doby was good, and that was enough for me to take notice of him. I was ignorant of the racial divide in this country. I had never been in the South and I knew little of Jim Crow. I was taught to treat others as I wanted to be treated myself, and I assumed everybody else did pretty much the same thing. Race was not something discussed in my home.

In the summer of 1956, the summer I spent with Bucky Bush in the west Texas oilfields, I got a crash course in racism. It was my first trip

245

to the South. The landmark Supreme Court case *Brown* v. *Board of Education* had been decided in 1954 and as a result "separate but equal" was no longer lawful. But in 1956 in Texas, separate and un-equal remained the guiding principle in the oilfields. There were no blacks in those fields: no black roughnecks, no black suppliers, ven-dors, or drivers. The mantra in the oilfields where I toiled was, "Yan-kee, ain't no blacks in this man's oilfield." Or any man's oilfields. Only they didn't say "blacks."

One day I was working on the rig with three other guys when an old black man drove up in a battered truck that was hissing and steaming. Obviously his truck was overheated and needed water. At the sight of him, the other roughnecks burst out of the shed, yelling, while the old black man stammered that all he wanted was a little water. At that, one of the other roughnecks grabbed a rifle and began firing while scream-ing, "Out of here, you nigger. You know you can't come here. Ain't no one like you out here." The poor old man, huddled over the wheel, hurried off. The one roughneck kept shooting, not to kill him but to scare him. He surely succeeded. He scared me, too.

"Why did you do that?" I asked.

"Yankee, you listen here," one of them said. "This man's oilfield is all white. Ain't no reason for anyone else out here. Any niggers or Mexi-cans come out here, we shoot 'em. Can't be no different."

I was silent. These were tough, ignorant men trying to hold on to their livelihood. It was the only one they had ever known. I found it frightening to be so near such hatred. I never forgot the look on the face of that old man in the truck. And I never forgot the roughnecks' blind fury. It was life-changing.

Before that, I had had no particular sensitivity to the country's racial divide. At Hotchkiss, the first black student in the school's history was one class ahead of me, a boy named Gus Winston, who was brilliant, an excellent athlete, and superb at everything he tried. After Hotch-kiss, he could have gone anywhere. He went to Harvard. He was typi-cal of the most talented Hotchkiss students, except that his skin was black. I gave that fact the attention I felt it deserved, which was not much. I never thought about what the Hotchkiss experience must have been like for Gus, the lone black kid in the school for a few years. "Benign neglect" wasn't a phrase then, but that's what I practiced; it was more gentlemanly than fussing over differences, and one of the guiding principles of Hotchkiss was to behave as a gentleman. I'm certain there were boys who did not behave in a gentlemanly manner toward Gus, but he was so powerful a person he seemed above the rest of us. We played football together and I never saw an untoward moment, but I'm certain there were some tough times for Gus. Sadly, he has disappeared from the alumni lists at Hotchkiss and we don't know what has become of him. Somehow, I know he has led a good life.

In my class, there were no blacks. Two classes behind me there was another black student named Barry Loncke, from New Haven, who, like me, attended Hotchkiss on a scholarship, his designed to get black kids to the school. He and I played basketball together, and he later became a distinguished judge in Los Angeles, much admired and respected. For me, the experience of being a teammate of his or of Gus's was unremarkable. Then came the summer of '56, in Texas, when my eyes were opened in so many ways.

In the fall of '56, I enrolled at Williams. Out of a student body that numbered around one thousand, there were perhaps a half-dozen black students, tops. I can't recall a single black faculty member. I found myself thinking—particularly after my accident, when my thinking took on new dimensions—how segregated my life experiences had been. I also began thinking about the admission and recruitment policies a place like Williams must have had to have so few blacks. There was a black student named Gordon Davis a year or two behind me, who later became the parks commissioner of New York City and the head of Lincoln Center. Years later, when I was on the board at Williams, he received an honorary doctorate from the college. He told a story about getting into the backseat of a car one day with some upperclassmen, going to a women's school for some sort of social. Gordy said: "One of the guys in the front seat said to me, 'How about that nigger kid in the freshman class. Have you gotten to know him?' What was I going to say, 'I am that nigger'?" Clearly, there was racism at Williams. At Yale Law School, again, in the entire student body there were maybe a half-dozen blacks and not a single black professor. As it happens, two of the black women in my class have become prominent: Eleanor Holmes Norton represents the District of Columbia in Congress, and Marian Wright Adelman started the Children's Defense Fund. Marian Wright was a law-school pal of mine, often seated next to me in alphabetical seating charts. One wonders how many more prominent leaders with black skin might have come out of Yale had there been more blacks there to begin with. But in those years Yale was at least making a start, and it was not long before things changed significantly there and all across the country.

When I was a partner in my Washington law firm, Caplin & Drysdale, in the early 1970s, we were fortunate to recruit a major legal talent who was black. His name was Tyrone Brown, from Newark, New Jersey. We worked on several projects together and became friends. He had graduated first in his class at Cornell Law School, was the second black law clerk at the United States Supreme Court, and he wrote as well as anyone I have ever known. He wrote lovely sentences. But, he confided to me, he worried that much of his success was due to his skin color. He was so intelligent I sought him out to learn more about issues of race. Ty Brown was (and is) one of the most talented people I have ever known, yet our society had made him feel insecure about his abilities. I am thankful that he helped me see the world through his eyes. I have never forgotten what I learned from him.

We often ate lunch together and on one particular occasion he insisted on treating me. We went to a steakhouse near our office and had a good lunch and a better talk. Then came the check. Ty found an error in it, a simple case of bad addition.

Ty said: "Look, Fay, here is a calculation in life I have to make that you never do. We're in a nice restaurant. The waiter added the check incorrectly. It's a mistake. If you call him over and say, 'There's a mistake here, could you please check your addition,' there will be no problem. You're white, he's white. But if I do the same thing, there might be a problem. I run the risk of turning an addition mistake into a racial incident. I can't ignore the risk unless I ignore the mistake. He might say, 'Are you accusing me of cheating you?' Or he might just think it. There's a fifty-fifty chance the situation will get ugly."

"Let's see what happens," I said.

The waiter came over, Brown explained the mistake in the gentlest manner possible. You could see the waiter bristle. There was no scene, but the waiter clearly resented being challenged by the black man he was serving. "You see, that's the calculation I always have to make and you never do." That lunch made a huge impact on me. I never forgot it.

When I became the president of Columbia Pictures in 1978, I was keenly aware there were very few blacks (and very few women) working in executive positions at Columbia or any of the other Hollywood studios. Not surprisingly, we were making few movies with black themes. We made a wonderful movie called *A Soldier's Story*, about black enlisted men, based on Charles Fuller's Pulitzer Prize–winning play. We didn't make any money on it. We made the Richard Pryor concert movies, and those made some money. Although they were vulgar, they were undeniably funny and his observations about race relations in this country were trenchant. We also made *Stir Crazy* with Pryor and Gene Wilder, directed by the wonderful Sidney Poitier. It was a big hit.

While at Columbia, I spoke one day at Yale Law School and met a young black man, Dennis Green, who impressed me so much I offered him a job on the spot. He remains a very close friend. He came to Columbia with one of the most extraordinary résumés I had ever seen. He was born in Harlem and went first to Hotchkiss and then to Columbia College, where he was a founder of the singing group Sha Na Na. Later, he went to Harvard to study business, and then to Yale Law School. He became a film executive at Columbia and is now a law professor at Florida State, teaching a class in racism and the media.

The group of blacks I knew was extraordinary—Gus Winston at Hotchkiss, Gordy Davis at Williams, Marian Wright Adelman at Yale Law School, Tyrone Brown at Caplin & Drysdale, Dennis Green at Columbia—but far too tiny. It made me wonder about how much untapped talent there must be in the black community. It made me also think how racism and the old boy network worked to keep elite schools and executive offices about as all white as the Texas oilfields.

Bart Giamatti had thought about these issues most of his life. He had dealt with issues of race at Yale for decades. We both felt race relations was the most pressing social problem in the United States, and when we got into baseball we vowed to do something about it. When Bart became commissioner, that left a vacancy in the National League presidency. We decided we would fill it with the best black person we could find. Is that fair to all the qualified nonblacks who wanted to be considered for that job? Was it fair for the hundreds of years before that when only whites would have been considered for such a job? We were doing what we could to correct a historic wrong. Reasonable people may argue whether our approach is sound and fair. Tyrone Brown might have argued against it; he might argue that for the rest of the chosen person's career he would wonder about his qualifications for the job, as would those working under him. I don't doubt that. That's a problem. But it's a bigger problem to have executive offices that are populated exclusively by white men. The decision-making that comes out of such an office will, almost by definition, be flawed and limited. Look at major-league baseball today.

Bart and I created a search committee to find a National League president and we really muscled it. We said, "Find us three candidates, one of whom must be black." We knew we would hire the black candidate. The committee came back and said it couldn't find a significant black candidate. Bart and I were discussing the subject in his office one day when he said, "What about that guy who announces for the Yankees? What's his name?"

"You mean Bill White?" I said.

"Yes, Bill White. He sounds like a good guy. He'd be good."

Bill White had tremendous knowledge of the game after decades as a wonderful ballplayer and as a broadcaster. He had no background as an executive, but as Bart knew firsthand, the job wasn't one where you set policy or managed large numbers of people. Basically, you supervised umpires and kept peace. The job required a good sense of people and a deep commitment to baseball. White had both those prerequisites.

His response when we called was: "The only reason you're thinking of me is because I'm black."

"In part, that's true," Bart said. "We want black executives in the game. But we also want you because you are smart and would do a fine job." Bill was impressed by Bart and vice versa.

Almost from the start, Bill and Bart and I had some rocky times. Bill was only doing what he saw as his job; he wanted the National League presidency to be a serious responsibility. He wanted to take on the head of the umpires union, Richie Phillips, and he wanted to oversee National League expansion, to give two examples. Bart and I knew those things had to be done in cooperation with our office and with considerable legal help. Bill did not have experience in handling such subjects. But the underlying problem was that Bill wanted the National League presidency to be independent of the commissioner. The problems had everything to do with turf and nothing to do with race.

On the subject of race relations in baseball, where we thought Bill would be helpful, he was reluctant. We had hoped he'd be a visible figure lobbying the owners to hire more black candidates for on-field and front-office positions. His position was a reasonable one, although unfortunate for us. "Look, I've been in baseball all my life, I've fought this topic for years," he said. "You're not going to get anywhere. I'm tired of it. I don't want to waste my time. You go try it."

"But you're important," Bart said.

"You guys do it. You haven't done it all your life. I have. I'm tired of it. I don't like losing. I don't like things coming out the wrong way."

When I became commissioner, Bill and I battled, and I said things I wish I hadn't. I have since apologized to him. I admire him greatly and he is a gentleman, first-class in every way, a strong man. He's also very independent, as am I. At one point he said, "When you guys hired me, I didn't tell you I have a real problem with authority. It has nothing to do with you two. I just don't like taking orders. I can't work for people."

I said: "I wish you had told us that earlier." It was a learning episode, for all of us.

I wound up taking on the role I'd hoped Bill would fill, talking about the importance of hiring blacks at every chance, with owners, general managers, field managers, with the umpires. I didn't have to talk about the subject with the players union. They knew what was going on. The nation is about 12 percent black. Eighteen percent of the players on the field were black. The front offices, however, were almost exclusively white.

I didn't find any overt racism among the owners. I think they all felt, in an ideal world, the black population in the country would be represented in the stands and in their front offices. But their commitment to change was negligible. The cliche "benign neglect" comes again to mind. I found the best way to appeal to the owners was at wallet level. I commissioned an extensive study to analyze what we all knew instinctively to be true: black fans were almost a rarity. The percentage of black fans in the stands was far below the percentage of blacks in the population at large, particularly when you consider there are often black neighborhoods within walking distance of many major-league ballparks. Hispanics, on the other hand, turned out at baseball games in numbers significantly greater than their population percentage. With the country 12 percent black, baseball attendance is only 5 percent black. Yet the nation was 9 percent Hispanic, and Hispanic baseball attendance is twice that number. Through our survey, we found that blacks continued to think of baseball as a white man's game, despite the number of blacks on the field. It was as if they knew the front offices were white, the managers were white, the third-base coaches were white, the *attitude* was white. In the black communities, among educators and church pastors in particular, there were very few cheerleaders for baseball, very few people organizing group trips to games, few black kids playing Little League baseball, little opportunity to play baseball in the inner cities. Blacks were negative about baseball. Given that, the 18 percent figure on the field—a number that is falling each year—was astounding. (It should be pointed out that many of the "blacks" in baseball are from the Dominican Republic, and some of them do not consider themselves black. I remember George Bell, the 1987 Most Valuable Player, who is from the great Dominican baseball capital of San Pedro de Macoris, making the point that he did not regard himself as black, even though his skin hue suggested otherwise.)

Nobody in baseball was reaching out to the black community. Part of the reason is that nobody knew how to. There were almost no blacks in the important front-office positions or in decision-making positions.

Bud Selig had Don Baylor, a dear friend of mine, as a coach for the Brewers in Milwaukee. I asked Selig to give serious consideration to Baylor the next time he was hiring a manager. Baylor was not hired. I talked to George Steinbrenner about hiring Chris Chambliss, who had been the Manager of the Year in AAA ball, as the Yankee manager. Nothing happened. I talked to Bob Lurie about hiring one of his Giant coaches, Dusty Baker, as manager. He did.

Baker became the Giants manager in December 1992. In 1993, he was the National League Manager of the Year, as he was again in 1997 and in 2000. For their inaugural season in 1993, the Colorado Rockies hired Don Baylor as manager. In 1995, he was the National League Manager of the Year. (I was touched when both Dusty and Don thanked me when they accepted their awards.) Steinbrenner eventually hired Bob Watson as general manager of the Yankees in 1995; Watson, who had been John McMullen's GM in Houston, laid the groundwork for the great Yankee teams of the late 1990s.

John McMullen of the Astros was probably the most progressive of the owners in my day, despite some of his views, which might have suggested he was a racist. He is a product of his time and place, but he is not racist. The truly important test for racist tendencies, of course, is how one behaves. McMullen offered Joe Morgan, the great second baseman for the Astros and the Cincinnati Reds who later became a superb broadcaster, the job as general manager in Houston. Morgan turned the job down only because he was so busy with all his other business ventures. McMullen didn't want Morgan because he is black; he wanted him because he knew he would be successful and because he didn't care he was black. Later, John hired Bob Watson for the same reasons, and Watson became the game's first black GM, making a series of brilliant moves for Houston. It was Watson who traded journeyman pitcher Larry Andersen to the Red Sox for Jeff Bagwell, a future Hall of Famer. Later he joined the Yankees, where he did more of the same, but with a far bigger budget.

The GM job is really the most important position on any club, because the GM has so much say about how the entire organization is run, from the low minor leagues right through the hiring of field managers for the big-league clubs. The general-manager slots generally go to baseball lifers as the culminating position in a career filled with low-level, low-paying jobs. Among many other things, the GM must be immersed in the minutiae of baseball operations, in trading deadlines and how the waiver wire works and the hiring of roving minor-league hitting instructors. Walter Haas, the late owner of the A's, once told me that Reggie Jackson wanted to be the GM in Oakland; Reggie certainly knew the game in the broadest sense, but he had not trained in the other areas, to get to know the organization inside-out. Walter's point was that you have to put in years to be a truly effective GM.

That's a legitimate view, and a wholly different one than the one expressed by Al Campanis, the Dodger lifer, one night on *Nightline* with Ted Koppel. That was in 1987, in Bart's first year as National League president, the fortieth anniversary of the season in which Doby and Robinson broke the color lines in their respective leagues. Koppel asked about the dearth of black executives in baseball, and Campanis said blacks lacked the "necessities" to make it in management. It was an ignorant statement from an uneducated man. Within a week he was out of baseball, after nearly a half-century with the Dodgers. But the Campanis episode should not be an indictment of one man; it was important because it revealed how deeply entrenched racist attitudes are in baseball, where a man can last as long as Campanis without his views being condemned or altered. Perhaps his comfort in his world view was so high he found himself talking on a live national television show just as he would behind the closed doors within baseball.

A few years later, as commissioner, I went on *Nightline* with several others, including Henry Aaron, to talk about racism in baseball. Aaron, the all-time home-run leader and an executive with the Braves, had been rightly outspoken in his criticism of baseball's racial lethargy. I was not there to defend baseball; I intended to cite the improvements baseball had made over the years and to acknowledge how much more needed to be done. But Koppel gave the opening statement to Henry, who stunned me by announcing baseball had made no progress in race relations since 1947. It was a ridiculous claim and obviously hyperbolic. It put me in a position of having to defend baseball. Defending an institution that has a long history of racism is an uncomfortable place to be, but I had no choice. He was being outrageous, I felt, to make a point, but I thought he was being dishonest. We had spent considerable time together on the subject; he knew there had been progress and he knew I was committed to bringing more change, but at that point in his life, I believe, he was feeling angry, shunted aside, ignored, and unsuccessful. I think he was saying things just so people would take notice of him. Koppel, interested in the show's ratings, in so-called good TV, allowed Henry to go on and on. Unlike his challenge of Campanis, Koppel never challenged Aaron's bizarre statements; I felt he was unwilling to take on a black man in public. When I challenged Koppel after the show, he said, "I knew you could defend yourself." Koppel, I know, has brought many important issues to the American public over the years. On my night with him, he dropped the ball.

It was a low moment for me, a through-the-looking-glass version of Bill White's sense that fighting racism in baseball was tilting at windmills. I was particularly upset because Henry Aaron had been a hero of mine, perhaps the most productive hitter in the history of the game and a strong and vital man who had endured more abuse than any human being should have to take. But the Henry Aaron on *Nightline* that night was a bitter man, I felt. Subsequent years have been kinder to him. He's made money, with the Braves and through a BMW dealership he owns in Atlanta. He's proven himself as a business executive. I think he feels like the accomplished man he is. We are, once again, friends.

What I had hoped to say on *Nightline* all those years ago still holds true: Despite the progress, baseball has done a woeful job in integrating the game in every aspect except on the field. Look at the history of black umpires. It is brief and not good. The first black umpire was a man named Emmett Ashford, who was not hired until 1966, nineteen years after Jackie Robinson and Larry Doby broke the color barrier for players. Ashford was fifty-one as a rookie umpire, more noted for his flashy jewelry than anything else. He worked only five seasons, to qualify for a pension, retired, and died ten years later, in 1980.

For a while during my term as commissioner, there were only two black umpires in the National League, Eric Gregg and Charlie Williams, and one in the American League, Chuck Meriweather. Things today are only a bit better. I think baseball should be embarrassed, but all you hear about is the on-field problems with umpires. No one seems to notice the absence of black umpires. The problem is not in finding qualified black umpires; it's deeper than that. The problem is developing a pool of umpiring talent among blacks. Umpires are hired out of umpiring schools run by former umpires. The schools are expensive and the culture is all white. Baseball should be running these schools and recruiting the best black umpires from the college level and every other level and offering scholarships and loans when necessary. It should offer opportunities to learn the umpiring trade to strong-minded black athletes whose baseball careers have stalled out in the minor leagues. It is a big issue and an ignored one. All race issues in baseball seem to be ignored these days, as the game obsessively focuses on its economic difficulties.

In the on-field hierarchy, the two most important jobs, just below the manager, are dugout coach and third-base coach. Most managers have worked either or both those jobs before becoming manager. Games are sometimes decided by third-base coaches who decide to send runners home in the blink of an eye. It is a visible and important job, and an important training job as well, and there were periods during my tenure as commissioner when there was not a single black third-base coach in the game. At one point I raised my concern with Lou Piniella, then the manager of the Reds. "Do you realize there's not a single black third-base coach in the game?" I asked.

"You know, Commissioner, I didn't. I guess I just don't notice things like that."

"Well there isn't, and there should be," I said.

"Look, I hire guys I like, guys I played with and know well, guys I'm close to. Most of my friends happen to be white. I don't have a really good black friend that I'm really comfortable with who I would think of for the third-base job."

"At some point, Lou, I'd like you to try to find one."

"If you're telling me it's really important, Commissioner, I'll do it."

"I am."

"Then I will."

It was a reminder of the difference between treating race relations with benign neglect and actively trying to do something. (Though I don't believe Lou Piniella ever did what he promised.)

The one place I could control the hiring was in baseball's executive offices. I decided half my hires for senior positions would be blacks or women. One of the people I hired was Len Coleman, who later became the president of the National League and one of George W. Bush's trusted friends. In 1997, when all of baseball celebrated the fiftieth anniversary of Jackie Robinson's major-league debut, Len Coleman was the ultimate organizer. I had hired Len away from Jack Welch at GE to head marketing for baseball. The basic challenge I posed to him was to plan how we could improve baseball's standing in the black community. Len was dedicated and brilliant. He said it would be difficult, but that change would come over the long term if we stayed with the program. He charted a fifteen-year plan to make it happen. "We start," he said, "with the publisher of *Ebony* and *Jet* magazines, John Johnson, because those magazines are influential. They don't cover baseball and baseball figures, and they should." That was news to me.

So Len and I flew to Chicago to see Mr. Johnson, one of the most successful and influential black businessmen. He was cordial but blunt: "I don't like baseball. Baseball has treated blacks shabbily and that's why our magazines don't bother with it. We write about basketball players and football players, because those sports pay attention to our magazines. Baseball has not. But I'm impressed that you're here—we certainly have never had a visit from a commissioner before—and I'll try to help you. You have a long way to go. We'll start to cover baseball. I'm certain we can help you fix your problems. If you stick with us, we'll stick with you."

Len and I did a lot of that together, planting seeds in black church groups and black publications and in inner-city youth leagues. As soon as I left, however, Len was all alone and the policy of benign neglect soon returned, much to my frustration. In Bud Selig's years as commissioner, baseball is once again ruled by white men. There are no blacks among the top five officials in baseball. There are no black owners. And no one, including the black community, seems to notice or care.

One of the very significant things Len did for me, along with my friend Joe Garagiola, the broadcaster and former Cardinal catcher, was to make me aware of the plight of the surviving generation of Negro Leaguers. Garagiola was for many years the president of BAT, the Baseball Assistance Team, an organization that helps old and needy ballplayers, widows of ballplayers, retired umpires and executives, and other baseball people who are in need of a helping hand. Peter Ueberroth created BAT and it is now a vitally important baseball institution and, to my mind, the finest contribution Ueberroth made to the game. Over the years, BAT has come to the aid of a good number of former Negro League players, most of whom had no formal affiliation with major-league baseball. As I became more aware of the plight of the Negro League alumni, I arranged for them to be included in the Major League Baseball Health Plan, at no cost to them; it was the least baseball and I could do to make small amends. Later, after I left baseball, Len created a plan by which each former Negro Leaguer receives an annual baseball pension of ten thousand dollars per year for life. The old ballplayers were and remain extremely grateful. In 2000, at their annual Negro League reunion, they honored Len and me for what we had done. I was proud to stand next to Len to be recognized. No honor has touched me more.

In 1990, Joe Garagiola came up with the idea that we should have a weekend at Cooperstown to honor the Negro Leaguers, to celebrate their role in baseball. I thought it was a wonderful idea and immediately asked Joe to help organize it, and he did so, magnificently, with a great assist from Frank Slocum, the ultimate insider baseball executive, and with friends from BellSouth. We invited about a hundred Negro League alumni for a June weekend in Cooperstown. It proved to be one of the highlights of my life. We flew them in—making certain they paid for nothing—to Syracuse or Albany, wherever was convenient for them. From there, our plan was to have them take buses into Cooperstown. That's when Joe said, "Fay, these guys rode buses all their lives. Can't we send limousines for them?"

To this day, whenever I see an old Negro Leaguer, he'll invariably say, "You were the one who sent the limos for us!" Most of them had never ridden in a limousine before, they thought it was a big deal, and they gave all the credit to me. In reality, the credit for the idea should go to Joe.

All of us stayed at the grand dame of the Cooperstown hotels, the Otesaga. It was a wonderful sight, seeing these aging black gents hanging out in the lobby and the dining rooms, with their dark skin and white hair, some of them in wheelchairs, telling marvelous stories, punctuated by bursts of laughter and obvious affection for one another and the times they had spent together. For the Friday and Saturday night dinners, the meals were served at big round tables. Before that weekend, I knew very little about Negro League baseball. I knew about Josh Gibson, the legendary catcher and home-run king of the Pittsburgh Crawfords and Homestead Grays, and I knew a number of celebrated players—Henry Aaron, Willie Mays, Ernie Banks, Jackie Robinson, Larry Doby, Satchel Paige, Joe Black—played in the Negro Leagues before they played in the majors, but that was about all I knew. So it was through pure good luck that for the Friday night dinner when I found an open seat it was next to a man I did not know who has become one of my dearest friends. He introduced himself: "Mr. Commissioner, I'm Slick Surratt." Since the day he said those words to me, Alfred "Slick" Surratt, formerly of the Kansas City Monarchs Negro League baseball club, has been one of my heroes. He is a joy to be with.

Before I get on to Slick Surratt, whose portrait in a Monarchs uniform now hangs in the den of my home, a few words about the man who happened to be sitting to my right that right. His name was Sam Jethroe and he played in the Negro League for seven years before becoming the National League Rookie of the Year in 1950, playing for the Boston Braves as a first-year player at the ripe old age of twenty-eight. (Some say he may have been older. *The Baseball Encyclopedia* states that he was born in 1918, which would make him a thirty-two-year-old rookie.) In other words, he lost his baseball youth, and his prime years with it, to racism. His second season was as good as his first, but he had vision problems in his third season and played poorly. He played two games for the Pittsburgh Pirates in 1954 and was out of baseball for good. He was a standout player in the Negro Leagues, but was only briefly on baseball's largest stage. When I met him, he was a courteous but bitter old man who felt his baseball pension was inadequate. After he retired, he had opened a bar in Pittsburgh, but the bar burned down. He struggled to make a living and he talked sadly about what could have been. He led the National League in steals in his first two seasons, and old-timers say he was among the fastest men ever to play in the Negro Leagues, as fast as Cool Papa Bell himself. And everyone knows how fast Cool Papa Bell was: He was so fast he once hit a ball up the middle and, the story goes, it hit him while he was sliding into second. I heard a lot of stories in Cooperstown that weekend, most of them delightful, some of them rooted in deep, sad truths, like the story of Sam Jethroe. There wasn't much I could say to console him. A few years later, I read of his death and recalled with sadness our single brief meeting.

Slick Surratt, sitting on the other side of me, could not have been more different. He was distinguished-looking, very slim, with an exceedingly pleasant face and a ready smile. He had a slight stammer that only enhanced his charm. He just oozed happiness, the way some people, a very few people, do. When you're around someone like that, it's magical. At one point, I said to him, "Slick, where did you get that nickname?"

"Commissioner," he said gently, "I don't know you well enough to answer that question."

What an answer! I said: "Then I'm going to have to get to know you better so you'll tell me."

He had a wonderful gentleness about him, and a playful use of language. I soon learned that Slick was a leadoff hitter for the Monarchs. I asked him if he could run. He said, "You know, I could, Commissioner, I truly could." I asked him what kind of bunter he was. "I could bunt into a teacup," he said. "If I bunt and you let the ball bounce twice, ain't no use pickin' it up. I'm already there."

I asked him what he notices when he watches baseball today. "Well, in our day," he said, "the bunt was big. We could all bunt and run. If a pitcher fell off the mound, didn't keep his feet even when he finished his delivery, we'd bunt him right out of our league. Commissioner, you watch pitchers today, those big righthanders fall off the mound toward first-base side, you couldn't do that in our league. We'd take advantage. We'd bunt you right out of the game. I could bunt and I could run. Yes, sir, I could."

Alfred Surratt was born in 1922, in Danville, Arkansas. He grew up in a world in which separate but unequal facilities and opportunities were the unwritten law of the land. "It says on the license plate in Arkansas, 'Land of Opportunity,' " Slick told me. "At the first opportunity I left!"

Over the years, I've asked him what it was like growing up in that rural town. "I lived on a hill," he said. "We had very little water, very little electricity. There was one school for black kids that went to the eighth grade. There wasn't no high school. There was no future for black kids at that time. The white folks said all a black man needed to do was read and write, and you got that by the eighth grade. I would liked to have gone to college. That was out of the question."

I asked Slick if there was a doctor in town.

"For white folks," he said.

"And how about for blacks?"

"No, sir."

"What would happen if a little black kid got an appendicitis attack?"

"He'd die," Slick said. "A black kid got sick bad, he died."

Slick served in World War II in the South Pacific and helped build Henderson Field at Guadalcanal. Japanese bullets bore down on him as he rode his bulldozer to build runways so the beleaguered Marines in the early days of that vital battle could get air support. He was a mechanic, first class, and he could break down a bulldozer and put it back together as fast as anybody. Later, after the war, he worked for the Ford Motor Company as a mechanic, welder, and instructor for over fifty years. He still works every day. In 1999, I wrote a short essay about Slick that was published in *The Philadelphia Inquirer*. Afterward, I received a call from a Ford executive, the head of minority relations for the company. He had read the article and learned of Slick's baseball background. Ford decided to name its annual award for the minority dealer of the year after Slick Surratt. Slick was filled with appreciation. He is an official of the Negro League Museum in Kansas City and I know that he, working with Joe Black, played a significant role in the decision to have me acknowledged there. There are only two white baseball executives recognized in the museum: Branch Rickey and me. Another honor for which I am grateful.

Over the years, since that night in Cooperstown, Slick and I have spent a lot of time together. I have traveled with him, Larry Doby, Joe Black (who died as I wrote this), and Claire Smith, the newspaper columnist, to college campuses to hold seminars on the Negro Leagues and the integration of baseball. Students often ask the old players, "What do you mean, you couldn't go into a restaurant—why didn't you just go in anyway?" They know nothing about the Jim Crow laws. I remember Larry responding to that question at Williams College by saying, "If I had gone into a restricted restaurant in those days, one of two things would have happened, and both were bad. Either I would have been arrested, or I would have been shot. Either way, I lost." These college visits were eye-opening experiences.

In 1991, I invited Slick and a dozen or so other Negro League alumni as my guests to the All-Star game in Toronto, where they met the first president Bush. Bush was about their age, a former ballplayer, and a war hero, so he was a hit with the Negro Leaguers and vice versa.

"That was pretty nice, wasn't it," I said to Slick afterward.

"Oh, yeah, that was special, Commissioner. I never met a president before."

"So how am I doing on that nickname?" I teased. He still hadn't told me where "Slick" came from. I was doing my job, trying to get to know him better.

"You're doing great, Commissioner. You're getting very close."

A year or two later, Slick was my guest at a World Series game. He had a wonderful time, sitting in excellent seats, meeting everybody, being treated royally. I asked him again about his nickname. He said, "You're getting very, very close, Commissioner, you sure are!"

That's when Larry Doby said to me, "Commissioner, if you haven't figured it out by now, you're nowhere near as smart as I think you are."

I said: "I think I just figured it out." At that moment I realized the nickname had nothing to do with his fielding. The man had lots of other moves.

After the Saturday night dinner at our Negro League weekend at Cooperstown, we gave each player a memento, a gold medallion, engraved with his name. Each player was introduced, and I said something about his playing career and life. They were honored in the same little upstate New York hamlet where baseball's greatest players have been honored for generations. There was much crying amid the laughter and the smiles.

In my formal remarks after dinner I said, "This recognition of you fine gentlemen is long overdue. We of baseball acknowledge our part in the shameful history of exclusion in this country. Baseball treated you badly and on behalf of baseball, I extend my sincere apologies. We want to recognize our wrong and your worth. It is my honor to be with you tonight and to have you here as our guests. We owe you very much. For you kept baseball alive in your black community and in so doing, you did baseball a magnificent service."

The next day, the event was a front-page story in *The New York Times*. Claire Smith wrote the story and she made a point I had never considered: The evening marked the first time baseball had ever formally apologized to the Negro Leaguers for the game's racist past. It never occurred to me that no other commissioner had ever apologized for so obvious and monumental a wrong.

In my library at home I have a wonderful, formal black-and-white portrait of Slick, wearing the baggy flannel uniform of the Kansas City Monarchs. Across the picture, in careful, neat penmanship, he wrote: "To Commissioner Vincent, my best friend. Slick Surratt." I can think of no greater compliment.

Lineup: Slick and Co.	
1.	Oscar Charleston
2.	Larry Doby
3.	Joe Black
4.	Ted "Double Duty" Radcliffe
5.	Alfred "Slick" Surratt
6.	Satchel Paige
7.	Buck O'Neil
8.	Jackie Robinson
9.	Jimmie Crutchfield

Slick and Co.

1. OSCAR CHARLESTON

WHEN I FIRST STARTED getting to know some of the old Negro Leaguers, they used to talk often about a ballplayer named Oscar Charleston. They all knew him, they had seen him play, they were in awe of him.

I had never heard of him.

"Never heard of him?" they'd say. "He was the greatest Negro League player ever!"

They said he could run the bases like Ty Cobb, could hit for power like Babe Ruth, and could play center like Tris Speaker. One season, 1921, he batted .434; in another he hit .445! Off the field, he would brawl with Klansmen, opposing players, umpires, anybody who got in his way.

He is the ultimate baseball legend. He may have been the greatest player of all time, but we'll never know, simply because the man had dark skin. The greatest Negro Leaguer ever, maybe the greatest *player* ever, and I had never heard of him until one weekend at Cooperstown in 1990, surrounded by dozens of men who knew the game in ways I did not.

"Willie Mays was truly great," Buck O'Neil told me once. "Oscar was a bigger Willie Mays. And Oscar was *handsome*. He could do it all. Greatest I ever saw, greatest player who ever lived, that was Oscar Charleston. Yes, sir, he was."

2. LARRY DOBY

LARRY DOBY WASN'T as colorful as Jackie Robinson, he wasn't as fast and he wasn't as flashy with the glove, but he was a formidable player in every way and he eventually made it to the Hall of Fame, even if his route to Cooperstown was far slower than his friend Jackie's. (Jackie was inducted six years after he retired; Larry finally got there in 1998, thirty-nine years after he retired.) Still, everything that Jackie endured, Larry endured, too, particularly in 1947, the first year, but Larry's story was not widely told. Fortunately, he told it to me. Over the years, we have become good friends.

When he was brought up to the Cleveland Indians, on July 5, 1947, in Chicago, the team owner, Bill Veeck, prepared him for what he would endure. "Look," Veeck said, "there will be guys in the clubhouse who will be unfriendly. They won't accept you. But never mind. They'll be gone next year. I'll get rid of them. You are my man. You and I are in this together."

Larry never forgot those words, especially the last sentence. Veeck really meant it. He brought Doby into the clubhouse, introduced him to the manager-shortstop, Lou Boudreau, and Boudreau brought him around to the players. "You'd put your hand out, expecting the other guy to put his out," Doby told me. "Some of them didn't. They would turn around and not say hello.

"So I got dressed and went out on the field to warm up. Everybody is playing catch, you know the way they do before a game. But nobody asks me. I'm all alone, standing there. I felt like I was standing there for hours. Probably, though, just a few minutes. Then Joe Gordon comes up to me.

"Joe Gordon was the second baseman, a great second baseman, and

I was a second baseman, too. He could have seen me as a threat. But Joe Gordon was all class. He had been with the Yankees, and the guys who played for the Yankees had class. They seemed to be a cut above everyone else. He said, 'Hey, kid, let's play catch.' That was a great moment. He sent out a message to everybody else. He was a leader and he was saying, 'This kid is on the team.' I'll never forget that. The others, I won't talk about. Never did, never will."

3. JOE BLACK

JOE BLACK was the first Negro Leaguer I got to know well. Bart admired him and hired him when he became commissioner. After pitching in the Negro Leagues for some ten years, Black pitched for the Brooklyn Dodgers from 1952, when he was a twenty-eight-year-old National League Rookie of the Year, through 1955. Those were storied Brooklyn teams and Bart knew the history and knew about Black and felt Joe had much to offer baseball. He had a college degree, from Morgan State, and he had managed his postplaying career well, working as a schoolteacher and later as an executive for Greyhound, eventually becoming the vice president in charge of personnel.

Bart asked Joe to go around clubhouses and talk to players about what they would do when they were done playing. Mookie Wilson of the Mets had once asked Bart what he should do when his playing days were over, and Bart was so impressed by the question he figured more ballplayers should be asking it of themselves. He thought Black could spur them to do so. Joe made strenuous efforts but never felt he was getting anywhere. He'd say, "I talk to a player about a job after baseball that pays thirty thousand dollars a year and they look at me like I'm a fat old Uncle Tom and say, 'Thirty a year? Hell, I make that in a month.' Bart kept sending him out. "If one guy listens to you, it will be worthwhile," he said.

But people did listen to him. The great Willie Mays could be difficult; I struggled to get him to agree to throw out the first pitch of the third game of the 1989 World Series, and eventually he agreed, but it was work getting there. When we were planning our Negro League Weekend at Cooperstown, however, Mays came without any arm-twisting. He had played for the Birmingham Barons of the Negro National League as a teenager in the late 1940s, but that's not why he came—I strongly suspect he came because he knew the weekend was important to Joe Black, and Mays had a deep and abiding respect for Joe Black, who played for the Dodgers when Mays played for the New York Giants.

Joe once told me about playing high-school ball at an integrated school in New Jersey in the early 1940s. He was a shortstop and he could run and hit and he had a good arm. Scouts came to the final game of the season to talk to and sign the good players on the team— the good white players, that is—but not Joe.

"Finally I said to one of the scouts, 'How come you guys aren't talking to me? I can play, too,' " Joe Black said, recounting for my benefit a seminal moment from his boyhood. "And the scout said, 'Because you're colored, and we can't sign colored kids.'

"I went home and cried all night. I looked at my scrapbook and sure enough, every face was white. So I ripped out the pictures of all my big-league heroes, DiMaggio and everybody else, everybody except Hank Greenberg. Greenberg I loved too much to rip out. Then I said to my mother, 'I hate all these white people.' I'm not proud of that, but that's how I felt. She told me not to hate. It was not the fault of all white people. But I ignored her. I hated.

"Then I got a scholarship to play football down in Maryland, at Morgan State. Now Morgan State, of course, is a black college, and the most wonderful thing happened there. They made me feel it was OK to be black. They made me feel proud to be black. They taught me black history I'd never known.

"The first Sunday morning my freshman year, I went to the big Presbyterian church in town in the center of Baltimore. I had been a Presbyterian all my life. I climbed the steps and was about to enter the church when a big white guy comes up to me and says, 'Hey, what are you doing here?'

"And I said, 'I'm going to church. I'm a Presbyterian.'

" 'Not here you're not. There's a church for your folks down the road. You can go to that church. You can't go here.' "

Joe was stunned. He figured white Presbyterians and black Presbyterians prayed to the same God. But on this occasion, slapped in the face with racism, he did not become filled with hate, as he had as a schoolboy. Instead, he realized the problem was not with himself and the color of his skin, but with the man at the door. Joe said his inner strength came from his college experience at Morgan State, and it served him well all the days of his life, in baseball and in his life beyond the game, too.

4. TED "DOUBLE DUTY" RADCLIFFE

AS I GOT TO KNOW SLICK SURRATT, and as I learned the lore of the Negro Leagues from him, I realized playful nicknames were an important part of the tradition of black baseball. They were common in the white game, too, but in the big leagues the nickname was just often a play from the player's name, like "Joltin' Joe" DiMaggio. The Negro League nicknames, it seemed, got to the essence of the player.

At one point in his career, Slick played for Theodore Roosevelt Radcliffe, who had a long career in the Negro Leagues as a player and manager. He did a tour of duty with practically every team: the Detroit Stars, the St. Louis Stars, the Homestead Grays, the Pittsburgh Crawfords, the Columbus Blue Birds, the New York Black Yankees, the Brooklyn Eagles, the Cincinnati Tigers, the Memphis Red Sox, the Birmingham Black Barons, the Chicago American Giants, the Louisville Buckeyes, the Detroit Wolves. He caught and pitched. (His brother, Alex, was considered one of the best third basemen in Negro League history.) Radcliffe, I learned, was a legend, and he had one of the best baseball nicknames I have ever heard.

In 1932, Radcliffe was pitching for the Pittsburgh Crawfords, in the Negro League World Series at Yankee Stadium. In the first game of a doubleheader, Radcliffe caught Satchel Paige in a 5–0 shutout. In the nightcap, Radcliffe pitched his own shutout. That night, Damon Runyon, the great New York newspaperman, wrote he had just seen a man do double duty, catching the first game and pitching the second. From that day on, he was Ted "Double Duty" Radcliffe. Sometimes it got shortened to just Duty, a nickname for a nickname. When I talk to the old-timers who knew him well—how lucky I am to able to say that—they'll say, "Remember when Duty . . ." They say that often, Duty was always up to something.

5. ALFRED "SLICK" SURRATT

SLICK TELLS THE STORY of playing for Duty up in Canada, sometime in the early 1950s. Duty was the player-manager and Slick was an outfielder. This is how Slick told it to me:

"Duty had promised me a raise, but I'm only getting fifty dollars a week and I needed some cash. I knew Duty had some because I saw him flashing a big old wad of it. Now Duty loved the ladies, so I waited until night when I knew he would be having dinner out, trying to impress some lovely lady. I found Duty and his lady friend sitting together, eating their dinner. I went up to him and said, 'Duty, can I speak to you?'

" 'Of course, my good friend, you can speak to me.'

"Now I knew I had him. He was trying to impress the lady.

"Duty says, 'What do you want, young man? Lookit here, you're a fine ballplayer. How can I help?'

" 'Well, Duty, I really need some money.'

" 'Well now, you just tell Duty how much you need.'

" 'Well, I could use $150. That would do me just fine.'

"Duty got out this big ole wad of cash and peeled off some bills for me. He said. 'You need one-fifty? Here's two. I want you to be happy and your family to be happy. You send some of that home to your missus and you make sure to tell her it comes from ole Double Duty Radcliffe.'

"I knew I was going to hear about it, but I got my cash. Sure enough, next day at the ballpark Duty grabs me and says, 'Don't you *ever* do that again. You do and ole Duty goin' to tear you up. Imagine, you talkin' like that to me when I'm with my lady. What you thinkin'?' Duty was good, but I beat him that night."

6. SATCHEL PAIGE

FOR A PERIOD, Larry Doby roomed with Satchel Paige—or, as he says, "I roomed with his luggage." When Larry or Slick or anybody tells

Satchel Paige stories, I am a totally captive audience. I saw Satchel Paige pitch for the Cleveland Indians in the 1948 season, when they said he was a forty-one-year-old rookie, having played in the Negro Leagues for decades. (Of course, no one knew his true age.) The Indians won the World Series that year, and I remember batters facing Paige's "hesitation" pitch. He'd go into a big windup, kick his left leg high in the air, and then everything would come to a stop: When he would decide to release the pitch was anybody's guess. He threw hard and with control. He was something.

Whitey Herzog, who in my years in baseball was the celebrated manager of the St. Louis Cardinals, tells the story of seeing Paige when he was a kid coming up in the minors. There was a hole in a scoreboard somewhere about the size of a big grapefruit. There was a local promotion: Anybody who hit a homer through the hole would win a free suit. No suits, of course, were ever given away. Herzog and some others approached Paige: "Satchel, could you throw a ball through that hole?"

"Oh, for sure."

"From sixty feet, six inches?"

"No problem. But not for free."

"How much you want?"

"A hundred bucks and I'll throw two balls out of three through that hole."

So Herzog and his boys went around and collected the hundred. They paced off sixty feet, six inches, from the scoreboard and gave Paige three balls. He went into his big windup and hit the wall with the first one.

"That's just to get your attention," he said.

The second ball went straight through. As did the third.

Satchel said, "You get another hundred, we'll do it all over."

Satchel had all sorts of game.

At one point in their careers, Paige had designated Slick as his driver. Paige didn't travel on the team bus with the others; he went around the country in a big white Cadillac.

"One night we're driving from Memphis to New Orleans and it's a long drive and it's right through the Deep South," Slick said. "Satchel says to me, 'Little 'un, you do the driving and I'll do the sleeping.' So I'm driving along, going pretty slow because we're two black guys in a Cadillac driving through the Deep South. All of sudden, Satch says, 'Pull over, little 'un.'

"So I pull over. We're somewhere in Mississippi at this point, I imagine. I said, 'Why do you want me to stop?'

" 'I want to let that old man with the wheelbarrow go by,' he says. I got the point.

"So now we're going seventy-five, eighty miles an hour down the highway and we hear the whir of the man's siren. This big ole police officer pulls us over and says, 'What in the hell are you boys doing? You know you can't drive like that.'

"I'm very quiet but Satch speaks up.

" 'Officer, you ever hear of the great Satchel Paige?'

" 'Yeah.'

" 'Well, look it here. I have a baseball for you signed by the great Satchel Paige. Little 'un here and me, we're hustling to New Orleans 'cause we got a game there tomorrow.'

"The officer looked closely at Satch and says, 'You mean you're Satchel Paige?'

" 'Yes, sir, the very one.'

" 'Well, I'll be damned. I'll tell you what I'm gonna do. I'm gonna radio ahead the rest of the way and let them know Satchel Paige is coming through in his white Cadillac and you won't have any trouble. You just go sailin' through now.'

"And we were off. No problems the rest of the way. Later, I saw that Satchel had a whole bag of signed balls with him. He was ready. It didn't matter how many times he got stopped. He could talk his way out of anything."

7. BUCK O'NEIL

BUCK O'NEIL, a tall, white-haired, elegant man with a kindly mahogany-colored face that time has aged with exceeding grace, played on and later managed the Kansas City Monarchs. The Monarchs were one of the great teams of Negro League baseball, and Kansas City, Missouri, where the league began, is the spiritual home of the Negro Leagues. The Negro League Museum is there and Buck O'Neil is the guiding force behind the place. He is a man of considerable charm, warmth, political skill, and a public relations genius. He is also a man of keen insight. He has told me, more than once, a story about Jackie Robinson, when Jackie was playing for the Monarchs, that reveals the character of the man incisively. The episode in question had a profound effect on Buck as well. This is how he told it:

"One day, the Monarch bus is on the road somewhere. This is back in the forties. I'm on the bus, Jackie's on the bus. We're traveling across Arkansas. The bus has a fifty-gallon gas tank. Fifty gallons of gas is a big piece of business for one of these tiny roadside filling stations. We stop at one of them and Jackie gets off to use the bathroom. The owner says, 'Hey, boy, that bathroom ain't for your kind.'

" 'Is that right?' Jackie says. 'Well, I guess your gas isn't for us, either.'

"The man looked at Jackie and then said: 'Well, OK, then, just this once.'

"Jackie used the bathroom and we got the gas. But he made his point, to all of us. He was smart. He was a college man. We learned from him."

8. JACKIE ROBINSON

STORIES ABOUT Jackie Robinson abound. The stories that interest me are the true ones. I'm fortunate that I've been able to hear Jackie Robinson stories directly from sources I trust who were on the scene, as Buck O'Neil was during Jackie's Negro League days, and as Robin Roberts, the Hall of Fame pitcher for the Phillies, was during Jackie's big-league career.

When Jackie came up in 1947, the Phillies were managed by a former Yankee outfielder of the thirties named Ben Chapman. Chapman was a Tennessean, growing up in a time and place where blacks were "coloreds" and worse. As the Phillies' manager he was vicious toward Robinson. In that 1947 season, he instructed his team to hurl the ugliest sort of racist invective at Robinson each time he came to the plate.

The worse the slurs became, the more determined Robinson got. His reputation for killing the Phillies is well-established.

Before the start of the next season, the National League president, Ford Frick, had Chapman and Robinson pose for a publicity picture together. Robinson went to his grave regretting that he ever cooperated with that picture. That's how much he despised Chapman.

In 1948, Roberts's rookie year, Chapman told his team, "Look, there's no point in calling him a nigger anymore. All he does is beat us to death. We'll shut up and see if he still plays so good."

"The team stopped yelling at him and he still went ten for fourteen over a three-game series," Roberts said. "He knew Chapman for what he was, he hated Chapman, and he was really motivated. He'd single, steal second, steal third, might even steal home. He did everything to destroy us. We couldn't get him out.

"One day we were playing the Dodgers at home, at Shibe Park. The Dodgers won and Robinson got his usual three hits. There's a tunnel underneath the stands that leads to the home clubhouse and the visitors' clubhouse. All of a sudden, Robinson comes out and heads right toward us. I'm right behind Chapman. Robinson looks at Chapman and says nothing. Chapman walks by him. As he does, Chapman says, 'You can really play this game, Robinson, but you're still a nigger.' Robinson looked at him and kept on going, didn't say a word. He kept killing us every time we played them. Before the season was out, Chapman was fired."

9. JIMMIE CRUTCHFIELD

IN 1991, A NEW BALLPARK with an old name was opened in Chicago, Comiskey Park. I was there for the opening, and on the field next to me was an elderly black man named Jimmie Crutchfield. We visited. Jimmie had been a Negro League star for various teams, including the Chicago American Giants, for whom he was an All-Star in 1941. But he was born in 1910, so by the time Jackie Robinson and Larry Doby integrated the game in 1947, he was an old man by baseball standards, and any chance he would have had to play in the big leagues had come and gone. He was a man who could have been bitter. He was anything but.

"Jimmie," I asked him, "did you ever play in the old Comiskey Park?"

"Oh, yes, played at Comiskey a lot. We also played on some rough fields. I grew up playing on outfields with stones in them and you never knew where the ball was going to go. When we played in the South in the Negro Leagues we played on some rough fields, but we played on some very good fields, too. We played at Yankee Stadium, the Polo Grounds, Comiskey."

Looking for conversation, I asked: "What are the things in your life you're proud of?"

I don't know if I had ever asked anybody that question before, but he was eighty-one years old and frail and I knew I might not have the chance to pose such a question again.

"The thing I'm proudest of," Jimmie Crutchfield said, "is that I never hated nobody."

I knew what a black man of his age had endured in his life. I have been struck by the eloquence of that answer ever since.

TOMORROW	0	0	0	0	0	0	0	0	9
HOME	0	0	0	0	0	0	0	0	

C H A P T E R   N I N E

Tomorrow

IT'S A COMMON misconception that I was fired as commissioner in 1992. I was not; I resigned. The resignation followed a vote of no confidence on the part of the owners, which made it seem as if I was about to be put out of office, but I left voluntarily. The distinction is an important one.

I thought then, and I think now, that the owners do not have the right to fire a commissioner. (We'll soon see, I suspect, Bud Selig agreeing with me.) The Major-League Agreement is clear on this. I looked very closely into it at the time, and I was sure that if I decided to fight any effort to fire me, I would prevail in court; it would have been an important fight, but it was one I ultimately decided not to make.

The most critical subject for any commissioner, and the most difficult, is labor relations. I would be very happy if it were possible to write this book without mentioning the words "lockout," "strike," "union," or "management," but they've been an unavoidable part of the game's recent history. When Bart became commissioner, baseball was just

277

coming out of the period when the owners colluded to hold down salaries in direct violation of their agreement with the players. I cannot underestimate the damage done to the game through that illegal action; it's not going too far to call that transgression baseball's Original Sin, at least as far as the relations between players and owners are concerned.

Discussion of player salaries causes a lot of fuzzy thinking. Fans approach me and say, "Don't you think it's outrageous how much the players make today?" When I was in the movie business I was asked the same question about the compensation of movie stars. I'm sympathetic to the question and what it implies, but my answer is no. Players, like movie stars, are not underpaid or overpaid; in our free market system, you and I are paid exactly what we should be paid. Ballplayers are paid what an owner is willing to pay and no more. The people who complain about player salaries ignore the beauties of capitalism.

When I go to a movie, I don't care what Julia Roberts is earning for her work; I go to enjoy the film and to watch her performance. When I was in the film business, I was responsible for what we paid the stars— Dustin Hoffman in *Tootsie,* for example. The calculation, the guess, was this: Can we earn back the salary at the box office? There's no reason for moviegoers to worry about such things, and for the most part they don't. As a baseball fan, I take that approach to the game and I suspect most fans try to do the same. When we watch a game, we don't care what Mike Piazza is earning; we want to see him fight off a series of full-count fastballs until he gets one he can drive. (Ted Williams used to say the secret to hitting is to get your pitch to hit and not to swing at the pitcher's pitch. Few understand that. Piazza does.)

Owners, too, can be unsophisticated when it comes to baseball economics, and more than a few are. When I was commissioner, the Indians were owned by Dick Jacobs, a Cleveland real-estate mogul. He was brilliant at real estate. He didn't understand the most basic principles of the baseball business.

He called me early in my tenure as commissioner to complain: "I'm stunned by the Mets! How can they sign Dwight Gooden for three years for $7 million? That's stupid. That's too much. I want you to call

Wilpon and Doubleday and fine them a million dollars for doing that. If you don't, you're useless."

"First of all, Dick, how do you know what too much is?" I asked him. "Obviously, the Mets think he is worth that money. More important, I can't do anything about it. To try to fine the Mets for a contract they've signed would be immediately challenged by the union. I can't set prices for ballplayers who I might think are paid too much. Can't be done. That would be illegal."

What was surprising was that Dick Jacobs didn't know I couldn't regulate salaries. Imagine buying into baseball without learning the fundamentals of how the game operates. He was fortunate, though, later selling the Indians for a tremendous profit.

When Peter Ueberroth was commissioner, he counseled the owners to decide—each on his own, of course—not to sign free agents. As long as each of you makes that decision independently, he said, it is legal and will keep your team salaries stable. But please remember, he said: It cannot be an orchestrated effort.

Of course, it immediately became an orchestrated effort, personified by the two owners who later pressed me to leave: Bud Selig and Jerry Reinsdorf. It was a direct violation of the collective-bargaining agreement that banned "collusion" among owners to set the players' salaries. Through most of the winters in the 1980s, it was obvious to even the ordinary fan that collusion among the owners was taking place. Name players, players with considerable track records, were not being signed by anybody. Shortly before he died, Walter Haas, the owner of the A's, told me, "Fay, if you ever have any doubt about collusion, don't, because I know. I was in on it. I'm sorry about it and I'm embarrassed by it, but it's true."

The owners got caught, of course. The players' union sued, documents were subpoenaed, notes of private conversations among owners were revealed, and the upshot was that a $280-million payment was made from the owners to the players. The most telling evidence was a note retained by Bill Giles, the president of the Phillies, who jotted down what Reinsdorf was telling him: not to sign Lance Parrish, the superb catcher who was then a free agent. That piece of paper was a

$280-million smoking gun. The owners had cheated. In the wake of this, I felt, the players were fully justified in their mistrust of the owners. Yet here is what the owners have done since the collusion settlement, when they should have been trying to repair their relationship with the union: They staged a lockout during spring training in 1990; they took a vote of no confidence in me in 1992 as a way of showing me the door because they feared I was "too soft" on the union; they shut down the 1994 baseball season in midsummer and robbed fans of the World Series; and they created four new teams, at a franchise fee of about $150 million each, to fund the $280-million collusion settlement, getting new owners to pay for the old owners' sins.

From the time Bart and I got into baseball, labor problems dominated the agenda. Bart's view as commissioner was that he would not be involved; he had endured a very bad go-round with the unions at Yale, and it hurt him. I told him he would never be able to hold to that; I used to remind him the last Italian who went up on a mountaintop and fiddled while the enterprise burned is not well regarded by history. (His usual and erudite reply was, "Go fuck yourself.") Bart's view aside, the overriding challenge for any commissioner is his relationship with the players union.

You'd think that by the late 1980s, when the union had been a major factor in baseball for over twenty years, the owners would recognize that this was a reality they had to deal with. And yet, you still had hardline owners who honestly believed they could break the union—a view that may still persist. The thinking is always, "If we lock the players out in spring training because we don't have a contract, enough players will come to work in the spring to undercut the union and cause it to fall." The owners constantly believe this will happen if they just stick together long enough—never mind that it has never happened, that the players have been very unified and well-financed and, in my experience, very bright. In 1990–91, when this debate was going on, I told the owners, "The single biggest reality you guys have to face up to is collusion. You stole $280 million from the players, and the players are unified to a man around that issue, because you got caught and many of you are still involved." Selig and Reinsdorf, two ringleaders of collusion, were the ones who were the most adamant in saying, "We've got to find some way to get around this union, we have to see if we can break them." I kept saying, "You're not going to break them, and if you try, the damage will be long-lasting. You must work with them. I'm not going to be a part of it."

After Bart died, I immediately hired Steve Greenberg to be my deputy commissioner. Steve was a lawyer and an agent, and he was very well-regarded by the union, especially by Donald Fehr. Fehr once said to me that if he had to pick one lawyer to hire if he were in trouble personally, it would be Steve Greenberg. I brought Steve into baseball thinking it was going to take a long time, but eventually, with Steve's help and skill, we would build a better relationship with the union, and out of the relationship would come some progress on important subjects. And we were clearly right.

For this and other transgressions, I became known as someone who was soft on the union. In baseball, if you try to be a moderate and say that the union isn't all bad, we have to work with them and they're not evil people, you lose a significant amount of ground with the hard-line owners. Doug Danforth, the silliest of the owners I knew—he was the managing partner in Pittsburgh and a former head of Westinghouse— used to tell me, "You shouldn't even meet with Fehr. He's beneath you. How can you have lunch or breakfast with him? It infuriates me when I hear that you're having a meal with him." And I'd say, "Doug, you don't understand, we can't do anything in baseball without talking to them or having their cooperation, and it doesn't do any good for you to take that view," and he'd say, "Well, I've broken more unions than you will ever know and we're going to break this union, and you can't be seen to be friendly with them, and every time you do that I get infuriated." I suspect that position, that attitude still exists, and it causes enormous trouble.

The hard-liners were absurd. I was trying to work with Don Fehr, to mend some of the lines of communication damaged by the battles of the past. Sometimes as a courtesy he would come up to my house because it's not easy for me to move around. We weren't socially friendly, but after he came for a meeting, and word got around, Jerry Reinsdorf started saying, "Fay Vincent is such a schmuck, he actually had Fehr at his house, Fehr helped his wife in with groceries one day"—which is true—and somehow that was considered to be one of my greatest sins.

In the summer of 1992, it was clear some of the owners didn't want me around for the upcoming negotiations with the players, the sequence of events that culminated in the cancellation of the 1994 World Series. Selig and Fred Wilpon of the Mets were leading the call for a new chief negotiator, and hired Richard Ravitch, presumably on the basis of the job he'd done on behalf of the city of New York in its dealings with the transit unions. Ravitch knew nothing about baseball—he once asked Steve Greenberg, "Which league has the designated hitter?"—but he led the hard-liners to believe that he was on the verge of a monumental breakthrough with the union, that he could achieve their goals if everybody let him handle things. Well, you know the fiasco that resulted.

In the meantime, Jerry Reinsdorf was spreading malicious and untruthful rumors about me, maintaining I had fudged my résumé and never held the job I'd claimed at the Securities and Exchange Commission, among other absurd claims. It would have been laughable— my career has been public and my moves and positions are all easily documented—except that Reinsdorf was persuasive with other owners. Selig was working the phones, which is one of the things he's best at. They were putting together a vote of no confidence in me, and Selig was telling people, "We have the votes, and if you're on the wrong side of this there'll be problems for you down the road." Their concern, simply stated, was that as commissioner I might act in the best interests of baseball rather than do what the owners wanted me to do. (Their specific fear was that if the upcoming negotiations led them to undertake a lockout of the players in spring training, I might order the camps opened, destroying their position; I promised not to intervene, but they didn't want to hear it. This seems to be the only arrow in the owners' strategic quiver, and the threat of it has repeatedly led the players to set strike dates late in the preceding season to prevent it from happening. The inevitability of this particular dance shows the ineffectiveness of the threat.)

The campaign against me culminated in a vote in September 1992, in which a majority of the owners expressed their lack of confidence in me and called upon me to resign. The implied threat was that if I didn't resign, they would force me out of office. And here I found myself the unhappy participant in a battle of principle, with some vociferous allies urging me to fight.

I firmly believed that under the Major-League Agreement, the owners do not have the power to fire a commissioner. (As far as I know, they still don't.) This part of the charter was written by Judge Kenesaw Mountain Landis when he first took the job; he knew his decisions might cause him trouble with the owners, and he put in provisions that would prevent a disgruntled group from forcing him out. He had been a federal judge, and he certainly wasn't going to give up a lifetime appointment for a job from which the people whose conduct he was judging could fire him whenever they wanted. The owners like to say that baseball is a business where the commissioner is the chief executive, and you can always fire the chief executive, but that analogy doesn't hold, because in business a chief executive is not expected to make rulings on the actions of his board of directors; a commissioner is in charge of keeping the owners in line with the game's rules and regulations.

My instinct was to stand up for this principle and to fight the owners' actions in court. I love and always will love baseball, and I believe a strong, independent commissioner is critical to its health. Part of me wanted to fight to continue Bart's legacy, and part of me believes quitters are weak. A lot of me didn't want to see the Seligs and Reinsdorfs get control of the game without a battle. I hired a brilliant litigator, Brendan Sullivan at Williams & Connolly, to look into my prospects. Sullivan told me, "We'll win this case, and you ought not to quit; let's go to court and I'll win it for you and you'll make a big point." (I had been impressed with Sullivan's efforts on behalf of his client Oliver North; I thought North and his secret arms deals were loathsome, but Sullivan's defense of him was outstanding. One Senator questioning North urged him to answer without consulting or listening to his attorney, who chimed in with, "What am I? A potted plant?" I admire lawyers who can make a point with humor, particularly when their legal talents are world-class.)

I had other counsel as well. George W. Bush was urging me to go to the next owners meeting and lay out my program for the future of the game. Wayne Huizenga of the Florida Marlins told me, "Go to St. Louis [where that meeting would be held], you'll blow 'em away and make everybody feel sheepish." Eli Jacobs of Baltimore and John Mc-Mullen of Houston also thought this was a live possibility, one I shouldn't overlook. I was less certain.

I went up to Cape Cod to think it over, and the more I thought about it, the more I realized this was the kind of fight where even if I won, I lost. A court case would probably drag on until the end of my term as commissioner, and the majority had already made it clear that I was not going to be reappointed. And even if I won, or if the speech went over so well that we never had to go to court, I would then have to go on working with Bud Selig and Jerry Reinsdorf, and Jackie Autry, and Doug Danforth. I truly could not stomach the thought of being in the same room with these people. The good thing about the circumstances of my life is that I had all the money I needed, so it was unnecessary for me to continue to be with and work with people whose standards of business and character I found appalling. It was time to go.

John McMullen flew up to the Cape to try to talk me out of resigning, but I never really had second thoughts. With Sullivan's help, I wrote a letter of resignation that read in part:

> As requested in the owners' resolution of Sept. 3, 1992, and in accordance with its terms, I tender my resignation as commissioner of baseball, effective immediately. . . .
>
> I strongly believe a baseball commissioner should serve a full term as contemplated by the Major League Baseball Agreement. Only then can difficult decisions be made impartially and without fear of political repercussions. Unfortunately, some want the commissioner to put aside the responsibility to act in the "best interests of baseball"; some want the commissioner to represent only owners, and to do their bidding in all matters. I haven't done that, and I could not do so, because I accepted the position believing the

commissioner has a higher duty and that sometimes decisions have to be made that are not in the interest of some owners.

Unique power was granted to the commissioner of baseball for sound reasons—to maintain the integrity of the game and temper owner decisions predicated solely on self-interest. The office should be maintained as a strong institution. My views on this have not changed. What has changed, however, is my opinion that it would be an even greater disservice to baseball if I were to precipitate a protracted fight over the office of the commissioner. . . .

A fight based solely on principle does not justify the disruption when there is not greater support among ownership for my views. While I would receive personal gratification by demonstrating that [my] legal position . . . is correct, litigation does nothing to address the serious problems of baseball. I cannot govern as commissioner without the consent of owners to be governed. I do not believe that consent is now available to me. Simply put, I've concluded that resignation—not litigation—should be my final act as commissioner "in the best interests" of baseball.

I can only hope owners will realize that a strong commissioner, a person of experience and stature in the community, is integral to baseball. I hope they learn this lesson before too much damage is done to the game, to the players, umpires and others who work in the game, and most importantly, to the fans . . . I remind them all that ownership of a baseball team is more than ownership of an ordinary business. Owners have a duty to take into consideration that they own a part of America's national pastime—in trust. This trust sometimes requires putting self-interest second.

When the news broke, one of the first calls I received was from then-president Bush; he wished me well and expressed his regret at what had happened. He was very sympathetic. I said to him, "You were kind enough to call me on my way in and now you are very nice to call me on my way out. Your first call meant a lot to me. This call means even more." When you're in the public eye you make decisions the public will weigh in on, and it's pointless to worry about what millions of people think; you can only hope that a few people, whom you respect, will understand what you are doing and why. I knew the

Bushes understood what I was doing and why, and that was important to me.

His call made me feel better, although I still felt pretty lousy. I felt then, and still believe, I failed. Nobody likes to leave any job under these circumstances: You like to leave at the top of your game with everything in order, and I left in a situation that was miserable, both for me and the game. I wasn't able to convince the owners that their method and style of attacking the union was deficient; I couldn't get them to agree that my strategy was correct. That's a big failure. At the same time, the bigger failure is theirs: They've tried it their way for ten years now, and they haven't made an inch of progress. I clearly was right, and I think I was also right that the effects of collusion so thoroughly polluted the whole relationship between the union and the owners that the impact is still being felt.

I am by no means saying that I was the perfect commissioner. I made mistakes, of course. (It was a mistake for me, among other mistakes, to have pressed hard for realignment in 1991, over the Cubs' objections.) I by no means had the cure to every baseball illness. As a traditional baseball fan, I was originally opposed to the concept of "wild-card" teams; in fact, I think the concept has worked well, creating late-season interest where there otherwise wouldn't be any. The traditionalist in me was opposed to interleague play because I worried it would diminish the World Series, historically the only time all year teams from the two different leagues faced one another. But that has worked well, too.

Baseball's biggest problem today is the same as it was when I came into the game fifteen years ago: The leadership in baseball thinks the players union is the enemy. I believe they have it completely wrong: The players union protects the owners from themselves. Because of the existence of the Basic Agreement between the players and the owners, hammered out amid great tension every five years or so, the owners have the right to come together and fix prices in a legally protected way. Under the terms of the Basic Agreement there is no free market for players until they become free agents after the players' sixth season. (Of the number of players who ever gain a place on a major-league roster, a tiny percentage plays for six years or more.) Owners can "underpay" players in their first five seasons, because the union agrees to let them do so. If the union disbanded and every player were a free agent, there would be a true free market for all players, and salaries—especially for younger players—would likely skyrocket. I once described that scenario to Gene Orza, Donald Fehr's deputy at the players union. I said the ultimate killing move for the players union would be to disband, with a provision that if average salaries ever fell below the current level the union would be reinstituted. He smiled at me knowingly. But for now the players union performs an important function, and it will continue to until players feel they can trust the commissioner and the owners.

Baseball's expansion in the 1990s was a poor idea, and I say that even though two of the four new teams were begun in my term. I tried to convince the owners not to expand, not to take that course. I asked them to think of baseball as a pie: Would you rather own one-twenty-sixth of it or one-twenty-eighth? They couldn't see that; they could only see the $10 million each would receive from a new franchise fee. Of course, that grand sum is now just enough money to pay one star player for one year, but they needed the money for the more mundane purpose of paying off their collusion debt. Their vision was short-sighted, and as contraction (the elimination of two or more teams) becomes a hot issue I feel vindicated; I tried to argue that rather than expanding, it made more sense to move two struggling teams—say Montreal and Houston—to cities where people were hungry for base-ball. One longtime owner, dismissing my argument, told me my idea was the single dumbest proposal he had heard in all his years in base-ball. I wondered where contraction and collusion rank on his list of the great ideas in baseball history.

o   o   o

AS THIS BOOK NEARS its publication date, yet another labor con-frontation is approaching. I wish I could be optimistic about the chances of avoiding dispute and disruption, but I cannot. The leaders on both sides are fixed in their approach and their views of their counterparts; there is simply too much history for there to be much trust.

Marvin Miller's genius, what helped him organize baseball players into one of the strongest unions we've ever seen, was that he portrayed the owners as an evil force and made the battle a moral fight instead of just an economic one. Any time you mix morality into an economic issue you make it very hard to resolve: If you are bad and I am good, it's difficult for us to come together to do something that's advantageous for both of us. There are solutions to baseball's problems that can aid both players and owners in the long run, but the relationship has been so contentious for so long that nobody has any inclination to think in those terms.

Baseball is heading for some very difficult times. I don't blame the players for not believing the owners' claims of economic distress: They've cried wolf over every change in the sport since the dawn of man. But baseball's current economic situation is dire; there is a real possibility that several teams could go under, and revenue sharing is only going to carry those weaker clubs so far. While I was commissioner, I worked with banks with which I had done business in the past, to put together a line of credit for the owners; Carl Pohlad, of the Minnesota Twins, told me, "If you get that bank line together, I'll eat my hat. It can't be done." But I did it, and it's one of the things I'm proudest of. The line of credit has been increased in the years since I left baseball; I understand there are currently $1.5 billion in loans outstanding, money that was used to bail out several clubs in the last few years. Without it, we'd have seen teams missing their payrolls during the season, and you can imagine the chaos that would have resulted.

The players make the seductive argument that all they want is the operation of the free marketplace, that their compensation should be determined by whatever the market will bear. But it's a weird kind of marketplace, because parts of it assume that, say, a first baseman for the Yankees should be paid on a comparable basis to a first baseman for Milwaukee—that's how arbitration works—when a TV weatherman in Milwaukee doesn't make nearly as much as a TV weatherman in New York, and those local TV stations are never in direct competition. Also, most marketplaces aren't subject to the kind of political pressure that baseball faces: If a department store in the Tampa/St. Petersburg area can't cut it economically, it closes; when its baseball team runs into equally severe losses, you have congressional hearings and lawsuits filed in state court to keep you from taking the similar necessary step. So while elements of baseball operate as if it's a free market, it's an anomalous market at best.

And yet, the kinds of problems baseball faces have been seen with increasing frequency in American business in general. As the situation in baseball grew more serious, the owners taking part in the 1994 negotiations cried, "We must grow the game, grow the game!" much as corporations looked to endless expansion as a panacea through the boom of the 1980s and 1990s. Seven years later, those same owners were talking about contracting the game—while Commissioner Selig reportedly doubled his annual salary from $3 million to somewhere around $6 million, much the way executive compensation exploded in the boom years regardless of the performance of the company. (Selig won't confirm the number, even though ballplayer salaries are public. Bart and I were paid $650,000.)

As commissioner, I advocated a partnership between the players and the owners, and I still believe that is the only long-term solution to baseball's constant, debilitating, and, from the perspective of many present and former fans, boring economic struggles.

The ultimate goal of the owners, in my opinion, should be to make the players their partners. The only way to accomplish that, in a free-market economy, is to identify common interests and joint economic objectives. The old model of owners as capitalists and players as employees no longer works. Something new has to emerge—and it will, over time.

The American business community has finally figured out what the Japanese have known for decades, that workers with an equity interest in their company are better and more loyal workers. Baseball should do the same.

In baseball, each team could take, say, 10 percent of its value, combine it with everybody else's 10 percent, and form a separate corporation to be owned by owners, players, and the general public. (Perhaps owners and players would get one class of stock—maybe only that class would pay a dividend—and the public would get another.) The players might contribute to this new corporation the interests they have in trading card revenue, and the owners might contribute the international business that is now developing. This would give the players a stake in helping to promote and build the game. The players would have equity in a business called Major League Baseball, just as executives or most ordinary workers do these days in the form of company stock plans.

One consistent fan complaint, post–free agency, is that players move too frequently. If everyone agrees it would help the business as a whole, there could be a provision in which players were rewarded in stock for staying with one club for a particular length of time. Maybe baseball could get the ticker symbol MLB. Instead of getting all their money up front, with a stock ownership plan players could defer some of their compensation, and that deferred compensation might very well increase in value tremendously over time. Historically it certainly has. Think how much wealthier the estates of Mickey Mantle and Roger Maris would have been had they received a piece of the Yankees in 1961. Teams may lose money year after year, but the overall value of most franchises has increased significantly and the big, storied franchises have skyrocketed in value. In this stock plan, players would participate more directly in television rights fees, merchandising fees, and spring-training revenues. Put that all together across the broad industry and you'd have, I believe, a solid stock. Above all else, the players would have a vested interest in the long-term welfare of the game, which they don't have now.

If baseball were a publicly traded company, I think it would make better decisions. In a publicly traded company, the largest issues ultimately come down to this: Is this good for the shareholders? The shareholders would be owners, players, fans—everybody. I have always believed that the proper role of the commissioner is to look out for the interests of those three groups, but at present, in part for legal reasons related to federal labor law, the players correctly say the commissioner is an owners' man and cannot represent them. That's not in the best interests of the game. Today, when a topic like speeding up the pace of ballgames or unifying the rules after thirty "experimental" years of the designated hitter comes forward, the adversarial relationship between ownership and players makes it almost impossible to take any action. But if both sides had a vested interest in keeping the game exciting and entertaining not just now but for years to come, reasonable people could make considerable progress. (For the record, I think games take far too long, and I tried to get players and managers and general managers and umpires together to discuss it, but the players were afraid that the umpires would punish them for speaking critically about anything any umpires have ever done. And as far as the DH goes, I would echo Bart's words when he was asked about this issue, as he was very, very often: "I'll soften my answer by saying it's appalling.")

People say, "In the old days, the clubs were owned by rich old gents in plaid sport coats and that was better." No, it wasn't. For one thing, the free-market rights of the players were trampled before 1976, when the reserve clause was finally eliminated. (Naturally, the owners fought to the bitter end, losing, in part, because of bad judgment by Bowie Kuhn and his legal advisers.) For another, the leagues had too many have-nots and too few haves—a disparity even greater than we see today.

I think the biggest genius in sports in the last thirty years was Ted Turner, because he identified first that it's not about the game in the stadium, but about television. He put together WTBS, created the first superstation, and it's taken three decades for George Steinbrenner to build his own TV network instead of selling the rights to someone who will profit further from them. A baseball franchise today has little value apart from its television rights. When the Boston Red Sox sold for $650 million to $700 million, people were shocked that so much could be paid for a franchise in a business that's supposedly struggling, but that's because they ignored the value of NESN (the New England Sports Network), which was a part of the purchase.

The day of the individual owner is dying, and ultimately that may be a good thing for baseball. The number of teams owned by media and cable companies will grow, because of the benefits of combining television programming distribution with club ownership. AOL Time Warner, on whose board I sit, owns the Atlanta Braves; the Tribune Media Company owns the Chicago Cubs; Fox owns the Los Angeles Dodgers; Disney owns the Anaheim Angels; The New York Times Company owns a piece of the Red Sox. Others will follow, because baseball provides media companies and cable companies with hundreds of hours of programming, and it's relatively cheap programming by television standards—if you think Alex Rodriguez was expensive, try paying the cast of *Friends* its $6 million *per half-hour episode*. Baseball turns out programming about 180 days a year, three hours a day. People who buy cars and lawnmowers like to watch it, so you can sell the programming to advertisers. You have dependable income that allows you to build nice stadiums, pay your stars to stay put, field competitive teams. The combination makes so much sense that it's almost inevitable that most clubs will ultimately be owned by media and cable companies.

Of course, networks are not evenly distributed across the nation. The Yankees can put one together; the Kansas City Royals can't. With costs being pegged to the revenues of the richest clubs, the numbers simply won't work for many individual owners, except for the occasional hobbyist who's willing to lose serious money out of a sense of civic obligation. A Bill Gates might want to buy a club, the way Ewing Kauffman did in Kansas City; but eventually those wealthy hobbyists pass away, and their heirs usually look to sell the club to stanch the flow of red ink. But who's going to buy a franchise in Houston, or Milwaukee, or Oakland, where there's no potential to put together a profitable television consortium?

One answer is to let those clubs go under, but it's not the only answer. I can envision the day when media companies will be permitted to own more than one team. Comcast, a big cable company based in Philadelphia with millions of subscribers in Pennsylvania and Maryland (and many other states), could own, for example, both the Phillies and the Baltimore Orioles. The Tribune Company could own the

Cubs, the White Sox, and the Milwaukee Brewers. Texas may be a rich enough market for broadcast owners to take on both the Rangers and the Astros, and perhaps even the Arizona Diamondbacks, in a huge southwestern regional network.

At first glance the idea might seem collusive and dangerous, but in reality it's no different than having one corporation own many competing brands, or several different chains of banks or department stores, or different distribution lines (think HBO and Cinemax) of any product. It would require close supervision, both inside the game and out, to keep a company from using one weak team to stock its stronger one with a steady line of prospects. But I think we can rely on the fact that such a company would be seriously devaluing one of its own assets, and it would benefit most from having all of its teams be strong and competitive.

Before the players cry out that such a system would put a drag on salaries, remember that under this vision of the game the players have stock ownership in the sport as a whole; if salaries really were held down by such a system—and I don't believe they would be—the players would own a share of the ultimate profits, so they'd share in any gains that resulted.

This is a radical vision of the future of the game, but it follows the model of so many other businesses that it may be not so much radical as inevitable. Logic tells you that every American business—every worldwide business—has decided that you can't have capital on one side opposed by labor on the other. As big owners become even bigger, the adversarial view of labor-management strife will give way to the corporate view of employee relations. Players should be interested, because the stock plan will give them something that may appreciate considerably down the road; owners will be interested because they can only benefit from having players care about the long-term good of the game. Unlike salaries, money that goes into the stock plan helps to build the business instead of flying out of it. You would certainly need union agreement to create a Major League Baseball stock ownership plan; the union would negotiate a certain number of seats on the board, agree who the chief executive would be, play a significant role, get the players on board. The CEO of MLB, Inc., would not be a tool of the owners. She or he would have to be responsible to all shareholders. I have some candidates: Condoleezza Rice, President Bush's national security adviser, is one. She told me once her ultimate dream was to be NFL commissioner, but I think she'd be great running baseball. Rudy Giuliani would be an excellent choice, too, as would Mario Cuomo, the former minor leaguer. Good candidates abound!

We're a long way from developing anything like this system, a long way from even considering such a sensible, inclusive plan. The solutions being suggested today, like revenue sharing, are a Band-Aid on a gaping wound. In the short term, we're facing an untidy, miserable period in which the owners will continue to pick fights and lose, will gain nothing, will probably call for Bud Selig's head—he led them down this path, and it's very hard to find anybody in baseball who doesn't think he's taken the wrong turn at every fork in the road; what, exactly, have been his successes?—and slowly, eventually, the owners in the biggest markets will say, Wait a minute, we're the ones who have the most at risk, why are we letting the small-market teams drive the negotiations? In addition, a new union leadership will have to emerge: Fehr and Orza have been enormously effective, but the new spirit of partnership will require a less ideological frame of mind. In the long run, baseball will wind up with some form of partnership between the owners and players—but as John Maynard Keynes said, in the long run we are all dead.

o   o   o

THAT'S QUITE ENOUGH about the structural side of the sport. I don't remember who said that examining the business of baseball is like looking at the sun, you can't do it for very long before you have to turn away, but I certainly know what he meant. The business is awful and ugly, but the game itself is so magical and lyrical that it keeps bringing you back. I hear all the talk of gloom and doom, and I always say, don't talk about the game being killed, because these guys today, however venal and stupid, can't kill it. You couldn't kill it if you tried, because the fans will come back the minute you resolve your little spats. Angry as they are, by and large they'll come back. Sure, some won't, but when you can put a really good product on the field, and it's Sosa and it's McGwire, and it's interesting, people come out. I love the game, I love watching, I enjoy all the parks, and I like the people very much. The business of the game is tawdry and miserable, so I try to ignore it, and I think most fans do too.

Baseball has a special place in the American soul. That was never clearer than in the days and weeks after September 11, 2001. In New York City, where I have lived and worked, a city I love deeply, two great towers were hideously razed and thousands of lives were lost on a day that gave new meaning to the word infamy. For a week and then some, the city's pulse was deadened. And then life started to come back. President Bush told us to get back to the business of living—just as Churchill had done sixty years earlier—and we did.

On September 21, a Friday night, baseball returned to New York City for the first time since the terrorist attacks. The Atlanta Braves came to Shea Stadium in beautiful downtown Flushing Meadow, Queens, to play the New York Mets. The Braves were in first place, but the Mets—my beloved Mets, managed by Bobby Valentine, son-in-law of my great friend Ralph Branca; owned by Fred Wilpon and Nelson Doubleday, old friends now—were still in the race. Forty thousand brave souls came out that night to watch the game, despite the fears generated by the activity of the ballpark's neighbor to the north, La Guardia Airport. Diana Ross, a neighbor of mine and still beautiful, sang "God Bless America," and in that open crescent of a stadium, in the stands and on the field, tears streamed down the faces of athletes and fans alike. For me, at home in Greenwich, Connecticut, watching on TV in a chair that knows me too well, the same: I sat with my eyes swelled with sorrow and grief and pride. We turn out for services and memorials to pay our respects, but ballfields are where we gather of our own accord. I was with those people at Shea; millions of us were. Many things brought us together that night, and baseball was not the least of them. And in just the correct ending, Mike Piazza, the New York catcher, hit a two-run homer in the eighth and the Mets won, 3–2.

My feelings about baseball have been complicated by my involvement in the game. My love for it is not as pure as the off-season snow, for I have seen its seedy side up so close I didn't need my glasses. But that September night, I was mesmerized by the game in the way I was in my World War II boyhood and in the mostly tranquil decade and a half that followed it, right through my high-school years, my college years, my law-school years.

As a child, you dream of becoming Tommy Henrich (in my case) or Joe DiMaggio or Ted Williams or Willie Mays or Brooks Robinson or Barry Bonds or Alex Rodriguez. It doesn't happen. One in a million, they used to say and still do, but the dream persists. The day comes when you no longer believe in Santa Claus, and the day comes, too, when you know you will never spit sunflower seeds from the on-deck circle in the late innings of a tense game. But you never forget you had the dream and what the dream felt like, and that makes the transition to fandom not only easy but comforting.

In my years at Yale Law School, from which I graduated in 1963, something happened to my rooting interest. I remained a devout Yankee fan through the famous '61 season, when Roger Maris broke Babe Ruth's record and the Yankees beat the Reds in five games in the World Series. I was twenty-three, and soon after I finally understood why my father admonished my support of such a bankerly club. The inept Mets were born in 1962, playing their games at the old Polo Grounds, losing far more often than winning, and they were lovable. I knew then my father was correct: rooting for the Yankees *was* like rooting for General Motors. The Mets' first skipper, the historic Casey Stengel, raised on skilled Yankee baseball, said of the children and the washouts on his Mets lineup card, "Can't anybody here play this game?" He said this mostly with mirth, certainly not with anger. It was about then I started to realize life is every bit as much about failure as it is success. I feel I have known both and I feel I am better for it. (Baseball, ultimately, is about failure: Hit safely one time in three for fifteen years and you're a legend.) In any event, ever since those heady Kennedy days, my team loyalties have pointed me toward Flushing, in good times and bad, except for the years 1988 through 1992 when I had no leanings whatsoever, or none to which I'll admit. In my baseball years, I'd go to Shea more frequently than anywhere else, with Fenway a close second. (It was easy to get to from my summer home on Cape Cod.) Yankee Stadium was more convenient to my midtown Manhattan office than Shea, but when George reigned at the Stadium I didn't want to be there. At Shea, I'd be greeted in pure Queens and I loved it: "Hey, Commish! How ya doin'?" Invariably, it was a guy with a beer, a working man, at home in the place he most wanted to be.

I have a young granddaughter and I hope her first trip to a big-league park moves her as my first visit did me. I can still see the bright green of the Yankee Stadium outfield grass against the bright white of the home-team uniforms worn by men shagging flies. The picture is in my mind's eye, a lingering color image from that inaugural journey. The top of my head is at my father's elbow as we walk through the dank cool air trapped in the Stadium's tunnel and into the open air of the stands, taking our seats in general admission. No reserved seats in the Vincent family budget. *What about here, Oscar?* (Great, Dad!)

The game is best at the ballpark. On TV, fly balls are rendered routine by announcers who don't understand how many things can go wrong. On TV, every deep fly seems like a home run. You cannot see the flight of the ball so you can't judge the distance. In person, every fly ball is dramatic; you can hear the sound and know, if your ear is trained, the quality of the hit. You can see the arc of the ball. You can guess whether it is reachable or not. TV cannot give you that. Radio, oddly, comes closer. Baseball is best when it gets in your mind's eye, and in your mind.

After World War II and through the 1950s, baseball had no real sporting competition. It was the national pastime, period. Basketball and football were major sports and they had their seasons, but baseball was the game that dominated TV and radio and sports sections and talk. My dear friend Isaac Stern, the great violinist and baseball fan, used to say that "music is what takes place between the notes." In baseball, every pitch is a note, and the more you understand the game, the more you realize how much is going on between the notes. Sometimes the game seems mind-bogglingly fast to me, there's so much calculating going on between pitches. Only to the unschooled person does it look as if nothing is happening.

The game and the ballparks in which it is played are part of our American heritage. We are proud of baseball, justifiably so. The buildings that house the game are important municipal edifices, and if you live in a city where there's a good one you show it off to your visiting cousin. Americans invented baseball and we nourished it and we have too much stock in it to let it wither. When you see the American flag, you flash back to your childhood; you see your former self saying the Pledge of Allegiance in school or joining Brownies or fishing with an uncle or going to a parade. Going to the ballpark nourishes the same emotions; you remember who first brought you and when, and you know why: to have a good time. Baseball memories are overwhelmingly positive: A steady drizzle, an undercooked hot dog, a bad seat, they can't diminish the joy of seeing DiMaggio hit a homer, Lou Brock steal a base, Derek Jeter field one deep in the hole. I know this, and I suspect you do, too.

Such ballplayers are magical to watch, but they are performing feats that many of us have also performed—just better, and with extraordinary consistency. We shouldn't think of them as superstars. They are everyday heroes, playing an everyday game. In our appreciation of their skill and daring, our understanding of the game and its subtleties, we join them as part of the century-plus-aged tapestry of the life of this beautiful sport. They who play, and we who watch, are all heroes of the game. In these perilous times, we need all the heroes we can get. We always have, and we always will.

	Lineup: Home
1.	Derek Jeter
2.	Ichiro Suzuki
3.	Cooperstown
4.	Camden Yards
5.	New England Collegiate Baseball League
6.	Alexander Cartwright
7.	Joe Garagiola
8.	Other Vincents
9.	The Fan

Home

1. DEREK JETER

AFTER JOE DIMAGGIO, I never imagined baseball would again have a figure who so combined grace and skill with success. It seems it does now. Derek Jeter, the Yankees' everyday shortstop since 1996, dazzles me. In his first six full seasons in the game, the Yankees went to the World Series five times and won four of those times. His career batting average through his first six seasons was .320. His career fielding percentage was .973. His ability to be at the right place at the right time on the field is matched only by his ability to say the right thing at the right time off the field. I have never met him, and that's my loss. But I think I know him. I have the very strong sense the player you see on the field *is* the handsome, polite young man you hear being interviewed on TV.

In the 2001 playoffs, when the Yankees were playing the Oakland A's for the American League pennant, Jeter made a play the likes of which I had never seen before. In Game Three, with the A's ahead two games to none and the Yankees holding a 1–0 lead in the seventh, Jeremy Giambi attempted to score from first on a single to right. For some reason—the genius of intuition—Jeter positioned himself between home and first, where he was in perfect position to make a brilliant stop on a wildly errant throw. With his body carrying him to first, he made a shovel pass home to the catcher, Jorge Posada, who tagged out Giambi (who failed to slide). The Yanks won the game and the series. When he was asked about it afterward, he said his manager Joe Torre had instructed him in spring training about the proper way to back up a cutoff man. "I was just doing what I was trained to do," he said. The answer was pure DiMaggio. He was saying, as Joe did all the time, *It's no big deal*. There's a lot of DiMaggio in Jeter. What he means, as Joe did, is, "It's no big deal for me."

Jeter plays with steady intensity, just as DiMaggio did, day in and day out. You don't see that much anymore. He's not into "styling." He seems motivated by something more than money. Like DiMaggio, he seems to be playing for somebody who might never have seen him play before. To me, he is a "classic" player, in the sense that he plays to fit the ideal, the model, and not to show off and not merely to win. Victory in the classical sense is only a moral good if properly achieved.

In DiMaggio's day, we never really got to know our heroes, and maybe it was just as well. The beat writers were more discreet, and so were the cops, and so were the players. Jeter doesn't have the luxury of a protective press; if he went out at night and made a fool of himself we'd know all about it. The fact he has held up so well under such intense inspection makes him even more remarkable. He has the stuff to surpass DiMaggio as the ultimate baseball icon. It will be difficult, but I'm hoping he does it.

2. ICHIRO SUZUKI

IN THE 2001 SEASON, the Seattle Mariners won 116 games during the regular season. In the history of baseball, no team has won more regular-season games. The Mariners rightfielder and leadoff hitter was a 156-pound twenty-seven-year-old rookie named Ichiro Suzuki.

Ichiro—nobody bothered with his motorcycle-conjuring last name—was no ordinary rookie.

He was a rookie who had played nine years of professional baseball, for the Orix Blue Wave, in his native Japan, where his career batting average was .353. In 2001, he became the first Japanese-born position player to sign with an American club. Over the course of a single season, he took American baseball by storm. He batted .350, caught everything that was hit at him and a lot of balls that weren't, threw out runners regularly, never missed a cutoff man, got his bunts down, ran the bases brilliantly, showed up ready to play every day, played the game the way it was meant to be played. He was the American League Rookie of the Year *and* the Most Valuable Player.

When I was young, Americans spoke of the Japanese attack on Pearl Harbor not in historic terms, but in personal terms. Men of my father's generation and even those younger routinely referred to the Japanese as Japs, never intending the term to be pejorative. I have friends to this day who won't consider buying a Japanese car. My friend Phil Knecht was among them: "I'm not driving a Japanese car, not after what they did to us." In the 1960s, my New York law firm had a long debate before admitting a talented young Japanese-American as a partner.

But 80 percent of the Americans alive today weren't alive in 1941, when Pearl Harbor was attacked. It is our nature to forgive and forget and now, finally, the American fan is ready to embrace a Japanese player. I'm sure we'll see many more Japanese position players in the United States in the future, especially if the dollar remains a much stronger currency than the yen.

I went on a baseball tour of Japan in 1990, when an American All-Star team played a series of exhibition games against Japanese teams. Don Zimmer was the American manager and he and I were amazed at what we saw. Hideo Nomo was then an eighteen-year-old pitcher and the American players found him unhittable. He threw one-hundred-mile-an-hour fastballs. The Japanese baseball was excellent, and the series could not have been closer: We won three, Japan won three, and one game was tied. At least we didn't lose the series! I was very much struck by the discipline with which the Japanese played. One night, I saw an outfielder miss a cutoff man and his manager walked onto the field and pulled him from the game. The player sprinted off in shame. Can you imagine that happening in American baseball? Maybe some of the discipline Ichiro demonstrates and represents will rub off on American baseball in the years to come. It would be nice to think that we could not only forgive another country, but actually learn from it.

3. COOPERSTOWN

I THINK COOPERSTOWN is a special place, a charming little hamlet in the middle of nowhere in upstate New York. I went there in the late 1940s with my father and uncle, and I went there again in the early 1990s as commissioner; I think it's an important trip for a baseball fan to make, because it makes baseball's past so meaningful to its present. Baseball and its history cannot be separated; every modern achievement is meaningful only when measured by what has happened before. Cooperstown understands this. The place is a time machine.

Bart had a dim view of Cooperstown, because he thought, correctly, that there was a fraudulent premise to its existence. Despite the legend, baseball was not invented there by Abner Doubleday, the Civil War veteran. (The game's birthplace is Hoboken, New Jersey, and its inventor, as much as the game can be said to have a single architect, was a New York City bank teller named Alexander Cartwright.) There is no historic basis for Cooperstown to be the baseball mecca.

Everything at Cooperstown is done beautifully. Cooperstown is the most important repository for historic baseball materials. When Bart died, Jean Yawkey, the owner of the Bart's beloved Red Sox, gave money to the Hall of Fame to dedicate a research library in his name.

Some years after I left baseball, an acquaintance gave me a series of tapes, interviews with ballplayers, recorded in the early 1960s. On them, Lawrence Ritter, a writer and professor, had interviewed some of the important historic baseball figures who were by then old men. It was the only source to hear "Smoky" Joe Wood talking in his own voice about the art of pitching in the Walter Johnson–Cy Young–Christy Mathewson era. (Later, he coached baseball for years at Yale, where my father played for him.) I was fascinated by these oral histories and I soon learned that nothing like them had been made since then. At the suggestion of Eli Jacobs, and with the support of Herbert Allen, we started a series of interviews called the Hall of Fame Oral History Project. So far, we've conducted about thirty videotaped interviews of important ballplayers, who talk about how they came to play the game and what it was like when they played it. I've conducted some of the interviews, sometimes with Claire Smith. It has given me the chance to spend days with marvelous old baseball people like Tommy Henrich, Bob Feller, Warren Spahn, Whitey Ford, Yogi Berra, Larry Doby, Joe Black, Tom Seaver, Brooks Robinson, Ralph Kiner, Johnny Pesky, and Dom DiMaggio. The men know this might be the last time they could get their stories down for the record and they know there's no commercial aspect to what we're doing, so they're open and relaxed. Their stories are great, often shooting off in unexpected ways, like Yogi telling of being off Omaha Beach on D-Day in a tiny rocket launcher. Priceless.

Anyone can write to the Hall of Fame and make arrangements to watch these videotapes in Cooperstown and use the material for non-commercial purposes. The address is 25 Main Street, Cooperstown, NY, 13326. They're fascinating pieces of baseball history, in a quaint little town that has a nice golf course and the most lovely sort of, as Bart would say, "ambience."

4. CAMDEN YARDS

MY WIFE, CHRISTINA, is a golfer, and many of her friends are golfers, and every once in a while I hear one of them ask the other, in a voice filled with *gravitas,* "If you could only play one golf course for the rest of your life, which would it be?" For a golfer, such a question evokes an astounding amount of emotion and consideration. It brings to mind a corollary baseball question, seldom asked: If you could watch baseball in only one ballpark for the rest of your life, which would it be? Now *there* is an important question.

I must make a nod to Fenway in Boston and Chicago's Wrigley, two antiques still holding on. Yankee Stadium makes too much of its grand history for my taste, plus there's the specter of George hanging over the place. No, if I had to pick a single ballpark in which to watch baseball for the rest of my life it would actually be one of the moderns, the first of the new ones to be built in the style of the old ones: Camden Yards, in Baltimore's Inner Harbor.

Camden Yards was built in the late 1980s under the watchful and nurturing eye of the man who owned the team at the time, my friend Eli Jacobs. It was the first of the post–World War II stadia that modeled itself on the classic lines of the old, intimate ballparks like Fenway and Ebbets Field in Brooklyn and the Polo Grounds on the outskirts of Harlem. Janet Marie Smith, the Orioles' architectural liaison, painstakingly studied photographs and blueprints of the old parks and talked to people who loved watching games there. She developed a tremendous insight, both technical and emotional, into what made them work. And then Eli and Janet, and scores of others, worked diligently to get all the modern conveniences just right. I recall Eli going to eight or ten different parks to study such fine points as the width of the chairs and aisles, and the design of the bathrooms and concession areas. Whenever you're at Camden Yards, you're aware that Babe Ruth was born in that neighborhood, that a flourishing city lies just beyond the ballpark's gates, that the team and its city are integrated in the most meaningful of ways. Thanks mostly to Eli, Camden Yards is everything a ballpark should be. It's become the model.

5. NEW ENGLAND COLLEGIATE BASEBALL LEAGUE

FOR YEARS, there has been a summer baseball league for college players on Cape Cod called, simply enough, the Cape Cod League. A movie called *Summer Catch,* which came out in the summer of 2001, depicts the league charmingly. I know the league well because I spent summer vacations on the Cape for years. The quality of the baseball is very, very high and dozens of former Cape Cod League players have gone on to the majors. They still use wooden bats in the Cape Cod League— collegiate baseball is played with metal bats—so scouts find Cape baseball instructive as to what a player can do with a real stick in his hands. The players come from all over the country to play in the league, they stay with local families, they often get daytime jobs. Sometimes, they fall in love.

In the early 1990s, a group of New England baseball buffs decided to start a similar league. The concept was much the same—wooden bats, summer nights—but this league was to be reserved for players from New England. George Foster, the wonderful outfielder for the Reds and Mets, lived in Connecticut and helped start the league. In 1995, I got involved in the league, mostly as a fundraiser and counselor; for those modest tasks they gave me the grand title of president, New England Collegiate Baseball League. Tom Hutton is the Commissioner and runs a great operation. There are ten teams throughout New England, and players now come from all over the country. One of the highlights of the season is a midsummer All-Star game against Cape Cod League All-Stars. At the end of the season the winning team is awarded something called the Fay Vincent Sr. Cup, named in memory of a former New England collegiate baseball player. One of the teams is in Torrington, Connecticut, my father's hometown. There's an umpire in the league, Eddie Rapuano, who umpired with my father in the 1970s; his son, also Eddie, is an umpire in the majors today. There's a pitcher, Keith Surkont, who went from Williams to the Rhode Island Reds of the NECBL to the minors; maybe someday he'll make it to the majors, as his grandfather did. I remember Max Surkont, a big righthander from Rhode Island who pitched for the Boston Braves in the early 1950s. There's a wonderful coziness, an interconnectedness, to the whole league. That's part of what New England is all about, at least in historic terms, a thousand little towns connected by two-lane roads and single-track train lines.

The midsummer baseball scene in Keene, New Hampshire, is particularly lovely. The whole town comes out to watch the team, or so it seems, one or two thousand people. There are dogs chasing frisbees and kids eating ice cream cones in foul territory between innings. The park the team plays in is beautiful, well-lighted, nice dirt in the infield, good grass in the outfield. I love being there.

When I became president, somebody said, "The only strikes you'll see in this league are the ones that go over the plate." The New England league is the amateur game at its purest. Only the umpires and coaches get paid. It's pure baseball.

6. ALEXANDER CARTWRIGHT

THERE'S A MYTH that when Alexander Cartwright laid out a baseball diamond and helped develop the first rule book in the 1840s, he got everything exactly correct the first time. He did not. He had the pitcher's box—no mound—a mere forty-five feet from home plate; it wasn't until 1893 that the distance was set at sixty feet, six inches. Can you imagine Randy Johnson throwing bullets at you from forty-five feet?

Nearly everything else Cartwright got right, both in the naming and in the numbers. Ninety feet between the bases. Three outs to an inning. Nine innings to a game. Four bases, but only one without a number attached to it: first base, second base, third base, home. Foul territory, fair territory. Nine to a side. How could you get that much right? Divine inspiration.

A batter hits a crisp grounder to short and it is fielded cleanly and the runner, even the speediest of runners, is out by a step. That was true in 1901 and was still true in 2001. If the shortstop bobbles the ball, the runner will be safe, if he's running hard. It was true then and it is true now.

Bart used to say to people, "Why don't they call it fourth base?" He was being Socratic; he had the answer. Baseball is generically rooted in the theme of all great literature, the idea of getting home. *The Odyssey,* the RBI, Bart didn't distinguish much between the two. He said, "You get *stranded* at second base, as far from home as there is. When you get home, your teammates—your family—rush out to welcome you. You are safe at home."

All that is bad in baseball is represented by a three or a multiple of three, Bart used to say. Fours are good. Four balls and you get to go to first. Advance four bases and you've brought home a run. Advance 360 feet and you're home. Four runs is the most that can be scored on a single swing of the bat. Three strikes and you're out. Make three outs and you're in the field. Get to third base, but no further, and you've accomplished nothing. Make the twenty-seventh out—three times three times three—and if your team is trailing, the game is over.

You could argue: But if you *get* that twenty-seventh out, your team has won. You could argue: When you're stranded at second, you've journeyed 180 feet, a multiple of three *and* four. The game is prone to arguments. (That's why baseball has such a popular hot-stove league.) It is filled with life. That's why it has endured.

7. JOE GARAGIOLA

OF ALL THE PEOPLE I've met through baseball—well over a thousand, I imagine—there is no one I admire more than Joe Garagiola. This is saying something, because there are many baseball people I admire deeply: Yogi Berra, Ralph Branca, Ted Williams, Bruce Froemming, John McMullen, Dusty Baker, Don Baylor, Cal Ripken, Jr., Warren Spahn, Murray Chass, Slick Surratt, Steve Greenberg, Claire Smith, to name just a baker's dozen. I could name many more.

I admire Joe for many reasons. He has bridged old-time baseball and the modern game with total grace. He talks about the old players, those he came up with in the 1940s, with great affection, yet he is deeply impressed by the skills and talents of today's players. He is amazed at what Barry Bonds can do at the plate, what Alex Rodriguez can do in the field, what Randy Johnson can do from the mound. He is not sentimental about the past. He appreciates it.

Joe was born in 1926 in St. Louis and became a professional baseball player sixteen years later. He grew up on the hill of that city with Yogi, who is a year older than Joe. They were both prominent catchers, they both have great wits, they both have led rich lives by not wavering from the good values with which they were raised. A devout Catholic, Joe likes to say, "We were put on this earth to keep each other warm."

Joe has found something good and useful to do at every stage of his life and that is no easy trick. He has gone from ballplayer to broadcaster to humanitarian to concerned senior citizen seamlessly. I think he has led a heroic life.

For years, he ran BAT, the Baseball Assistance Team. He raised millions for it, he found old players and widows and others who were in need and got money to them quietly and unobtrusively. He has, I know, saved lives. His ear is always to the rail. He'll hear about a World Series ring for sale and know that something is wrong. Maybe the player is living under a bridge, or threatening to kill himself, or on a suicidal drinking binge; he finds the player and gets help to him, no questions asked, no names named.

Years ago, he was talking to Bill Tuttle, the old Detroit Tiger outfielder, who always played with a huge plug of tobacco stuck in his cheek, like Nellie Fox. Now half his jaw was missing, because of cancer of the mouth. He chewed tobacco for years and paid the price for it horrifically. Bill said to Joe, "You ought to talk to these kids about chewing tobacco." Joe took the advice seriously: He single-handedly spearheaded baseball's public service announcements about the dangers of chewing tobacco. (I banned chewing in the minors but the union blocked any similar rule in the majors, citing civil liberty considerations. Sad.) I suspect Joe has saved lives with that campaign.

Joe knows the game inside and out and backward and forward. When you hear him broadcast a game, or when you sit with him at one, you learn. He's a good teacher. He must be: His son, Joe Jr., was the general manager of the Arizona Diamondbacks in 2001. All they did was beat the New York Yankees in seven games in the World Series. That doesn't happen by luck. Much of the credit must go to Joe Jr. And some of the credit must go to Joe.

He is deserving of it.

8. OTHER VINCENTS

A LOVE FOR BASEBALL is not handed down, generation to generation, from father to son, father to son, like a fine watch. That is an enduring myth from a sexist era. I am blessed with three wonderful adult children: a daughter, Anne, and twin boys, Bill and Ted. When the boys were young and Earl Weaver's Orioles were good, I used to take them to games at Memorial Stadium in Baltimore. Why I did not also bring Anne, I cannot tell you; instead, I took her to hockey games. Today she has no interest in hockey; it's baseball she loves. She lives in San Diego and she roots for the Padres and when Tony Gwynn, the affable Padres hitting machine for two decades, announced his retirement in 2001, I imagine she got a little lump in her throat, just as I did when DiMaggio announced his retirement a half-century earlier. Nothing drives home how relentlessly time marches on than seeing a ballplayer, one you've watched most of your life, step back into the shadows. You ask yourself, where did the time go?

The 2001 season was a tough one in the retirement department. My son Bill, a teacher in Baltimore, is devoted to the Orioles, and as Gwynn was making his farewell, the ultimate Oriole symbol, Cal Ripken, Jr., did the same after playing in 2,978 games, 2,632 of which he started consecutively.

Bill, who in the summer after he graduated from college made a cross-country tour with a friend and visited every major-league park in the country, is old-school. He'd rather take the overnight train to Florida than fly. He has an abundance of patience, as all good teachers do. He can sit all day at a spring-training camp, watching ballplayers go through their preseason drills, sitting among the pensioners, knowing that he might be able to bring home something useful to the kids he coaches in Baltimore. He's an umpire, too, like his father's father. It's in the blood.

Ted is a husband and a father and a financial adviser living just up the road from Greenwich, in Stamford. He worked for a while in hockey, his favorite sport, but baseball is not a part of his life. As I write this, his daughter Laura is making the march from infant to toddler. Maybe she'll find her way to the game and maybe she won't. There's a genetic predisposition for baseball there, but there are other factors, too. Maybe her tastes will run to dance or computers or music or soccer. Baseball may be a primary thing in her life, a secondary thing, or nothing at all.

I strongly suspect the game will be there for her if she is interested in it, ten years from now, twenty years from now, fifty years from now. The game has proved it has staying power; not many things from the popular culture of the Civil War era live on so unadulterated. Ultimately, there's only a single source for that power. It comes from the people who follow the game, who are attached to the game, who love the game. It has never been for everyone, but there will always be those for whom the game touches the soul.

9. THE FAN

WHEN ROGER ANGELL first started writing about baseball for *The New Yorker* in the 1960s, he did something novel. Most sportswriters, then and now, were writing about the game from the players' perspective. They would try to get inside the head of the player, or manager, and explain what was really happening for the fan who watched the game from a seat in the stands or at home. Roger wrote about the game from our lookout, from the perspective of the fan who is knowledgeable and enthusiastic about the game and who happens to have a press pass, giving him access to players and managers and clubhouses. That approach has served him well for decades.

He did one other important thing: He never claimed too much for the game. Baseball is an entertainment, an escape. It is moving and dramatic, and for millions of us, it's an important part of our lives. But it is not life itself. For the well-adjusted person, no one thing is life itself. I have learned that. I think we all do, sooner or later.

It would be a mistake to think baseball is permanent. What is permanent? The ancient Greeks played sports we do not. Of course, they ran marathons, too, and we still do today. One might be inclined to say that the marathon has a permanent place in the culture of sports. Maybe. Baseball has been around for a mere eyeblink of time, 160 years or so. Does it have a chance to become a permanent part of our civilization? I'm tempted to say yes, but I think we'd do well to take it one century at a time.

It will last if the players and owners and other stewards of the game keep their eye on the ball—and on the fan. What is baseball without its fans? Nothing, not a thing.

The fan applauds—gingerly, politely—when a player on the opposing team catches a ball no mortal could get a glove on. In his mind, he can field, pitch, bat, manage, umpire. He knows the game so well he can call balls and strikes from a bleacher seat, a living-room sofa, over the car radio. When the season is over and the World Series trophy—

ugly in one pose, regal in another—is hoisted and once again his team is not spraying champagne, he gets out the next year's calendar and marks up a square four months hence, a weekday in mid-February, with the letters "P. & C.," noting the date that pitchers and catchers are due to report for spring training. Next year, next year, there's always next year.

INDEX

313